CALIFORNIA

Made in the United States
Text printed on 90%
recycled paper

Houghton Mifflin Harcourt

CALIFORNIA

Printed in the U.S.A.

ISBN 978-0-544-20391-4

12 13 14 15 16 17 18 19 0029 27 26 25 24 23 22 21 20

4500790729   B C D E F G

Dear Students and Families,

Welcome to **California Go Math!**, Grade 2! In this exciting mathematics program, there are hands-on activities to do and real-world problems to solve. Best of all, you will write your ideas and answers right in your book. In **California Go Math!**, writing and drawing on the pages helps you think deeply about what you are learning, and you will really understand math!

By the way, all of the pages in your **California Go Math!** book are made using recycled paper. We wanted you to know that you can Go Green with **California Go Math!**

Sincerely,

The Authors

Made in the United States
Text printed on 90% recycled paper

CALIFORNIA

GO MATH!

Authors

Juli K. Dixon, Ph.D.
Professor, Mathematics Education
University of Central Florida
Orlando, Florida

Edward B. Burger, Ph.D.
President, Southwestern University
Georgetown, Texas

Steven J. Leinwand
Principal Research Analyst
American Institutes for
  Research (AIR)
Washington, D.C.

Contributor

Rena Petrello
Professor, Mathematics
Moorpark College
Moorpark, CA

Matthew R. Larson, Ph.D.
K-12 Curriculum Specialist for
  Mathematics
Lincoln Public Schools
Lincoln, Nebraska

Martha E. Sandoval-Martinez
Math Instructor
El Camino College
Torrance, California

English Language Learners Consultant

Elizabeth Jiménez
CEO, GEMAS Consulting
Professional Expert on English
  Learner Education
Bilingual Education and
  Dual Language
Pomona, California

© Houghton Mifflin Harcourt Publishing Company • Image Credits: (bg) ©Jeff Oishan/Getty Images; (bg) ©Mark Karrass/Corbis; (b) ©Allan Vernon/Flickr/Getty Images; (t) ©Mark Karrass/Corbis; (b) ©Allan Vernon/Flickr/Getty Images

Number Sense and Place Value

 COMMON CORE Critical Area Extending understanding of base-ten notation

Critical Area

GO DIGITAL

Go online! Your math lessons are interactive. Use *iTools*, Animated Math Models, the Multimedia *e*Glossary, and more.

Chapter 1 Overview

In this chapter, you will explore and discover answers to the following **Essential Questions**:

- How do you use place value to find the values of numbers and describe numbers in different ways?
- How do you know the value of a digit?
- What are some different ways to show a number?
- How do you count by 1s, 5s, 10s, and 100s?

v

2 Numbers to 1,000   53

Domain Number and Operations in Base Ten

CALIFORNIA COMMON CORE STANDARDS 2.NBT.1, 2.NBT.1a, 2.NBT.1b, 2.NBT.3, 2.NBT.4, 2.NBT.8

Addition and Subtraction

 COMMON CORE Critical Area Building fluency with addition and subtraction

GO DIGITAL

Go online! Your math lessons are interactive. Use *iTools*, Animated Math Models, the Multimedia *e*Glossary, and more.

Chapter 3 Overview

In this chapter, you will explore and discover answers to the following **Essential Questions**:

• How can you use patterns and strategies to find sums and differences for basic facts?

• What are some strategies for remembering addition and subtraction facts?

• How are addition and subtraction related?

Chapter 4 Overview

In this chapter, you will explore and discover answers to the following **Essential Questions**:

- How do you use place value to add 2-digit numbers, and what are some different ways to add 2-digit numbers?
- How do you make an addend a ten to help solve an addition problem?
- How do you record the steps when adding 2-digit numbers?
- What are some ways to add 3 numbers or 4 numbers?

4 2-Digit Addition 169

Domain Number and Operations in Base Ten
CALIFORNIA COMMON CORE STANDARDS 2.OA.1, 2.NBT.5, 2.NBT.6, 2.NBT.9

Measurement and Data

COMMON CORE Critical Area Using standard units of measure

Chapter 9 Overview

In this chapter, you will explore and discover answers to the following **Essential Questions**:
- What are some of the methods and tools that can be used to estimate and measure length in metric units?
- What tools can be used to measure length in metric units and how do you use them?
- What metric units can be used to measure length and how do they compare with each other?
- If you know the length of one object, how can you estimate the length of another object?

Chapter 10 Overview

In this chapter, you will explore and discover answers to the following **Essential Questions**:
- How do tally charts, picture graphs, and bar graphs help you solve problems?
- How are tally marks used to record data for a survey?
- How is a picture graph made?
- How do you know what the bars in a bar graph stand for?

Geometry and Fractions

 COMMON CORE **Critical Area** Describing and analyzing shapes

Essential Question

What objects match three-dimensional shapes?

Start

Chapter 11 Overview

In this chapter, you will explore and discover answers to the following **Essential Questions**:

- What are some two-dimensional shapes and three-dimensional shapes, and how can you show equal parts of shapes?

- How can you describe some two-dimensional and three-dimensional shapes?

- How can you describe equal parts of shapes?

Whales

by John Hudson

CRITICAL AREA Extending understanding of base-ten notation

Some scientists study whales. Different kinds of whales swim along the west coast of the United States of America.

A scientist sees 8 blue whales.

Blue whales are the largest animals on Earth.

Social Studies

Where is the United States of America on the map?

Alaska

Pacific
Ocean

Canada

Atlantic
Ocean

N
W — E
S

United States
of America

0   500   1,000 Miles
0   500 1,000 Kilometers

Mexico

Map Legend
—— Border

The scientist also sees 13 humpback whales.

Humpback whales sing underwater.

Did the scientist see more humpback whales or

more blue whales?   more _____ whales

Social Studies

Where is the Pacific Ocean on the map?

3

Whales also swim along the east coast of Canada and the United States of America. Pilot whales swim behind a leader, or a *pilot*. A scientist sees a group of 29 pilot whales.

Where is Canada on the map?

Social Studies

Alaska

Pacific
Ocean

Canada

Atlantic
Ocean

N

W—O—E

S

United States
of America

0   500   1,000 Miles
0   500 1,000 Kilometers

Mexico

Map Legend
— Border

Fin whales are fast swimmers. They are
the second-largest whales in the world.
A scientist sees a group of 27 fin whales.
How many tens are in the number 27?

_____ tens

Social Studies

Where is the Atlantic Ocean on the map?

5

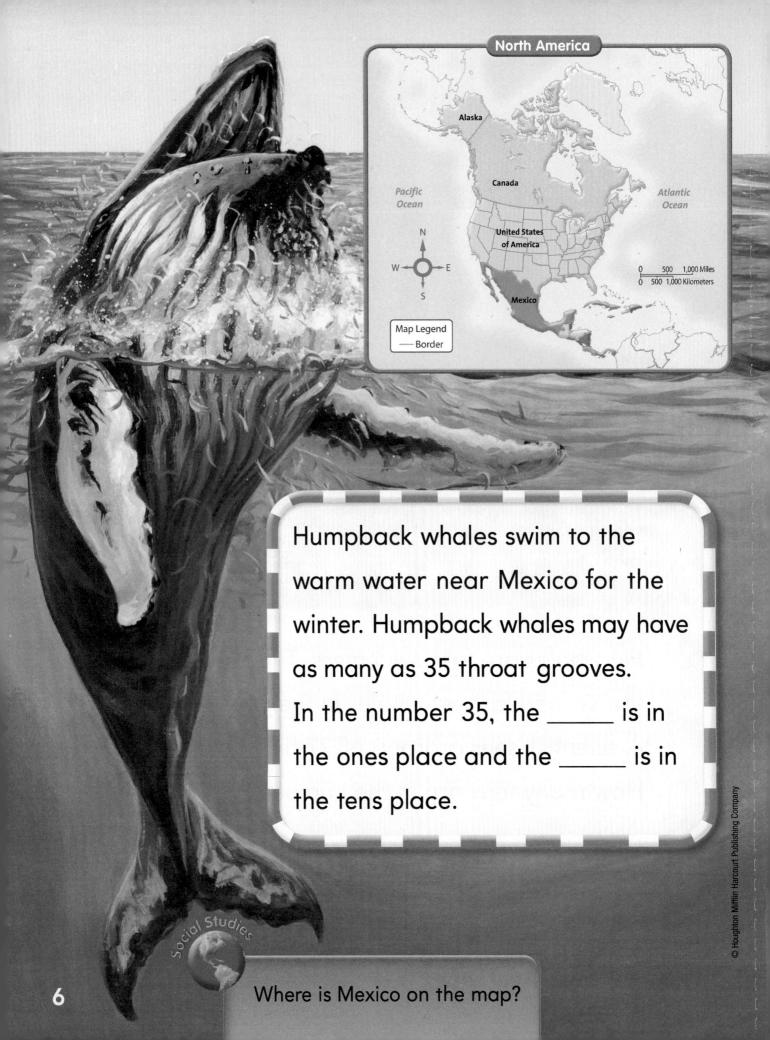

Alaska

Canada

Pacific
Ocean

United States
of America

Atlantic
Ocean

N

W   E

S

0   500   1,000 Miles
0   500   1,000 Kilometers

Mexico

Map Legend
— Border

Humpback whales swim to the warm water near Mexico for the winter. Humpback whales may have as many as 35 throat grooves.

In the number 35, the _____ is in the ones place and the _____ is in the tens place.

Social Studies

Where is Mexico on the map?

Write About the Story

Look at the pictures. Draw and write your own story. Compare two numbers in your story.

Vocabulary Review

more	fewer
tens	greater than
ones	less than

WRITE ▸ Math

_____

_____

_____

_____

_____

_____

The Size of Numbers

The table shows how many young whales were seen by scientists.

Young Whales Seen	
Whale	**Number of Whales**
Humpback	34
Blue	13
Fin	27
Pilot	43

1. Which number of whales has a 4 in the tens place?

   _____

2. How many tens and ones describe the number of young blue whales seen?

   _____ ten _____ ones

3. Compare the number of young humpback whales and the number of young pilot whales seen. Write > or <.

   34 ◯ 43

4. Compare the number of young fin whales and the number of young blue whales seen. Write > or <.

   27 ◯ 13

MATH BOARD Write a story about a scientist watching sea animals. Use some 2-digit numbers in your story.

Number Concepts

Curious about Math

At a farmers' market, many different fruits and vegetables are sold.

If there are 2 groups of 10 watermelons on a table, how many watermelons are there?

Show What You Know ✓

Model Numbers to 20

Write the number that tells how many.

1.

_____

2.

_____

Use a Hundred Chart to Count

Use the hundred chart.

3. Count from 36 to 47. Which of the numbers below will you say? Circle them.

42   31   48   39   37

1	2	3	4	5	6	7	8	9	10
11	12	13	14	15	16	17	18	19	20
21	22	23	24	25	26	27	28	29	30
31	32	33	34	35	36	37	38	39	40
41	42	43	44	45	46	47	48	49	50
51	52	53	54	55	56	57	58	59	60
61	62	63	64	65	66	67	68	69	70
71	72	73	74	75	76	77	78	79	80
81	82	83	84	85	86	87	88	89	90
91	92	93	94	95	96	97	98	99	100

Tens

Write how many tens. Write the number.

4. _____ tens

_____

5. _____ tens

_____

This page checks understanding of important skills needed for success in Chapter 1.

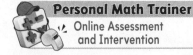

Personal Math Trainer
Online Assessment and Intervention

Name _____

Vocabulary Builder

Review Words
ones
tens
count on
count back

Visualize It

Fill in the boxes of the graphic organizer.
Write sentences about **ones** and **tens**.

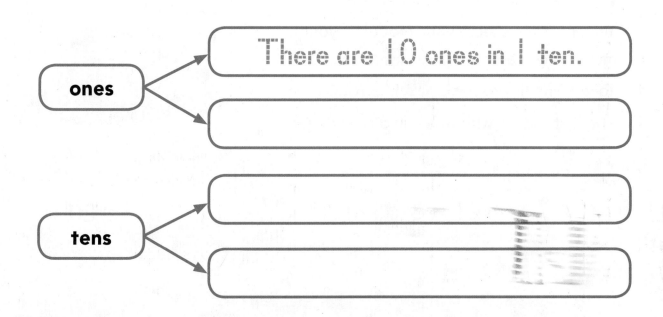

There are 10 ones in 1 ten.

Understand Vocabulary

1. Start with I. **Count on** by ones.

   I, ____, ____, ____, ____, ____

---

2. Start with 8. **Count back** by ones.

   8, ____, ____, ____, ____, ____

GO DIGITAL
• Interactive Student Edition
• Multimedia eGlossary

Game # Three in a Row

Materials • 15 • 15 ○ • ▬▬▬▬▬

Play with a partner.

1. Choose a leaf. Read the number on the leaf. Use ▬▬▬▬ to model the number.

2. Your partner checks your model. If your model is correct, put your ● on the leaf.

3. Take turns. Try to get 3 ● in a row.

4. The first player with 3 ● in a row wins.

5	21	13	19	20
25	15	7	8	12
11	9	14	16	24
22	23	17	18	10

Name ______________________________

Algebra • Even and Odd Numbers

Essential Question How are even numbers and odd numbers different?

HANDS ON
Lesson 1.1

Operations and Algebraic Thinking—2.OA.3
MATHEMATICAL PRACTICES
MP.3, MP.5, MP.7

Listen Real World · Hands On

Use ▪ to show each number.

Math Talk **Mathematical Practices**

When you make pairs for 7 and for 10, how are these models different? **Explain.**

FOR THE TEACHER • Read the following problem. Beca has 8 toy cars. Can she put her cars in pairs on a shelf? Have children set pairs of cubes vertically on the ten frames. Continue the activity for the numbers 7 and 10.

Count out cubes for each number. Make pairs.
Even numbers show pairs with no cubes left over.
Odd numbers show pairs with one cube left over.

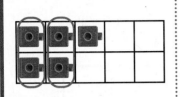

5 _odd_

8 _even_

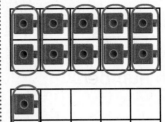

12 _____

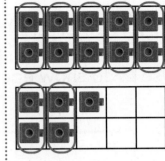

15 _____

Share and Show

Use cubes. Count out the number of cubes.
Make pairs. Then write **even** or **odd**.

1. 6 _____

2. 3 _____

3. 2 _____

4. 9 _____

5. 4 _____

6. 10 _____

7. 7 _____

8. 13 _____

 9. 11 _____

10. 14 _____

Name _____

Shade in the ten frames to show the number.
Circle **even** or **odd**.

11.   17
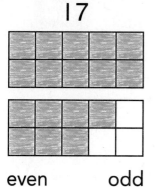
even   odd

12.   16
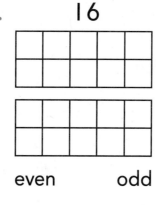
even   odd

13.   19
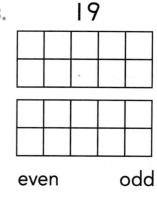
even   odd

14.   15
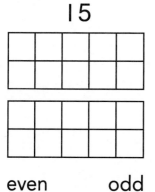
even   odd

15.   20
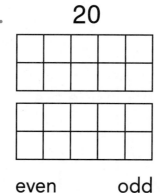
even   odd

16.   18
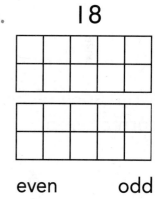
even   odd

17.   **MATHEMATICAL PRACTICE ③**   **Make Arguments**
Which two numbers in the box
are even numbers?

_____ and _____

Explain how you know that they
are even numbers.

_____

_____

_____

Chapter 1 • Lesson 1

Problem Solving • Applications

WRITE ▶ Math

18. **THINK SMARTER** Fill in the blanks to describe the groups of numbers. Write **even** or **odd**.

_____ numbers   _____ numbers

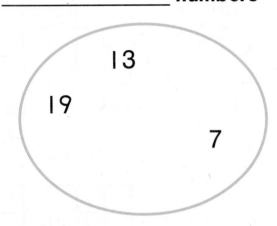

13

19

7

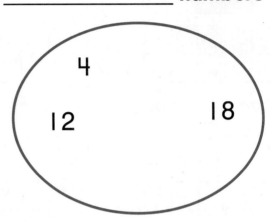

4

12   18

Write each of these numbers inside the correct loop.

5   6   10   11   24   25

19. **THINK SMARTER** Does each ten frame show an even number? Choose Yes or No.

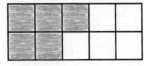   ○ Yes   ○ No

   ○ Yes   ○ No

TAKE HOME ACTIVITY • Have your child show you a number, such as 9, using small objects and explain why the number is even or odd.

FOR MORE PRACTICE: Standards Practice Book

Name _____

Algebra • Represent Even Numbers

Essential Question Why can an even number be shown as the sum of two equal addends?

Operations and Algebraic Thinking—2.OA.3
MATHEMATICAL PRACTICES
MP.7, MP.8

Listen and Draw

Make pairs with your cubes. Draw to show the cubes. Then write the numbers you say as you count to find the number of cubes.

_____ _____ cubes

FOR THE TEACHER • Give each small group of children a set of 10 to 15 connecting cubes. After children group their cubes into pairs, have them draw a picture of their cubes and write their counting sequence for finding the total number of cubes.

Math Talk **Mathematical Practices**

Do you have an odd number or even number of cubes? **Explain.**

Model and Draw

An even number of cubes can be shown as two equal groups.

> You can match each cube in the first group with a cube in the second group.

$$6 = 3 + 3$$

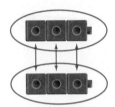

$$10 = 5 + 5$$

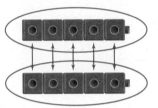

Share and Show

 MATH BOARD

How many cubes are there in all? Complete the addition sentence to show the equal groups.

1. ___ = ___ + ___

2. ___ = ___ + ___

3. ___ = ___ + ___

4. ___ = ___ + ___

Name _____

Shade in the frames to show two equal groups
for each number. Complete the addition sentence
to show the groups.

5. 10

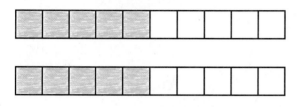

___ = ___ + ___

6. 16

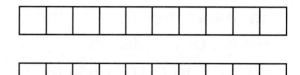

___ = ___ + ___

7. 20

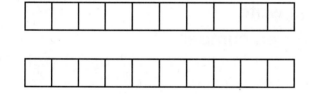

___ = ___ + ___

8. 18

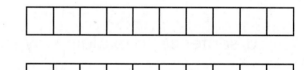

___ = ___ + ___

THINK SMARTER The number 7 is an odd number.
Marc showed 7 with this addition sentence.
Use Marc's way to show these odd numbers
with addition sentences.

$7 = 3 + 3 + 1$

9. 5 = ___ + ___ + ___

10. 11 = ___ + ___ + ___

11. 9 = ___ + ___ + ___

12. 13 = ___ + ___ + ___

Problem Solving • Applications  WRITE ▸ Math

Solve. Write or draw to explain.

13. **MATHEMATICAL PRACTICE ②** **Use Reasoning**
Jacob and Lucas each have
the same number of shells.
Together they have 16 shells.
How many shells do
Jacob and Lucas each have?

Jacob: _____ shells

Lucas: _____ shells

Personal Math Trainer

14. *THINK SMARTER* ✚ Choose an even number between
10 and 19. Draw a picture and then write
a sentence to explain why it is an even number.

 TAKE HOME ACTIVITY • Have your child explain what he or she learned in this lesson.

FOR MORE PRACTICE:
Standards Practice Book

Name _____

Understand Place Value

Essential Question How do you know the value of a digit?

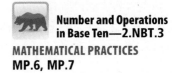
Number and Operations in Base Ten—2.NBT.3
MATHEMATICAL PRACTICES
MP.6, MP.7

Write the numbers. Then choose a way to show the numbers.

Tens	Ones

Tens	Ones

FOR THE TEACHER • Read the following problem. Have children write the numbers and describe how they chose to represent them. Gabriel collects baseball cards. The number of cards that he has is written with a 2 and a 5. How many cards might he have?

Math Talk Mathematical Practices

Explain why the value of 5 is different in the two numbers.

0, 1, 2, 3, 4, 5, 6, 7, 8, and 9 are **digits**.
In a 2-digit number, you know the value of
a digit by its place.

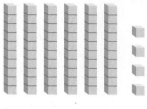

64

Tens	Ones
6	4

6 tens   4 ones

The digit **6** is in the tens place. It tells you there are 6 tens, or 60.

The digit **4** is in the ones place. It tells you there are 4 ones, or 4.

Share and Show

Circle the value of the red digit.

1. 26

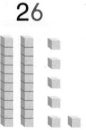

60   ⬭6⬭

2. 58

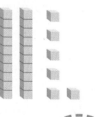

5   50

3. 40

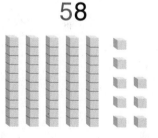

40   4

4. 73

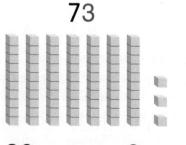

30   3

☑ 5. 24

2   20

☑ 6. 61

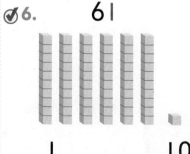

1   10

© Houghton Mifflin Harcourt Publishing Company

On Your Own

Circle the value of the red digit.

7.   5 1

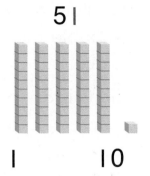

1   10

8.   49

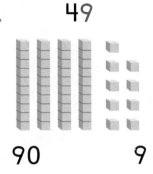

90   9

9.   70

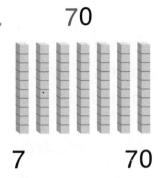

7   70

10.   1 8

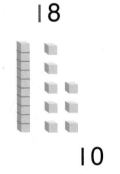

1   10

11.   65

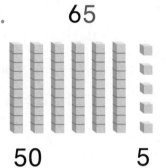

50   5

12.   33

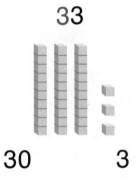

30   3

13.   30

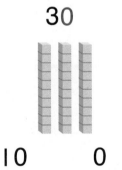

10   0

14.   46

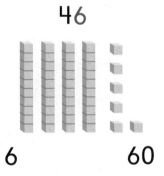

6   60

15.   54

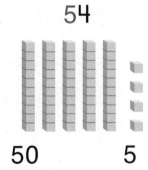

50   5

16. THINK SMARTER Look at the digits of the numbers. Draw quick pictures for the missing blocks.

47

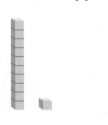

52

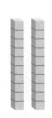

Math on the Spot

Problem Solving • Applications

WRITE ▸ Math

Write the 2-digit number that matches the clues.

17. My number has 8 tens.

The digit in the ones place is greater than the digit in the tens place.

My number is _____.

18. In my number, the digit in the ones place is double the digit in the tens place.

The sum of the digits is 3.

My number is _____.

---

19. **MATHEMATICAL PRACTICE ①** Make Sense of Problems

In my number, both digits are even numbers.

The digit in the tens place is less than the digit in the ones place.

The sum of the digits is 6.

My number is _____.

20. **THINK SMARTER** What is the value of the digit 4 in the number 43?

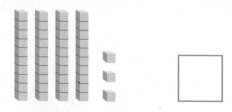

TAKE HOME ACTIVITY • Write the number 56. Have your child tell you which digit is in the tens place, which digit is in the ones place, and the value of each digit.

FOR MORE PRACTICE: Standards Practice Book

Name _____

Expanded Form

Essential Question How do you describe a
2-digit number as tens and ones?

Number and Operations in
Base Ten—2.NBT.3
MATHEMATICAL PRACTICES
MP.4

Use ▭▭▭▭ ▭ to model each number.

Tens	Ones

FOR THE TEACHER • After you read the following
problem, write 38 on the board. Have children
model the number. Emmanuel put 38 stickers on
his paper. How can you model 38 with blocks?
Continue the activity for 83 and 77.

Math Talk **Mathematical Practices**

Explain how you know
how many tens and ones
are in the number 29.

Chapter 1

What does 23 mean?

Tens	Ones

The 2 in 23 has a value of 2 tens, or 20.
The 3 in 23 has a value of 3 ones, or 3.

___2___ tens ___3___ ones

___20___ + ___3___

Share and Show

Draw a quick picture to show the number.
Describe the number in two ways.

1. 37

_____ tens _____ ones

_____ + _____

2. 54

_____ tens _____ ones

_____ + _____

3. 16

_____ ten _____ ones

_____ + _____

4. 60

_____ tens _____ ones

_____ + _____

Name _____

Draw a quick picture to show the number.
Describe the number in two ways.

5. 48

_____ tens _____ ones

_____ + _____

6. 31

_____ tens _____ one

_____ + _____

7. 59

_____ tens _____ ones

_____ + _____

8. 75

_____ tens _____ ones

_____ + _____

Solve. Write or draw to explain.

9. **THINK SMARTER** Eric has 4 bags
of 10 marbles and 6 single
marbles. How many marbles
does Eric have?

_____ marbles

Problem Solving • Applications   WRITE ▸ Math

MATHEMATICAL PRACTICE ⑥ **Make Connections**

Use crayons. Follow the steps.

10. Start at 51 and draw a green line to 43.

11. Draw a blue line from 43 to 34.

12. Draw a red line from 34 to 29.

13. Then draw a yellow line from 29 to 72.

1 ten 5 ones	30 + 2
4 tens 3 ones	20 + 9
10 + 2	3 tens 4 ones
	5 tens 1 one
70 + 2	7 + 2 ·

14. **THINK SMARTER** Draw a picture to show the number 26. Describe the number 26 in two ways.

_____ tens _____ ones

_____ + _____

TAKE HOME ACTIVITY • Ask your child to write 89 as tens plus ones. Then have him or her write 25 as tens plus ones.

FOR MORE PRACTICE: Standards Practice Book

Name _____

Different Ways to Write Numbers

Essential Question What are different ways to write a 2-digit number?

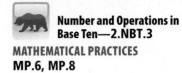

Number and Operations in Base Ten—2.NBT.3

MATHEMATICAL PRACTICES
MP.6, MP.8

Write the number. Then write it as tens and ones.

_____ tens _____ ones

_____ + _____

_____ + _____

_____ tens _____ ones

Math Talk

Mathematical Practices

In 44, do both digits have the same value? **Explain.**

FOR THE TEACHER • Read the following problem. Taryn counted 53 books on the table. How many tens and ones are in 53? Continue the activity with the numbers 78, 35, and 40.

A number can be written in different ways.

fifty-nine
5 tens 9 ones
50 + 9
59

ones	teen words	tens
0 zero	11 eleven	10 ten
1 one	12 twelve	20 twenty
2 two	13 thirteen	30 thirty
3 three	14 fourteen	40 forty
4 four	15 fifteen	50 fifty
5 five	16 sixteen	60 sixty
6 six	17 seventeen	70 seventy
7 seven	18 eighteen	80 eighty
8 eight	19 nineteen	90 ninety
9 nine		

Share and Show

Look at the examples above.
Then write the number another way.

1. thirty-two

_____

2. 20 + 7

_____

3. 63

_____ tens _____ ones

4. ninety-five

_____ + _____

5. 5 tens 1 one

_____

6. seventy-six

_____ + _____

7. twenty-eight

_____ tens _____ ones

8. 8 tens 0 ones

_____

30 thirty

Name _____

On Your Own

Write the number another way.

9. 2 tens 4 ones

_____

10. thirty

_____ tens _____ ones

11. eighty-five

_____

12. 54

_____ + _____

13. twelve

_____ + _____

14. 90 + 9

_____ tens _____ ones

15. 7 tens 8 ones

_____

16. 39

_____

THINK SMARTER Fill in the blanks to make the sentence true.

17. Sixty-seven is the same as _____ tens _____ ones.

_____

18. 4 tens _____ ones is the same as _____ + _____.

_____

19. 20 + _____ is the same as _____.

TAKE HOME ACTIVITY • Write 20 + 6 on a sheet of paper. Have your child write the 2-digit number. Repeat for 4 tens 9 ones.

FOR MORE PRACTICE: Standards Practice Book

✓ Mid-Chapter Checkpoint

Concepts and Skills

Shade in the ten frames to show the number.
Circle **even** or **odd**. (2.OA.3)

1. 15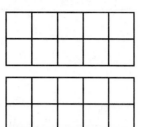

even   odd

2. 18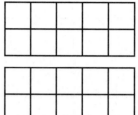

even   odd

Draw a quick picture to show the number.
Describe the number in two ways. (2.NBT.3)

3. 35

_____ tens _____ ones

_____ + _____

4. 53

_____ tens _____ ones

_____ + _____

5. **THINK SMARTER** Write the number 42 in another way. (2.NBT.3)

_____

Algebra • Different Names for Numbers

Essential Question How can you show the value of a number in different ways?

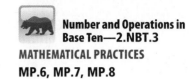

Number and Operations in Base Ten—2.NBT.3
MATHEMATICAL PRACTICES
MP.6, MP.7, MP.8

Listen and Draw Real World  Hands On

Use ▭▭▭ ▭ to show the number different ways.
Record the tens and ones.

_____ tens _____ ones

_____ tens _____ ones

_____ tens _____ ones

Math Talk

Mathematical Practices

Describe how you made the different models for 26.

FOR THE TEACHER • Read the following problem. Syed has 26 rocks. What are some different ways to show 26 with blocks? Have children start with 26 ones blocks. Then have them use base-ten blocks and record the number of tens and ones in each of their models.

Model and Draw

These are some different ways to show 32.

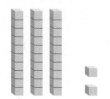   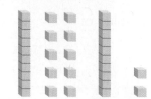   

__3__ tens __2__ ones   __2__ tens __12__ ones   __1__ ten __22__ ones

__30__ + __2__   __20__ + __12__   __10__ + __22__

Share and Show

The blocks show the numbers in different ways.
Describe the blocks in two ways.

✓ 1. **28**

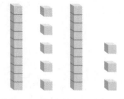   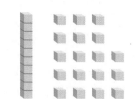

____ tens ____ ones   ____ ten ____ ones   ____ tens ____ ones

____ + ____   ____ + ____   ____ + ____

✓ 2. **35**

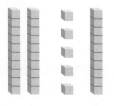   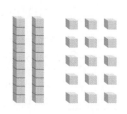   

____ tens ____ ones   ____ tens ____ ones   ____ tens ____ ones

____ + ____   ____ + ____   ____ + ____

34 thirty-four

Name _____

The blocks show the numbers in different ways.
Describe the blocks in two ways.

3. 43

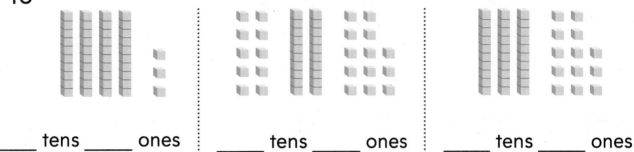

_____ tens _____ ones   _____ tens _____ ones   _____ tens _____ ones

_____ + _____   _____ + _____   _____ + _____

4. 30

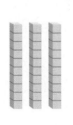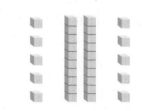

_____ tens _____ ones   _____ tens _____ ones   _____ tens _____ ones

_____ + _____   _____ + _____   _____ + _____

5. **THINK SMARTER**   I have 2 bags of 10 oranges.
I also have 24 single oranges.
How many oranges do I have?

I have _____ oranges.

Draw a quick picture to
show the number.

Problem Solving • Applications   WRITE ▸ Math

6. **MATHEMATICAL PRACTICE 6** Make Connections Fill in the blanks to make each sentence true.

_____ tens _____ ones is the same as 90 + 3.

_____

2 tens 18 ones is the same as _____ + _____.

_____

5 tens _____ ones is the same as _____ + 17.

_____

7. **GO DEEPER** A number has the digit 4 in the ones place and the digit 7 in the tens place. Which of these is another way to write this number? Circle them.

40 + 7   70 + 4   seventy-four

4 tens 34 ones   4 + 7   4 tens 7 ones

8. **THINK SMARTER** Which of these is another way to show the number 42? Choose Yes or No for each.

1 ten 42 ones	○ Yes	○ No
30 + 12	○ Yes	○ No
2 tens 22 ones	○ Yes	○ No
3 tens 2 ones	○ Yes	○ No

TAKE HOME ACTIVITY • Write the number 45. Have your child write or draw two ways to show this number.

FOR MORE PRACTICE:
Standards Practice Book

Name _____

Problem Solving • Tens and Ones

Essential Question How does finding a pattern help you find all the ways to show a number with tens and ones?

Number and Operations in Base Ten—2.NBT.3
MATHEMATICAL PRACTICES
MP.1, MP.4, MP.7

Gail needs to buy 32 pencils. She can buy single pencils or boxes of 10 pencils. What are all of the different ways Gail can buy 32 pencils?

🔑 Unlock the Problem (Real World)

What do I need to find?

ways Gail can buy
32 pencils

What information do I need to use?

She can buy _single_ pencils

or _boxes of 10_ pencils.

Show how to solve the problem.
Draw quick pictures for 32. Complete the chart.

Boxes of 10 pencils	Single pencils
3	2
2	12
1	
0	

HOME CONNECTION • Your child found a pattern in the different combinations of tens and ones. Using a pattern helps to make an organized list.

Find a pattern to solve.

1. Sara has 36 crayons. She can pack them in boxes of 10 crayons or as single crayons. What are all of the ways Sara can pack the crayons?

Boxes of 10 crayons	Single crayons
3	6

2. Mr. Winter is putting away 48 chairs. He can put away the chairs in stacks of 10 or as single chairs. What are all of the ways Mr. Winter can put away the chairs?

Stacks of 10 chairs	Single chairs
4	8

Math Talk   **Mathematical Practices**

Describe the pattern that helped you solve Exercise 2.

Share and Show

Find a pattern to solve.

☑ 3. Philip is putting 25 markers into a bag. He can put the markers in the bag as bundles of 10 or as single markers. What are all of the ways Philip can put the markers in the bag?

Bundles of 10 markers	Single markers

☑ 4. Stickers are sold in packs of 10 stickers or as single stickers. Miss Allen wants to buy 33 stickers. What are all of the ways she can buy the stickers?

Packs of 10 stickers	Single stickers

5. **THINK SMARTER** Devin had 32 baseball cards. He gets 7 more cards. He can pack them in boxes of 10 cards or as single cards. What are all of the ways Devin can sort the cards?

Boxes of 10 cards	Single cards

On Your Own

Solve. Write or draw to explain.

6. **MATHEMATICAL PRACTICE ⑦ Look for Structure**
   Lee can pack her toy cars in boxes of 10 cars
   or as single cars. Which of these is a way that
   she can pack her 24 toy cars? Circle your answer.

   | 4 boxes of 10 cars and 2 single cars | 1 box of 10 cars and 24 single cars | 2 boxes of 10 cars and 4 single cars |

Personal Math Trainer

7. **THINK SMARTER ➕** Mr. Link needs
   30 cups. He can buy them in
   packs of 10 cups or as single cups.
   What are all of the different
   ways he can buy the cups?
   Find a pattern to solve.

   Choose two of the ways
   from the chart. Explain how
   these two ways show the
   same number of cups.

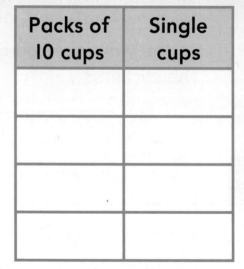

Packs of 10 cups	Single cups

TAKE HOME ACTIVITY • Have your child explain how
he or she solved one of the exercises in this lesson.

FOR MORE PRACTICE:
Standards Practice Book

Counting Patterns Within 100

Essential Question How do you count by 1s, 5s, and 10s with numbers less than 100?

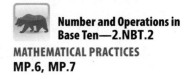

Number and Operations in Base Ten—2.NBT.2
MATHEMATICAL PRACTICES
MP.6, MP.7

Name _____

Listen and Draw

Look at the hundred chart. Write the missing numbers.

1	2	3		5	6		8		10
11		13	14	15	16		18	19	20
	22	23	24		26	27	28	29	30
31	32		34	35	36		38	39	
41		43	44	45	46	47		49	50
51		53		55		57		59	60
	62		64	65	66	67	68		70
71	72	73	74		76		78	79	
81		83		85	86	87	88	89	90
	92		94	95	96		98		100

Math Talk

Mathematical Practices

Describe some different ways to find the missing numbers in the chart.

FOR THE TEACHER • Have children complete the hundred chart to review counting to 100.

Model and Draw

You can count on by different amounts.
You can start counting with different numbers.

Count by ones.

1, 2, 3, 4, __5__, __6__, ___, ___

29, 30, 31, 32, __33__, ___, ___, ___

Count by fives.

5, 10, 15, 20, ___, ___, ___, ___

50, 55, 60, 65, ___, ___, ___, ___

Share and Show

Count by ones.

1. 15, 16, 17, _____, _____, _____, _____, _____

Count by fives.

2. 15, 20, 25, _____, _____, _____, _____, _____

3. 60, 65, _____, _____, _____, _____, _____

Count by tens.

4. 10, 20, _____, _____, _____, _____, _____

5. 30, 40, _____, _____, _____, _____, _____

On Your Own

Count by ones.

6. 77, 78, _____, _____, _____, _____, _____

7. 52, _____, _____, _____, _____, _____, _____

Count by fives.

8. 35, 40, _____, _____, _____, _____, _____

9. 70, _____, _____, _____, _____, _____, _____

Count by tens.

10. 20, 30, _____, _____, _____, _____, _____

11. **THINK SMARTER** Dinesh counts by fives to 100.
Gwen counts by tens to 100.
Who will say more numbers? Explain.

_____

_____

_____

_____

Problem Solving • Applications   WRITE ▶ Math

MATHEMATICAL PRACTICE ① Analyze

12. Andy counts by ones. He starts at 29 and stops at 45. Which of these numbers will he say? Circle them.

31   20
    47   35
    46
40   39

13. Camila counts by fives. She starts at 5 and stops at 50. Which of these numbers will she say? Circle them.

55   25
    6   40
        18
10   45

14. **THINK SMARTER** Grace starts at the number 40 and counts three different ways.
Write to show how Grace counts.

Count by ones. 40, _____, _____, _____, _____, _____, _____

Count by fives. 40, _____, _____, _____, _____, _____, _____

Count by tens. 40, _____, _____, _____, _____, _____, _____

 TAKE HOME ACTIVITY • With your child, practice counting by ones to 100, starting with numbers such as 58 or 62.

FOR MORE PRACTICE: Standards Practice Book

Name _____

Counting Patterns Within 1,000

Essential Question How do you count by 1s, 5s, 10s, and 100s with numbers less than 1,000?

Number and Operations in Base Ten—2.NBT.2
MATHEMATICAL PRACTICES
MP.6, MP.7

Listen and Draw

Write the missing numbers in the chart.

401		403	404		406	407	408		410
411				415	416	417	418	419	
421	422	423	424	425		427	428	429	430
	432		434	435	436	437	438		
441	442	443	444		446	447		449	450
			454	455	456	457	458	459	460
461	462						468	469	470
	472	473	474	475	476	477		479	480
481	482		484	485	486				490
	492	493		495	496	497	498		

Math Talk **Mathematical Practices**

What are the next three numbers that follow the counting in this chart? **Explain** how you know.

FOR THE TEACHER • Have children complete the number chart to practice counting with 3-digit numbers.

Counting can be done in different ways.
Use patterns to count on.

Count by fives.

95, 100, 105, __110__, __115__, _____, _____

140, 145, 150, __155__, _____, _____, _____

Count by tens.

300, 310, 320, _____, _____, _____, _____

470, 480, 490, _____, _____, _____, _____

Share and Show

Count by fives.

1. 745, 750, 755, _____, _____, _____, _____

Count by tens.

2. 520, 530, 540, _____, _____, _____, _____

3. 600, 610, _____, _____, _____, _____, _____

Count by hundreds.

4. 100, 200, _____, _____, _____, _____, _____

5. 300, 400, _____, _____, _____, _____, _____

On Your Own

Count by fives.

6. 215, 220, 225, _____, _____, _____, _____

7. 905, 910, _____, _____, _____, _____, _____

8. 485, _____, _____, _____, _____, _____

Count by tens.

9. 730, 740, 750, _____, _____, _____, _____

10. 160, 170, _____, _____, _____, _____, _____

11. 850, _____, _____, _____, _____, _____

Count by hundreds.

12. 200, 300, _____, _____, _____, _____, _____

13. **THINK SMARTER** Martin starts at 300 and counts by fives to 420. What are the last 6 numbers Martin will say?

_____, _____, _____, _____, _____, _____

Problem Solving • Applications WRITE Math

 **Look for a Pattern**

14. Lisa counts by fives. She starts at 120 and stops at 175. Which of these numbers will she say? Circle them.

170   135
   151
155   200   180

15. George counts by tens. He starts at 750 and stops at 830. Which of these numbers will he say? Circle them.

755   780
   690
760   795   810

16. THINK SMARTER Carl counts by hundreds. Which of these show ways that Carl could count? Choose Yes or No for each.

100, 110, 120, 130, 140	○ Yes	○ No
100, 200, 300, 400, 500	○ Yes	○ No
500, 600, 700, 800, 900	○ Yes	○ No
300, 305, 310, 315, 320	○ Yes	○ No

 TAKE HOME ACTIVITY • With your child, count by fives from 150 to 200.

FOR MORE PRACTICE:
Standards Practice Book

Name _____

1. Does the ten frame show an
   even number? Choose Yes or No.

   ○ Yes   ○ No

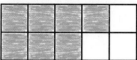   ○ Yes   ○ No

2. Write an even number between 7 and 16.
   Draw a picture and then write a sentence to
   explain why it is an even number.

_____

_____

3. What is the value of the digit 5 in the
   number 75?

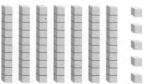   _____

4. Ted has an even number of yellow markers and an odd number of green markers. Choose all the groups of markers that could belong to Ted.

○   8 yellow markers and 3 green markers

○   3 yellow markers and 6 green markers

○   4 yellow markers and 2 green markers

○   6 yellow markers and 7 green markers

5. Jeff starts at 190 and counts by tens. What are the next 6 numbers Jeff will say?

190, _____, _____, _____, _____, _____, _____

6. Megan counts by ones to 10. Lee counts by fives to 20. Who will say more numbers? Explain.

_____

_____

_____

7. Draw a picture to show the number 43.

Describe the number 43 in two ways.

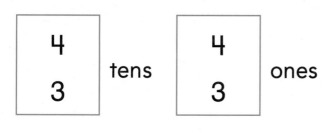

4
3 tens

4
3 ones

_____ + _____

---

8. Jo lives on Maple Road.
Her address has the digit 2 in
the ones place and the digit
4 in the tens place. What is
Jo's address?

_____ Maple Road

---

9. Do the numbers show counting by fives?
Choose Yes or No.

76, 77, 78, 79, 80	○ Yes	○ No
20, 30, 40, 50, 60	○ Yes	○ No
70, 75, 80, 85, 90	○ Yes	○ No
35, 40, 45, 50, 55	○ Yes	○ No

10. Mrs. Payne needs 35 notepads. She can buy them in packs of 10 notepads or as single pads. What are all the different ways Mrs. Payne can buy the notepads? Find a pattern to solve.

Packs of 10 notepads	Single notepads

Choose two of the ways from the chart. Explain how these two ways show the same number of notepads.

11. Ann has a favorite number. It has a digit less than 4 in the tens place. It has a digit greater than 6 in the ones place. Could the number be Ann's number? Choose Yes or No.

30 + 9   ○ Yes   ○ No

sixty-seven   ○ Yes   ○ No

2 tens 8 ones   ○ Yes   ○ No

Write another number that could be Ann's favorite. _____

Curious about Math

The White House has 412 doors and 147 windows. Look at the digit 1 in each of these numbers. How do the values of these digits compare?

Name _____

Show What You Know ✓

Identify Numbers to 30

Write how many.

1.  _____ leaves

2. 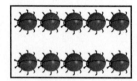   _____ bugs

Place Value: 2-Digit Numbers

Circle the value of the red digit.

3. **47**

    40   4

4. **84**

    4   40

5. **65**

    6   60

Compare 2-Digit Numbers Using Symbols

Compare. Write >, <, or =.

6.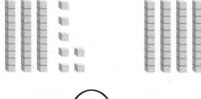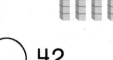

    37 ◯ 42

7.

    40 ◯ 33

This page checks understanding of important skills needed for success in Chapter 2.

Personal Math Trainer
Online Assessment and Intervention

© Houghton Mifflin Harcourt Publishing Company

Vocabulary Builder

Review Words

more

fewer

digits

tens

ones

Visualize It

Fill in the boxes of the graphic organizer.
Write sentences using **fewer** and **more**.

fewer

9 pens is fewer than 11 pens.

more

Understand Vocabulary

Use the review words. Complete the sentences.

1. 3 and 9 are _____ in the number 39.

2. 7 is in the _____ place in the number 87.

3. 8 is in the _____ place in the number 87.

GO DIGITAL
• Interactive Student Edition
• Multimedia eGlossary

Game

Fish for Digits

Materials

- 12 ● • 12 ○ • 1 🎲

Play with a partner.

1 Name a place for a digit. You can say **tens place** or **ones place**. Toss the 🎲.

2 Match the number on the 🎲 and the place that you named with a fish.

3 Put a ● on that fish. Take turns.

4 Match all the fish. The player with more ● on the board wins.

14

56

12

46

25

23

32

53

65

61

41

34

Name _____

Group Tens as Hundreds
Essential Question How do you group tens as hundreds?

Number and Operations in Base Ten—2.NBT.1.a, 2.NBT.1.b
MATHEMATICAL PRACTICES
MP.6, MP.7, MP.8

Circle groups of ten. Count the groups of ten.

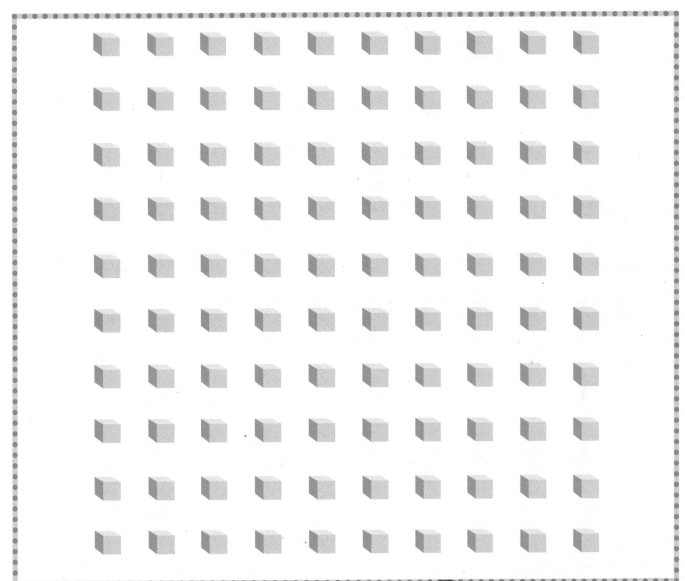

FOR THE TEACHER • Read the following problem and have children group ones blocks to solve. Marco has 100 cards. How many groups of 10 cards can he make?

Math Talk
Mathematical Practices
How many ones are in 3 tens? How many ones are in 7 tens? **Explain.**

Model and Draw

10 tens is the same as 1 **hundred**.

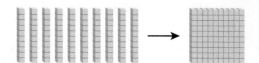 →

_____10_____ tens

_____1_____ hundred

_____100_____

Share and Show

MATH BOARD

Write how many tens. Circle groups of 10 tens.
Write how many hundreds. Write the number.

1.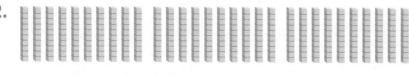

_____20_____ tens

_____ hundreds

_____

2.

_____ tens

_____ hundreds

_____

☑ 3.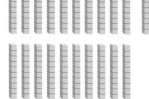

_____ tens

_____ hundreds

_____

☑ 4.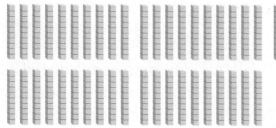

_____ tens

_____ hundreds

_____

On Your Own

Write how many tens. Circle groups of 10 tens.
Write how many hundreds. Write the number.

5.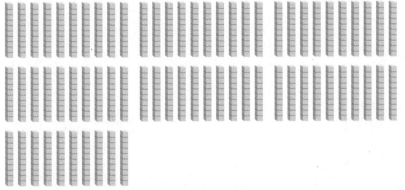

_____ tens

_____ hundreds

_____

6.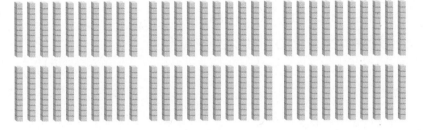

_____ tens

_____ hundreds

_____

7.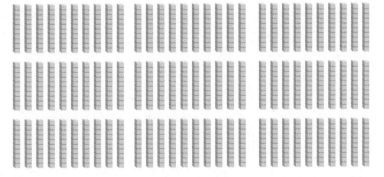

_____ tens

_____ hundreds

_____

8. **THINK SMARTER** Wally has 400 cards.
How many stacks of 10 cards
can he make?

_____ stacks of 10 cards

Problem Solving • Applications

WRITE ▸ Math

Solve. Write or draw to explain.

9. Mrs. Martin has 80 boxes of paper clips. There are 10 paper clips in each box. How many paper clips does she have?

_____ paper clips

10. **THINK SMARTER** Pencils are sold in boxes of 10 pencils. Mr. Lee needs 100 pencils. He has 40 pencils. How many boxes of 10 pencils should he buy?

_____ boxes of 10 pencils

Draw a picture to explain your answer.

TAKE HOME ACTIVITY • Ask your child to draw a quick picture of 20 tens and then tell you how many hundreds there are.

FOR MORE PRACTICE:
Standards Practice Book

© Houghton Mifflin Harcourt Publishing Company

Name _____

Explore 3-Digit Numbers

Essential Question How do you write a 3-digit number for a group of tens?

Number and Operations in Base Ten—2.NBT.1
MATHEMATICAL PRACTICES
MP.7, MP.8

Listen and Draw Real World

Circle groups of blocks to show hundreds.
Count the hundreds.

_____ hundreds

_____ straws

FOR THE TEACHER • Read the following problem and have children circle groups of tens blocks to solve. Mrs. Rodriguez has 30 bundles of straws. There are 10 straws in each bundle. How many straws does Mrs. Rodriguez have?

Math Talk

Mathematical Practices

Describe how the number of hundreds would be different if there were 10 more bundles of straws.

Model and Draw

What number is shown with 11 tens?

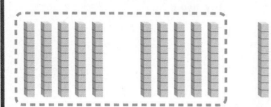

_11_ tens

_1_ hundred _1_ ten

_110_

In the number 110, there is a 1 in the hundreds place and a 1 in the tens place.

Share and Show

Circle tens to make 1 hundred. Write the number in different ways.

1.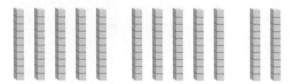

_____ tens

_____ hundred _____ tens

_____

☑ 2.

_____ tens

_____ hundred _____ tens

_____

☑ 3.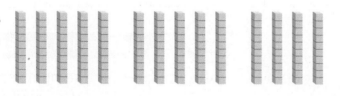

_____ tens

_____ hundred _____ tens

_____

On Your Own

Circle tens to make I hundred. Write the number in different ways.

4.

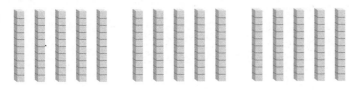

_____ tens

_____ hundred _____ tens

_____

5.

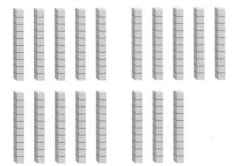

_____ tens

_____ hundred _____ tens

_____

6.

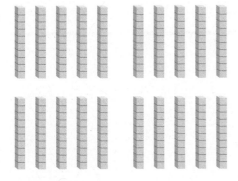

_____ tens

_____ hundreds _____ tens

_____

7. THINK SMARTER Kendra has 120 stickers. 10 stickers fill a page. How many pages can she fill?

_____ pages

Problem Solving • Applications

Solve. Write or draw to explain.

8. **MATHEMATICAL PRACTICE ①** **Analyze** There are 16 boxes of crackers. There are 10 crackers in each box. How many crackers are in the boxes?

_____ crackers

9. **GO DEEPER** Simon makes 8 towers of 10 blocks each. Ron makes 9 towers of 10 blocks each. How many blocks did they use?

_____ blocks

10. **THINK SMARTER** Ed has 150 marbles. How many bags of 10 marbles does he need to get so that he will have 200 marbles in all?

_____ bags of 10 marbles

 TAKE HOME ACTIVITY • Have your child draw 110 Xs by drawing 11 groups of 10 Xs.

FOR MORE PRACTICE:
Standards Practice Book

Name _____

Model 3-Digit Numbers

Essential Question How do you show a 3-digit number using blocks?

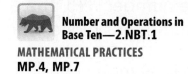

Number and Operations in Base Ten—2.NBT.1
MATHEMATICAL PRACTICES
MP.4, MP.7

Use ▭▭▭▭. Draw to show what you did.

```



```

FOR THE TEACHER • Read the following problem. Jack has 12 tens blocks. How many hundreds and tens does Jack have? Have children show Jack's blocks and then draw quick pictures. Then have children circle 10 tens and solve the problem.

Math Talk
Mathematical Practices

If Jack had 14 tens, how many hundreds and tens would he have? **Explain.**

Chapter 2

sixty-five **65**

Model and Draw

In the number 348, the 3 is in the hundreds place, the 4 is in the tens place, and the 8 is in the ones place.

Write how many hundreds, tens, and ones.	__3__ hundreds + __4__ tens + __8__ ones
Show the number 348 using blocks.	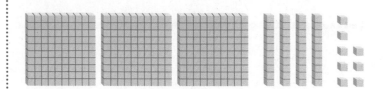
Draw a quick picture.	

Share and Show

MATH BOARD

Write how many hundreds, tens, and ones.

Show with _____ . Then draw a quick picture.

☑ 1. 234

__ hundreds + __ tens + __ ones

☑ 2. 156

__ hundred + __ tens + __ ones

Name _____

Write how many hundreds, tens, and ones.

Show with [image]. Then draw a quick picture.

3. 125

__ hundred + __ tens + __ ones

4. 312

__ hundreds + __ ten + __ ones

5. 245

__ hundreds + __ tens + __ ones

6. 103

__ hundred + __ tens + __ ones

7. 419

__ hundreds + __ ten + __ ones

8. 328

__ hundreds + __ tens + __ ones

Problem Solving • Applications

WRITE ▶ Math

9. **THINKSMARTER** How are the numbers 342 and 324 alike? How are they different?

_____

_____

_____

_____

MATHEMATICAL PRACTICE ④ Model Mathematics

Write the number for the clue.

10. A model for my number has 2 hundreds blocks, no tens blocks, and 3 ones blocks.

My number is _____.

11. A model for my number has 3 hundreds blocks, 5 tens blocks, and no ones blocks.

My number is _____.

12. **THINKSMARTER** There are 2 boxes of 100 pencils and some single pencils on the table. Choose all the numbers that show how many pencils could be on the table.

- ○ 200
- ○ 106
- ○ 203
- ○ 207

TAKE HOME ACTIVITY • Write the number 438. Have your child tell you the values of the digits in the number 438.

FOR MORE PRACTICE: Standards Practice Book

Hundreds, Tens, and Ones

Essential Question How do you write the 3-digit number that is shown by a set of blocks?

Number and Operations in Base Ten—2.NBT.1 *Also 2.NBT.3*
MATHEMATICAL PRACTICES
MP.7, MP.8

Listen and Draw Real World

Write the number of hundreds, tens, and ones.
Then draw a quick picture.

Hundreds	Tens	Ones

Hundreds	Tens	Ones

FOR THE TEACHER • Read the following to children. Sebastion has 243 yellow blocks. How many hundreds, tens, and ones are in this number? Repeat for 423 red blocks.

Math Talk **Mathematical Practices**

Describe how the two numbers are alike. **Describe** how they are different.

Write how many hundreds, tens,
and ones there are in the model.
What are two ways to write this number?

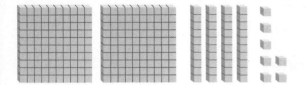

Hundreds	Tens	Ones
2	4	7

247

200 + 40 + 7

Share and Show

Write how many hundreds, tens, and ones are
in the model. Write the number in two ways.

1.

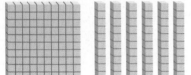

Hundreds	Tens	Ones

_____

_____ + _____ + _____

2.

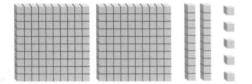

Hundreds	Tens	Ones

_____

_____ + _____ + _____

3.

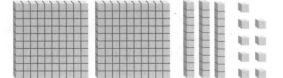

Hundreds	Tens	Ones

_____

_____ + _____ + _____

70 seventy

Name _____

Write how many hundreds, tens, and ones are in the model. Write the number in two ways.

4.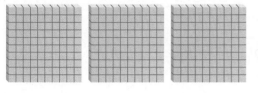

Hundreds	Tens	Ones

_____

_____ + _____ + _____

5.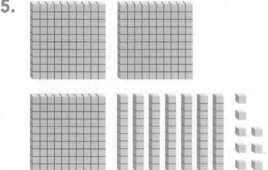

Hundreds	Tens	Ones

_____

_____ + _____ + _____

6.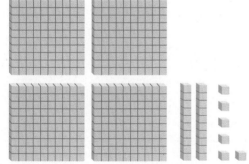

Hundreds	Tens	Ones

_____

_____ + _____ + _____

Solve. Write or draw to explain.

7. **THINK SMARTER** A model for my number has 4 ones blocks, 5 tens blocks, and 7 hundreds blocks. What number am I?

_____

Problem Solving • Applications WRITE ▸ Math

8. **GO DEEPER** The hundreds digit of my number is greater than the tens digit. The ones digit is less than the tens digit. What could my number be? Write it in two ways.

_____ + _____ + _____

_____

9. **THINK SMARTER** Karen has these bags of marbles. How many marbles does Karen have?

_____ marbles

Explain how you used the picture to find the number of marbles Karen has.

_____

_____

_____

TAKE HOME ACTIVITY • Say a 3-digit number, such as 546. Have your child draw a quick picture for that number.

FOR MORE PRACTICE: Standards Practice Book

Place Value to 1,000

Essential Question How do you know the values of the digits in numbers?

Number and Operations in Base Ten—2.NBT.1

MATHEMATICAL PRACTICES
MP.6, MP.7

Write the numbers. Then draw quick pictures.

_____ sheets of color paper

Hundreds	Tens	Ones

_____ sheets of plain paper

Hundreds	Tens	Ones

Math Talk
Mathematical Practices

Describe how 5 tens is different from 5 hundreds.

FOR THE TEACHER • Read the following. There are 245 sheets of color paper in the closet. There are 458 sheets of plain paper by the table. Have children write each number and draw quick pictures to show the numbers.

© Houghton Mifflin Harcourt Publishing Company

The place of a digit in a number tells its value.

327

The 3 in 327 has a value of 3 hundreds, or 300.

The 2 in 327 has a value of 2 tens, or 20.

The 7 in 327 has a value of 7 ones, or 7.

There are 10 hundreds in 1 **thousand**.

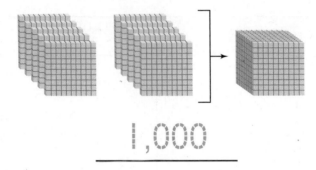

1,000

The 1 is in the thousands place and has a value of 1 thousand.

Share and Show

Circle the value or the meaning of the red digit.

1. 702	2 ones	2 tens	2 hundreds
2. 459	500	50	5
3. 362	3 hundreds	3 tens	3 ones

On Your Own

Circle the value or the meaning of the red digit.

4. 549	400	40	4
5. 607	7 ones	7 tens	7 hundreds
6. 1,000	1 one	1 hundred	1 thousand
7. 914	90	900	9,000
8. 380	800	80	8
9. 692	6 ones	6 tens	6 hundreds

10. **Go DEEPER** Write the number that matches the clues.

- The value of my hundreds digit is 300.
- The value of my tens digit is 0.
- The value of my ones digit is an even number greater than 7.

The number is _____.

Problem Solving • Applications | WRITE ▶ Math

Math on the Spot

11. **THINK SMARTER** Ty is making a Venn diagram. Where in the diagram should he write the other numbers?

Numbers with a 5
in the Tens Place

Numbers with a 2
in the Hundreds Place

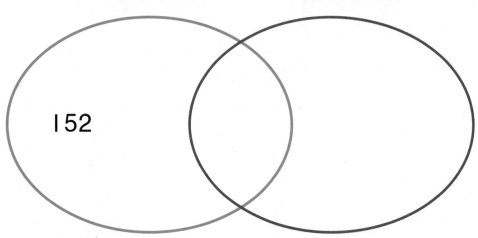

152

| ~~152~~ |
| 215 |
| 454 |
| 257 |
| 352 |
| 205 |
| 250 |

12. **MATHEMATICAL PRACTICE ③** **Apply** Describe where 752 should be written in the diagram. Explain your answer.

_____

_____

_____

Personal Math Trainer

13. **THINK SMARTER +** Fill in the bubble next to all the numbers that have a digit 4 in the tens place.

○ 764

○ 149

○ 437

○ 342

TAKE HOME ACTIVITY • Ask your child to write 3-digit numbers, such as "a number with 2 hundreds" and "a number with a 9 in the ones place."

FOR MORE PRACTICE:
Standards Practice Book

© Houghton Mifflin Harcourt Publishing Company

Name _____

Number Names

Essential Question How do you write 3-digit numbers using words?

Number and Operations in Base Ten—2.NBT.3
MATHEMATICAL PRACTICES
MP.7

Listen and Draw

Write the missing numbers in the chart. Then find and circle the word form of these numbers below.

	12	13		15	16	17	18	19	20
21	22	23	24	25	26	27	28		30
31	32	33	34		36	37	38	39	40
41	42	43	44	45		47	48	49	50
51		53	54	55	56	57	58	59	60

forty-one   ninety-two   fourteen

eleven   thirty-five   forty-six

fifty-three   twenty-nine   fifty-two

Math Talk **Mathematical Practices**

Describe how to use words to write the number with a 5 in the tens place and a 7 in the ones place.

HOME CONNECTION • In this activity, your child reviewed the word form of numbers less than 100.

You can use words to write 3-digit numbers.
First, look at the hundreds digit. Then, look at
the tens digit and ones digit together.

245

two hundred forty-five

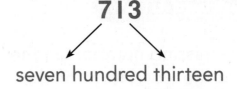

713

seven hundred thirteen

Share and Show

Write the number using words.

1. 506

   ~~five hundred six~~

   _____

2. 189

   _____

☑ 3. 328

   _____

Write the number.

4. four hundred fifteen

   _____

5. two hundred ninety-one

   _____

6. six hundred three

   _____

☑ 7. eight hundred forty-seven

   _____

78 seventy-eight

Name _____

Write the number.

8. seven hundred seventeen

_____

9. three hundred ninety

_____

10. six hundred forty-three

_____

11. nine hundred twelve

_____

12. four hundred twenty-six

_____

13. eight hundred seventy-one

_____

Write the number using words.

14. 632

_____

15. 568

_____

16. 321

_____

17. Alma counts two hundred sixty-eight leaves. Which is another way to write this number? Circle your answer.

$2 + 6 + 8$

$200 + 60 + 8$

$2 + 60 + 8$

Problem Solving • Applications  WRITE ▸ Math

MATHEMATICAL PRACTICE ② Connect Symbols and Words

Circle the answer for each problem.

18. Derek counts one hundred ninety cars. Which is another way to write this number?

119

190

910

19. Beth counted three hundred fifty-six straws. Which is another way to write this number?

3 + 5 + 6

30 + 50 + 60

300 + 50 + 6

20. THINK SMARTER There are 537 chairs at the school. Write this number using words.

_____

Show the number in two other ways.

Hundreds	Tens	Ones

_____ + _____ + _____

 TAKE HOME ACTIVITY • Ask your child to write the number 940 using words.

FOR MORE PRACTICE:
Standards Practice Book

Name _____

Different Forms of Numbers

Essential Question What are three ways
to write a 3-digit number?

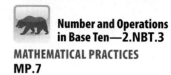

**Number and Operations
in Base Ten—2.NBT.3**

MATHEMATICAL PRACTICES
MP.7

Listen and Draw Real World

Write the number. Use the digits to write
how many hundreds, tens, and ones.

_____ hundreds _____ tens _____ ones

_____ hundreds _____ tens _____ ones

_____ hundreds _____ tens _____ one

FOR THE TEACHER • Read the following: Evan has
426 marbles. How many hundreds, tens, and ones
are in 426? Continue the activity for 204 and 341.

 Math Talk

Mathematical Practices

How many hundreds are
in 368? **Explain.**

© Houghton Mifflin Harcourt Publishing Company

You can use a quick picture to show a number.
You can write a number in different ways.

five hundred thirty-six

_5_ hundreds _3_ tens _6_ ones

_500_ + _30_ + _6_

_536_

Share and Show

Read the number and draw a quick picture.
Then write the number in different ways.

1. four hundred seven

_____ hundreds _____ tens _____ ones

_____ + _____ + _____

_____

☑ 2. three hundred twenty-five

_____ hundreds _____ tens _____ ones

_____ + _____ + _____

_____

☑ 3. two hundred fifty-three

_____ hundreds _____ tens _____ ones

_____ + _____ + _____

_____

Name _____

Read the number and draw a quick picture.
Then write the number in different ways.

4. one hundred seventy-two

_____ hundred _____ tens _____ ones

_____ + _____ + _____

_____

5. three hundred forty-six

_____ hundreds _____ tens _____ ones

_____ + _____ + _____

_____

6. two hundred sixty-four

_____ hundreds _____ tens _____ ones

_____ + _____ + _____

_____

7. **THINK SMARTER** Ellen used these blocks to show 452.
What is wrong? Cross out blocks and draw
quick pictures for missing blocks.

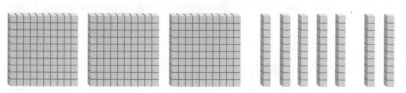

TAKE HOME ACTIVITY • Ask your child to show
the number 315 in three different ways.

© Houghton Mifflin Harcourt Publishing Company

FOR MORE PRACTICE:
Standards Practice Book

Name _____

Concepts and Skills

Circle tens to make 1 hundred. Write the number
in different ways. (2.NBT.1)

1.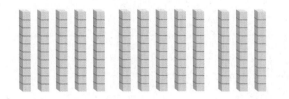

_____ tens

_____ hundred _____ tens

_____

Write how many hundreds, tens, and ones are in
the model. Write the number in two ways. (2.NBT.1)

2.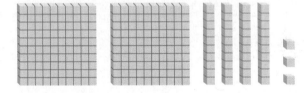

Hundreds	Tens	Ones

_____

_____ + _____ + _____

Circle the value or the meaning of the red digit. (2.NBT.1)

3. 528   5   50   500

4. 674   4 ones   4 tens   4 hundreds

5. THINK SMARTER Write the number
six hundred forty-five in another way. (2.NBT.3)

_____

Chapter 2

Algebra • Different Ways to Show Numbers

Essential Question How can you use blocks or quick pictures to show the value of a number in different ways?

Number and Operations
in Base Ten—2.NBT.3
MATHEMATICAL PRACTICES
MP.3, MP.6, MP.7

 **Listen and Draw** Real World

Draw quick pictures to solve.
Write how many tens and ones.

_____ tens _____ ones

_____ tens _____ ones

 FOR THE TEACHER • Read this problem to children. Mrs. Peabody has 35 books on a cart to take to classrooms. She can use boxes that each hold 10 books. She can also place single books on the cart. What are two different ways she can put the books on the cart?

 Math Talk **Mathematical Practices**

Describe how you found different ways to show 35 books.

Here are two ways to show 148.

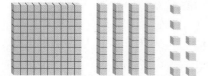

Hundreds	Tens	Ones
1	4	8

Hundreds	Tens	Ones
0	14	8

Share and Show

Write how many hundreds, tens, and ones are in the model.

✓ 1. 213

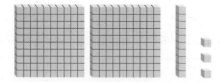

Hundreds	Tens	Ones

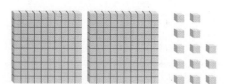

Hundreds	Tens	Ones

✓ 2. 132

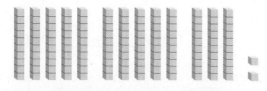

Hundreds	Tens	Ones

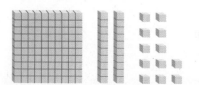

Hundreds	Tens	Ones

On Your Own

Write how many hundreds, tens, and ones are in the model.

3. 144

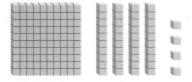

Hundreds	Tens	Ones

Hundreds	Tens	Ones

4. 204

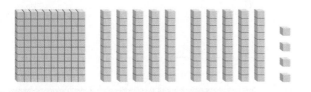

Hundreds	Tens	Ones

Hundreds	Tens	Ones

5. **MATHEMATICAL PRACTICE ③** Make Arguments

Sue said that 200 + 20 + 23 is the same as 200 + 30 + 3. Is she correct? Explain.

_____

_____

_____

Problem Solving • Applications

 WRITE Math

Marbles are sold in boxes, in bags, or as single marbles. Each box has 10 bags of marbles in it. Each bag has 10 marbles in it.

6. **THINK SMARTER** Draw pictures to show two ways to buy 324 marbles.

Use the marble information above.

7. **THINK SMARTER** There is only one box of marbles in the store. There are many bags of marbles and single marbles. Draw a picture to show a way to buy 312 marbles.

How many boxes, bags, and single marbles did you show?

TAKE HOME ACTIVITY • Write the number 156. Have your child draw quick pictures of two ways to show this number.

FOR MORE PRACTICE: Standards Practice Book

Name _____

Count On and Count Back by 10 and 100

Essential Question How do you use place value to find 10 more, 10 less, 100 more, or 100 less than a 3-digit number?

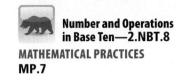

Number and Operations in Base Ten—2.NBT.8
MATHEMATICAL PRACTICES
MP.7

Draw quick pictures for the numbers.

Girls

Hundreds	Tens	Ones

Boys

Hundreds	Tens	Ones

FOR THE TEACHER • Tell children that there are 342 girls at Center School. Have children draw quick pictures for 342. Then tell them that there are 352 boys at the school. Have them draw quick pictures for 352.

Math Talk

Mathematical Practices

Describe how the two numbers are different.

You can show 10 less or 10 more than a number by changing the digit in the tens place.

10 less than 264

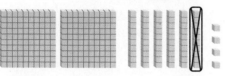

Hundreds	Tens	Ones
2	5	4

10 more than 264

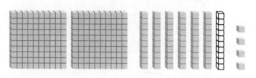

Hundreds	Tens	Ones
2	7	4

You can show 100 less or 100 more than a number by changing the digit in the hundreds place.

100 less than 264

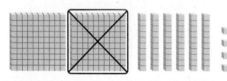

Hundreds	Tens	Ones
1	6	4

100 more than 264

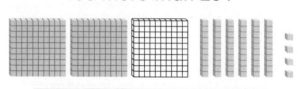

Hundreds	Tens	Ones
3	6	4

Share and Show

Write the number.

1. 10 more than 648

   _____

2. 100 less than 513

   _____

✓ 3. 100 more than 329

   _____

✓ 4. 10 less than 827

   _____

On Your Own

Write the number.

5. 10 more than 471

_____

6. 10 less than 143

_____

7. 100 more than 555

_____

8. 100 less than 757

_____

9. 100 more than 900

_____

10. 10 less than 689

_____

11. 100 less than 712

_____

12. 10 less than 254

_____

13. 10 more than 986

_____

14. 100 less than 392

_____

15. **THINK SMARTER** Rick has 10 more crayons than Lori. Lori has 136 crayons. Tom has 10 fewer crayons than Rick. How many crayons does each child have?

Red

Rick: _____ crayons

Tom: _____ crayons

Lori: _____ crayons

Problem Solving • Applications  WRITE) Math

 **Analyze Relationships**

16. Juan's book has 248 pages. This is 10 more pages than there are in Kevin's book. How many pages are in Kevin's book?

_____ pages

17. There are 217 pictures in Tina's book. There are 100 fewer pictures in Mark's book. How many pictures are in Mark's book?

_____ pictures

18. **GO DEEPER** Use the clues to answer the question.

- Shawn counts 213 cars.

- Maria counts 100 fewer cars than Shawn.

- Jayden counts 10 more cars than Maria.

How many cars does Jayden count?   _____ cars

19. **THINK SMARTER** Rico has 235 stickers.
Gabby has 100 more stickers than Rico.
Thomas has 10 fewer stickers than Gabby.
Write the number of stickers each child has.

_____   _____   _____
   Rico   Gabby   Thomas

 TAKE HOME ACTIVITY • Write the number 596. Have your child name the number that is 100 more than 596.

FOR MORE PRACTICE:
Standards Practice Book

Name _____

Algebra • Number Patterns

Essential Question How does place value help you identify and extend counting patterns?

Number and Operations in Base Ten—2.NBT.8
MATHEMATICAL PRACTICES
MP.7

Shade the numbers in the counting pattern.

801	802	803	804	805	806	807	808	809	810
811	812	813	814	815	816	817	818	819	820
821	822	823	824	825	826	827	828	829	830
831	832	833	834	835	836	837	838	839	840
841	842	843	844	845	846	847	848	849	850
851	852	853	854	855	856	857	858	859	860
861	862	863	864	865	866	867	868	869	870
871	872	873	874	875	876	877	878	879	880
881	882	883	884	885	886	887	888	889	890
891	892	893	894	895	896	897	898	899	900

FOR THE TEACHER • Read the following problem and discuss how children can use a counting pattern to solve. At Blossom Bakery, 823 muffins were sold in the morning. In the afternoon, four packages of 10 muffins were sold. How many muffins were sold that day?

Math Talk **Mathematical Practices**

What number is next in the counting pattern you see? **Explain.**

Chapter 2

ninety-three **93**

Model and Draw

Look at the digits in the numbers. What two numbers are next in the counting pattern?

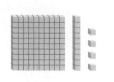 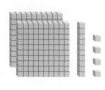 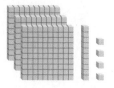 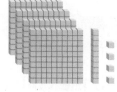

H T O   H T O   H T O   H T O

114,   214,   314,   414,   ▨,   ▨

The ___hundreds___ digit changes by one each time.

The next two numbers are __514__ and __614__.

Share and Show

MATH BOARD

Look at the digits to find the next two numbers.

1. H T O H T O H T O H T O
   137, 147, 157, 167, ▨7, ▨

   The next two numbers are __177__ and __187__.

2. H T O H T O H T O H T O
   245, 345, 445, 545, ▨, ▨

   The next two numbers are __645__ and __745__.

3. H T O H T O H T O H T O
   421, 431, 441, 451, ▨, ▨

   The next two numbers are __461__ and __472__.

4. H T H T O H T O H T O
   389, 489, 589, 689, ▨, ▨

   The next two numbers are __699__ and __700__.

On Your Own

Look at the digits to find the next two numbers.

5. HTO HTO HTO HTO 193, 293, 393, 493,  ■, ■

   The next two numbers are _543_ and _693_.

6. HTO HTO HTO HTO 484, 494, 504, 514, ■, ■

   The next two numbers are _524_ and _534_.

7. HTO HTO HTO HTO 500, 600, 700, 800, ■, ■

   The next two numbers are _900_ and _1000_.

8. HTO HTO HTO HTO 655, 665, 675, 685, ■, ■

   The next two numbers are _695_ and _765_.

9. **THINK SMARTER** Mark read 203 pages.
   Laney read 100 more pages than Mark.
   Gavin read 10 fewer pages than Laney.
   How many pages did Gavin read?

_293_ pages

Problem Solving • Applications  WRITE ▶ Math

Solve.

10. **GO DEEPER** There were 135 buttons in a jar. After Robin put more buttons into the jar, there were 175 buttons in the jar. How many groups of 10 buttons did she put into the jar?

_____ groups of 10 buttons

Explain how you solved the problem.

_____

_____

_____

_____

11. **THINK SMARTER** Write the next number in each counting pattern.

162, 262, 362, 462, _____

347, 357, 367, 377, _____

609, 619, 629, 639, _____

 TAKE HOME ACTIVITY • With your child, take turns writing number patterns in which you count on by tens or by hundreds.

FOR MORE PRACTICE:
Standards Practice Book

Name _____

Problem Solving • Compare Numbers

Essential Question How can you make a model
to solve a problem about comparing numbers?

**Number and Operations in
Base Ten—2.NBT.4**
MATHEMATICAL PRACTICES
MP.2, MP.4

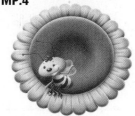

Children bought 217 boxes of chocolate milk
and 188 boxes of plain milk. Did they buy
more boxes of chocolate milk or plain milk?

⚷ Unlock the Problem (Real World)

What do I need to find?

if the children bought ___more___

~~boxes of chocolate milk~~

~~or plain milk~~

What information do I need to use?

_____ boxes of chocolate
milk

_____ boxes of plain milk

Show how to solve the problem.
Model the numbers. Draw quick pictures of your models.

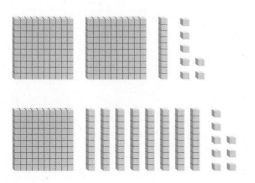

The children bought more boxes of _____ milk.

HOME CONNECTION • Your child used base-ten blocks to represent the
numbers in the problem. These models were used as a tool for comparing
numbers to solve the problem.

Model the numbers. Draw quick pictures to show how you solved the problem.

- What do I need to find?
- What information do I need to use?

1. At the zoo, there are 137 birds and 142 reptiles. Are there more birds or more reptiles at the zoo?

more _____

2. Tom's book has 105 pages.
Delia's book has 109 pages.
Whose book has fewer pages?

_____ book

Math Talk **Mathematical Practices**

Explain what you did to solve the second problem.

Name _____

Share and Show

Model the numbers. Draw quick pictures
to show how you solved the problem.

✓3. Mary's puzzle has
164 pieces. Jake's puzzle
has 180 pieces. Whose
puzzle has more pieces?

_____ puzzle

✓4. There are 246 people at
the game. There are
251 people at the museum.
At which place are there
fewer people?

at the _____

5. There are 131 crayons in a
box. There are 128 crayons in
a bag. Are there more crayons
in the box or in the bag?

in the _____

6. There are 308 books in
the first room. There are
273 books in the second
room. In which room are
there fewer books?

in the _____ room

Problem Solving • Applications WRITE Math

7. **THINK SMARTER** There are 748 children at Dan's school. There are 651 children at Karen's school. There are 763 children at Jason's school. Which school has more than 759 children?

_____ school

8. **MATHEMATICAL PRACTICE ①** Analyze There are 136 crayons in a box. Use the digits 4, 1, and 2 to write a number that is greater than 136.

_____

9. **THINK SMARTER** Becky has 134 stamps. Sara has 129 stamps. Who has more stamps?

_____

Sara buys 10 more stamps. Who has more stamps now?

_____

Draw quick pictures to show the stamps Becky and Sara have now.

 TAKE HOME ACTIVITY • Ask your child to explain how he or she solved one of the problems on this page.

FOR MORE PRACTICE: Standards Practice Book

Name _____

Algebra • Compare Numbers

Essential Question How do you compare 3-digit numbers?

Number and Operations in Base Ten—2.NBT.4
MATHEMATICAL PRACTICES
MP.6, MP.8

 **Listen and Draw** **Real World**

Draw quick pictures to solve the problem.

More _____ were at the park.

 FOR THE TEACHER • Read the following problem and have children draw quick pictures to compare the numbers. There were 125 butterflies and 132 birds at the park. Were there more butterflies or more birds at the park?

 Math Talk **Mathematical Practices**

Explain how you compared the numbers.

Chapter 2

one hundred one **101**

Use place value to **compare** numbers. Start by looking at the digits in the greatest place value position first.

> is greater than
< is less than
= is equal to

Hundreds	Tens	Ones
4	8	3
5	7	0

4 hundreds < 5 hundreds

483 ⊘ 570

Hundreds	Tens	Ones
3	5	2
3	4	6

The hundreds are equal.

5 tens > 4 tens

352 ⊘ 346

Share and Show

Compare the numbers. Write >, <, or =.

1.

Hundreds	Tens	Ones
2	3	9
1	7	9

239 ◯ 179

2.

Hundreds	Tens	Ones
4	3	5
4	3	7

435 ◯ 437

✓3.   764
     674

764 ◯ 674

✓4.   519
     572

519 ◯ 572

On Your Own

Compare the numbers. Write $>$, $<$, or $=$.

5.
378

504

378 $\bigcirc$ 504

6.
821

821

821 $\bigcirc$ 821

7.
560

439

560 $\bigcirc$ 439

8.
934

943

934 $\bigcirc$ 943

9.
475

475

475 $\bigcirc$ 475

10.
736

687

736 $\bigcirc$ 687

MATHEMATICAL PRACTICE ② **Use Reasoning** Write a 3-digit number in the box that makes the comparison true.

11. $526 <$ ☐

12. $319 >$ ☐

13. ☐ > 782

14. ☐ < 131

Problem Solving • Applications

 WRITE ▸ Math

Solve. Write or draw to explain.

15. **THINK SMARTER** Mrs. York has 300 red stickers, 50 blue stickers, and 8 green stickers. Mr. Reed has 372 stickers. Who has more stickers?

_____

16. **MATHEMATICAL PRACTICE ①** Analyze Jasmine has some number cards. Use the digits on these cards to make two 3-digit numbers. Use each digit only once. Compare the numbers.

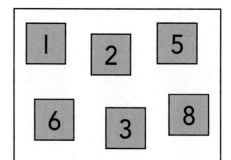

_____ ◯ _____

Personal Math Trainer

17. **THINK SMARTER +** Is the comparison true? Choose Yes or No.

453 > 354   ○ Yes   ○ No

253 < 164   ○ Yes   ○ No

391 > 417   ○ Yes   ○ No

490 < 528   ○ Yes   ○ No

 TAKE HOME ACTIVITY • Have your child explain how to compare the numbers 281 and 157.

FOR MORE PRACTICE: Standards Practice Book

Chapter 2 Review/Test

1.

Do the choices show a way to represent the blocks? Choose Yes or No.

3 hundreds	○ Yes	○ No
30 ones	○ Yes	○ No
30 hundreds	○ Yes	○ No
30 tens	○ Yes	○ No

2. Robin has 180 stickers. How many pages of 10 stickers does she need so that she will have 200 stickers in all?

_____ pages of stickers

3. Sanjo has 348 marbles. Harry has 100 fewer marbles than Sanjo. Ari has 10 more marbles than Harry. Write the number of marbles each child has.

_____ _____ _____
  Sanjo   Ari   Harry

GO DIGITAL Assessment Options Chapter Test

4. Write the next number in each counting pattern.

214, 314, 414, 514, _____

123, 133, 143, 153, _____

5. Is the comparison true? Choose Yes or No.

$787 < 769$	○ Yes	○ No
$405 > 399$	○ Yes	○ No
$396 > 402$	○ Yes	○ No
$128 < 131$	○ Yes	○ No

6. Cody is thinking of the number 627. Write Cody's number in words.

_____

Show Cody's number in two other ways.

Hundreds	Tens	Ones

_____ + _____ + _____

7. Matty needs 200 buttons. Amy gives her 13 bags with 10 buttons in each bag. How many buttons does she need now?

_____ buttons

---

8. There are 4 boxes of 100 sheets of paper and some single sheets of paper in the closet. Choose all the numbers that show how many sheets of paper could be in the closet.

○ 348   ○ 324

○ 406   ○ 411

---

9. Blocks are sold in boxes, in bags, or as single blocks. Each box has 10 bags in it. Each bag has 10 blocks in it. Tara needs 216 blocks. Draw a picture to show a way to buy 216 blocks.

How many boxes, bags, and single blocks did you show?

_____

_____

10. Dan and Hannah collect toy cars. Dan has 132 cars. Hannah has 138 cars. Who has more cars?

_____

Dan gets 10 more cars. Hannah gets 3 more cars. Who has more cars now?

_____

Draw quick pictures to show how many cars Dan and Hannah have now.

Dan's Cars	Hannah's Cars

11. Choose all the numbers that have the digit 2 in the tens place.

- ○ 721
- ○ 142
- ○ 425
- ○ 239

12. Ann has 239 shells. Write the number in words.

_____

© Houghton Mifflin Harcourt Publishing Company

All About Animals

by John Hudson

CRITICAL AREA Building fluency with addition and subtraction

The giraffe is the tallest land animal in the world. Adult giraffes are 13 to 17 feet tall. Newborn giraffes are about 6 feet tall.

A group of 5 giraffes drinks water at a watering hole. A group of 5 giraffes eats leaves from trees. How many giraffes are there in all?

_____ giraffes

How do giraffes care for their young?

The ostrich is the largest bird in the world. Ostriches cannot fly, but they can run fast. Ostrich eggs weigh about 3 pounds each! Several ostriches will lay eggs in a shared nest.

There are 6 eggs in a nest. Then 5 more eggs are put in that nest. How many eggs are in the nest now?

_____ eggs

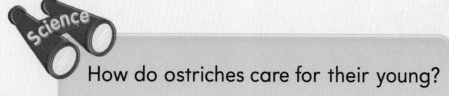

How do ostriches care for their young?

Kangaroos can move quickly by jumping with their two back legs. When they are moving slowly, they use all four legs.

Western gray kangaroos live in groups called mobs. There are 8 kangaroos in a mob. 4 more kangaroos join the mob. How many kangaroos are in the mob in all?

_____ kangaroos

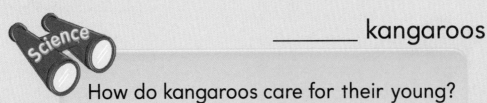

How do kangaroos care for their young?

Wild boars like to eat roots. They use their tough snouts to dig. Wild boars can be up to 6 feet long.

Wild boars live in groups called sounders. There is one sounder of 14 boars. If 7 of the boars are eating, how many boars are not eating?

_____ boars

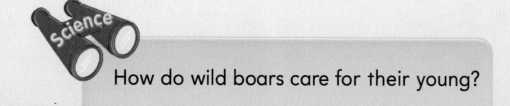

How do wild boars care for their young?

Moose are the largest kind of deer. Male moose have antlers that may be 5 to 6 feet wide. Moose can trot and gallop. They are also good swimmers!

A ranger saw 7 moose in the morning and 6 moose in the afternoon. How many moose did the ranger see that day?

_____ moose

Science

How do moose care for their young?

Write About the Story

Choose one kind of animal.
Draw a picture and write your own
story about that kind of animal.
Use addition in your story.

Vocabulary Review

add   in all

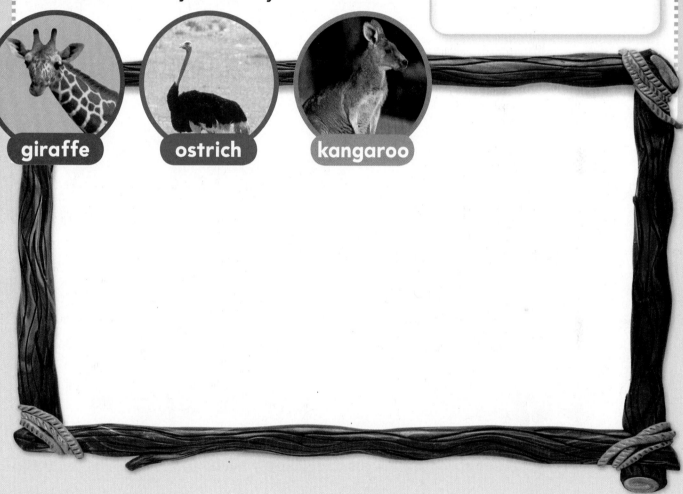

giraffe   ostrich   kangaroo

WRITE ▸ Math

_____

_____

_____

_____

How many eggs are there?

Draw more ostrich eggs in each nest.
Write an addition sentence below each
nest to show how many eggs are in
each nest now.

_____

_____

 Choose a different animal from the story.
Write another story that uses addition.

Basic Facts and Relationships

Curious
about
Math

Parrot fish live near coral reefs in tropical ocean waters. They use their sharp teeth to scrape food off of the coral.

Suppose 10 parrot fish are eating at a coral reef. 3 of the fish swim away. How many fish are still eating?

Name _____

Use Symbols to Add

Use the picture. Use + and = to complete
the addition sentence.

1.    3 ◯ 1 ◯ 4

2.    2 ◯ 3 ◯ 5

Sums to 10

Write the sum.

| 3. | 4
+3 | 4. | 5
+0 | 5. | 2
+7 | 6. | 6
+2 | 7. | 9
+1 |

Doubles and Doubles Plus One

Write the addition sentence.

8.

____ ◯ ____ ◯ ____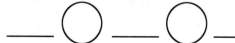

9.

____ ◯ ____ ◯ ____

This page checks understanding of important skills needed
for success in Chapter 3.

Personal Math Trainer
Online Assessment
and Intervention

Vocabulary Builder

Review Words

addition
subtraction
plus
minus
equals
count on
count back

Visualize It

Sort the review words in the graphic organizer.

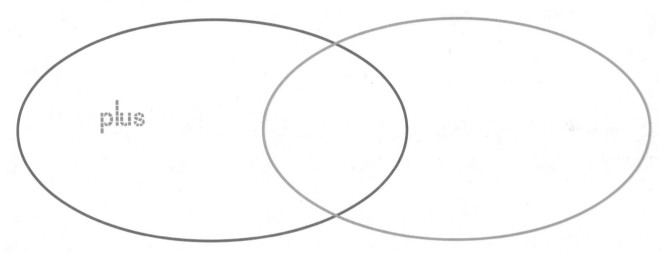

Addition Words   **Subtraction** Words

plus

Understand Vocabulary

1. Circle the **addition** sentence. $3 + 6 = 9$ $9 - 6 = 3$

2. Circle the **subtraction** sentence. $8 + 2 = 10$ $10 - 2 = 8$

3. Circle the **count on** fact. $5 - 1 = 4$ $4 + 1 = 5$

4. Circle the **count back** fact. $8 - 2 = 6$ $6 + 2 = 8$

GO DIGITAL
• Interactive Student Edition
• Multimedia eGlossary

Game Caterpillar Chase

Materials

- 1 🔲
- 1 🔲
- 1 🎲

Play with a partner.

1. Put your cube on START.
2. Toss the 🎲, and move that many spaces.

3. Say the sum or difference. Your partner checks your answer.
4. Take turns. The first person to get to FINISH wins.

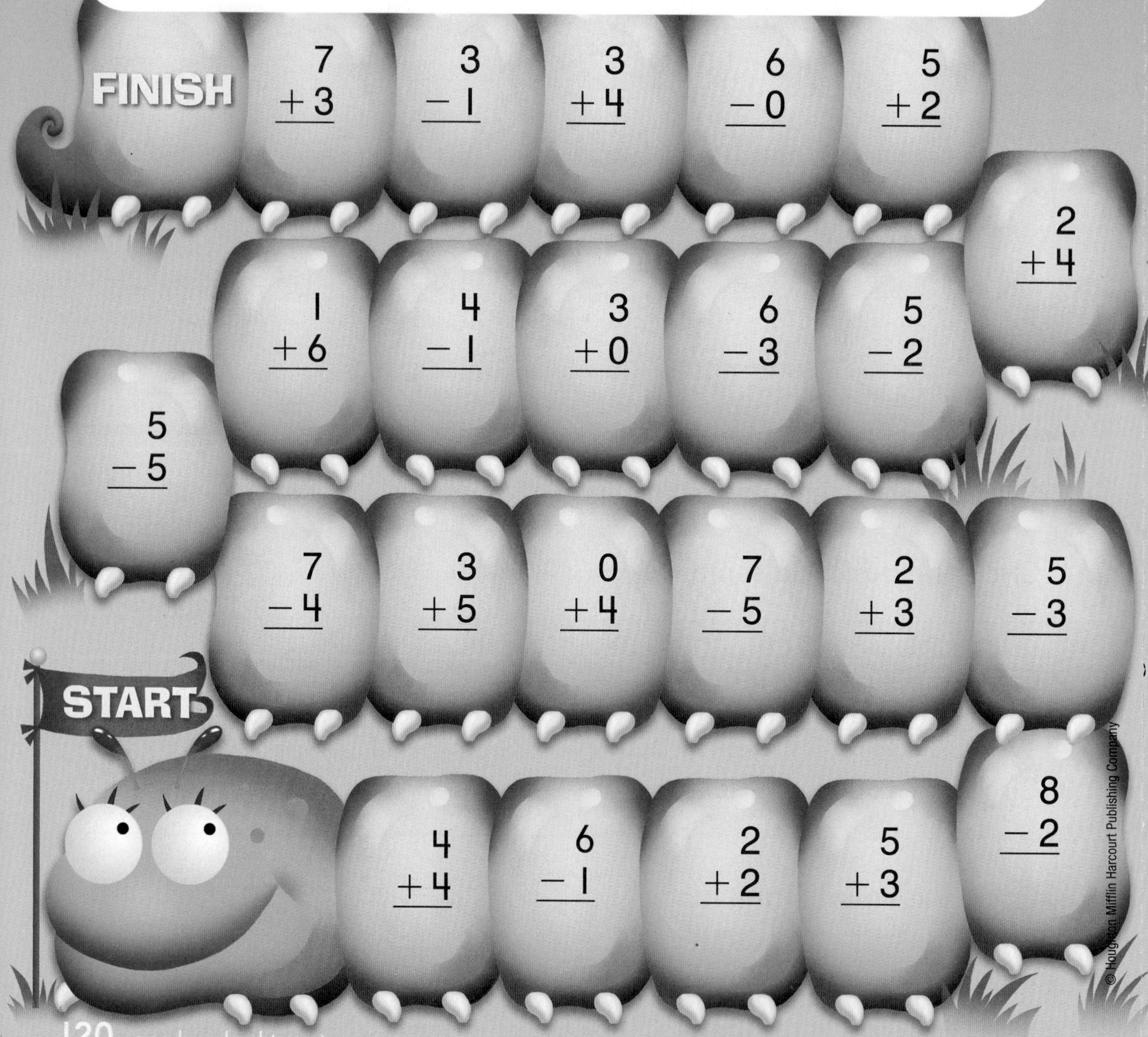

FINISH

| $7 + 3$ | $3 - 1$ | $3 + 4$ | $6 - 0$ | $5 + 2$ |

$2 + 4$

| $1 + 6$ | $4 - 1$ | $3 + 0$ | $6 - 3$ | $5 - 2$ |

$5 - 5$

| $7 - 4$ | $3 + 5$ | $0 + 4$ | $7 - 5$ | $2 + 3$ | $5 - 3$ |

START

| $4 + 4$ | $6 - 1$ | $2 + 2$ | $5 + 3$ | $8 - 2$ |

Name _____

Use Doubles Facts

Essential Question How can you use doubles facts to find sums for near doubles facts?

Operations and Algebraic Thinking—2.OA.2
MATHEMATICAL PRACTICES
MP.7, MP.8

Listen and Draw *Real World*

Draw a picture to show the problem. Then write an addition sentence for the problem.

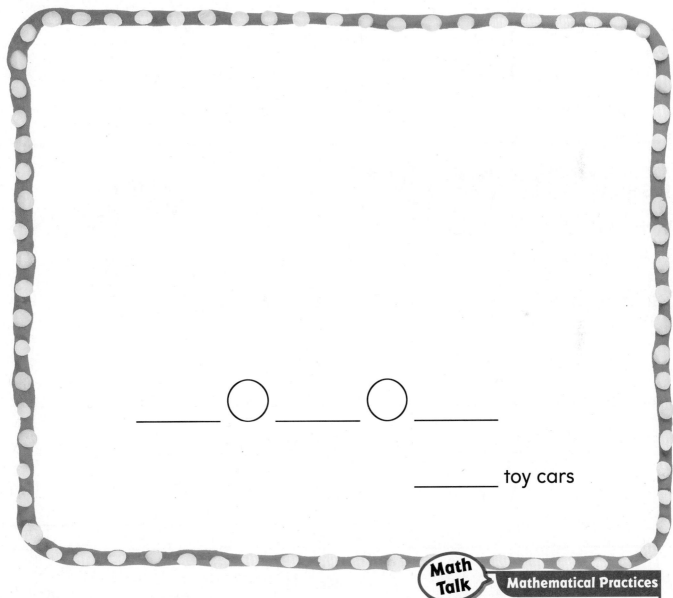

_____ ◯ _____ ◯ _____

_____ toy cars

FOR THE TEACHER • Read this problem and have children draw a picture for the problem. Nathan has 6 toy cars. Alisha gives him 6 more toy cars. How many toy cars does Nathan have now? After children write an addition sentence, have them name other doubles facts that they know.

Math Talk

Mathematical Practices

Explain why 4 + 4 = 8 is called a doubles fact.

You can use doubles facts to find sums for other facts.

3 + 4 = ?

↓

3 + 3 + 1 = ?

3 + 3 = 6

6 + 1 = 7

So, 3 + 4 = _____.

7 + 6 = ?

↓

7 + 7 − 1 = ?

7 + 7 = 14

14 − 1 = 13

So, 7 + 6 = _____.

Share and Show   MATH BOARD

Write a doubles fact you can use to find the sum. Write the sum.

1. 2 + 3 = _____

_____ + _____ = _____

2. 4 + 5 = _____

_____ + _____ = _____

3. 4 + 3 = _____

_____ + _____ = _____

4. 6 + 7 = _____

_____ + _____ = _____

☑5. 5 + 6 = _____

_____ + _____ = _____

☑6. 8 + 7 = _____

_____ + _____ = _____

Name _____

Write a doubles fact you can use
to find the sum. Write the sum.

7. 5 + 4 = _____

____ + ____ = ____

8. 6 + 5 = _____

____ + ____ = ____

9. 6 + 7 = _____

____ + ____ = ____

10. 7 + 8 = _____

____ + ____ = ____

11. 8 + 9 = _____

____ + ____ = ____

12. 5 + 6 = _____

____ + ____ = ____

13. 7 + 6 = _____

____ + ____ = ____

14. 9 + 8 = _____

____ + ____ = ____

15. THINK SMARTER Mr. Norris wrote a doubles fact.
It has a sum greater than 6. The numbers that
he added are each less than 6. What fact
might he have written?

Math on the Spot

_____

Problem Solving • Applications

Solve. Write or draw to explain.

16. **MATHEMATICAL PRACTICE ①** Analyze
Andrea has 8 red buttons and 9 blue buttons. How many buttons does Andrea have?

_____ buttons

---

17. **GO DEEPER** Henry sees 3 rabbits. Callie sees double that number of rabbits. How many more rabbits does Callie see than Henry?

_____ more rabbits

---

18. **THINK SMARTER** Could you use the doubles fact to find the sum for 4 + 5? Choose Yes or No.

$4 + 4 = 8$	○ Yes	○ No
$5 + 5 = 10$	○ Yes	○ No
$9 + 9 = 18$	○ Yes	○ No

 TAKE HOME ACTIVITY • Ask your child to write three different doubles facts with sums less than 17.

FOR MORE PRACTICE:
Standards Practice Book

Name _____

Practice Addition Facts

Essential Question What are some ways
to remember sums?

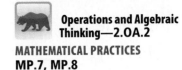

**Operations and Algebraic
Thinking—2.OA.2**
MATHEMATICAL PRACTICES
MP.7, MP.8

Draw pictures to show the problems.

_____

_____

FOR THE TEACHER • Read the following two
problems. Have children draw a picture and write
a number sentence for each. On Monday, Tony
saw 3 dogs and 6 cats. How many animals did
he see? On Tuesday, Tony saw 6 dogs and 3 cats.
How many animals did he see?

**Math
Talk** **Mathematical Practices**

Explain how the two
problems are alike.
Explain how they are
different.

Chapter 3

These are some ways to remember facts.

> You can count on
> 1, 2, or 3.

$6 + 1 = \underline{7}$

$6 + 2 = \underline{8}$

$6 + 3 = \underline{9}$

> Changing the
> order of the
> **addends** does not
> change the sum.

$\underline{8} = 2 + 6$

$\underline{8} = 6 + 2$

Share and Show

Write the sums.

1. $4 + 4 = \underline{}$

   $4 + 5 = \underline{}$

2. $5 + 0 = \underline{}$

   $2 + 0 = \underline{}$

3. $3 + 8 = \underline{}$

   $8 + 3 = \underline{}$

4. $\underline{} = 5 + 5$

   $\underline{} = 5 + 4$

5. $5 + 7 = \underline{}$

   $7 + 5 = \underline{}$

6. $\underline{} = 7 + 7$

   $\underline{} = 7 + 8$

7. $\underline{} = 3 + 7$

   $\underline{} = 7 + 3$

✓8. $9 + 3 = \underline{}$

   $3 + 9 = \underline{}$

✓9. $\underline{} = 6 + 6$

   $\underline{} = 6 + 5$

Name _____

Write the sums.

10. 7 + 1 + ____

1 + 7 = ____

11. ____ = 4 + 0

____ = 9 + 0

12. 5 + 5 = ____

5 + 4 = ____

13. 8 + 2 = ____

2 + 8 = ____

14. 3 + 3 = ____

3 + 4 = ____

15. 7 + 8 = ____

8 + 7 = ____

16. ____ = 4 + 1

____ = 1 + 4

17. 0 + 7 = ____

0 + 6 = ____

18. 8 + 8 = ____

8 + 9 = ____

19. 5 + 3 = ____

3 + 5 = ____

20. ____ = 9 + 9

____ = 9 + 8

21. 6 + 7 = ____

7 + 6 = ____

22. **THINK SMARTER** Sam painted 3 pictures. Ellie painted double that number of pictures. How many pictures did they paint?

_____ pictures

Problem Solving • Applications  WRITE ▶ Math

Solve. Write or draw to explain.

23. **GO DEEPER** Chloe draws 8 pictures. Reggie draws 1 more picture than Chloe. How many pictures do they draw?

_____ pictures

24. **MATHEMATICAL PRACTICE ①** **Analyze** Joanne made 9 clay bowls last week. She made the same number of clay bowls this week. How many clay bowls did she make in the two weeks?

_____ clay bowls

Personal Math Trainer

25. **THINK SMARTER +** There are 9 raisins in the bowl. Devon puts 8 more raisins in the bowl. Complete the addition sentence to find how many raisins are in the bowl now.

_____ + _____ = _____

_____ raisins

 TAKE HOME ACTIVITY • Ask your child to write several addition facts that he or she knows.

FOR MORE PRACTICE: Standards Practice Book

Name _____

Algebra • Make a Ten to Add

Essential Question How is the make a ten strategy used to find sums?

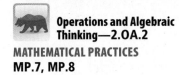

Operations and Algebraic Thinking—2.OA.2

MATHEMATICAL PRACTICES
MP.7, MP.8

Write the fact below the ten frame when you hear the problem that matches the model.

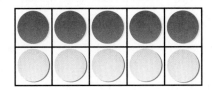

_____

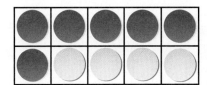

_____

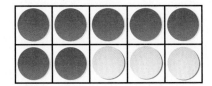

_____

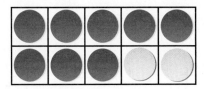

_____

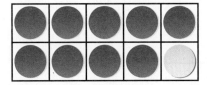

_____

FOR THE TEACHER • Read the following problem. There are 6 large dogs and 4 small dogs. How many dogs are there? Have children find the ten frame that models the problem and write the addition sentence. Repeat by revising the story for each addition fact represented by the other ten frames.

Math Talk **Mathematical Practices**

Describe a pattern you see in these make a ten facts.

Chapter 3

7 + 5 = ?

You need to add 3 to 7 to make a ten. Break apart 5 as 3 and 2.

7 + 5

7 + 3 + 2

10 + 2 = _12_

So, 7 + 5 = _____.

Share and Show

MATH BOARD

Show how you can make a ten to find the sum.
Write the sum.

1. 8 + 3 = _____

10 + _____ = _____

2. 2 + 9 = _____

10 + _____ = _____

3. 8 + 5 = _____

10 + _____ = _____

4. 4 + 7 = _____

10 + _____ = _____

5. 3 + 9 = _____

10 + _____ = _____

6. 7 + 6 = _____

10 + _____ = _____

Name _____

Show how you can make a ten to find the sum.
Write the sum.

7. $4 + 9 =$ _____

  3 1

  $10 +$ _____ $=$ _____

8. $9 + 8 =$ _____

  1 7

  $10 +$ _____ $=$ _____

9. $8 + 6 =$ _____

  $10 +$ _____ $=$ _____

10. $5 + 9 =$ _____

  $10 +$ _____ $=$ _____

11. $7 + 9 =$ _____

  $10 +$ _____ $=$ _____

12. $8 + 4 =$ _____

  $10 +$ _____ $=$ _____

13. $9 + 9 =$ _____

  $10 +$ _____ $=$ _____

14. $8 + 7 =$ _____

  $10 +$ _____ $=$ _____

15. **THINK SMARTER** There were 5 bees in a hive. How many more bees need to go in the hive for there to be 14 bees?

_____ more bees

Problem Solving • Applications  WRITE ▸ Math

Solve. Write or draw to explain.

16. **MATHEMATICAL PRACTICE ①** **Analyze** There are 9 large bicycles at the store. There are 6 small bicycles at the store. How many bicycles are at the store?

_____ bicycles

17. **GO DEEPER** Max is thinking of a doubles fact. It has a sum that is greater than the sum of 6 + 4 but less than the sum of 8 + 5. What fact is Max thinking of?

_____ + _____ = _____

18. **THINK SMARTER** Natasha had 8 shells. Then she found 5 more shells. Draw to show how to find the number of shells Natasha has now.

How many shells does she have now? _____ shells

 TAKE HOME ACTIVITY • Ask your child to name pairs of numbers that have a sum of 10. Then have him or her write the addition sentences.

FOR MORE PRACTICE: Standards Practice Book

Name _____

Algebra • Add 3 Addends

Essential Question How do you add three numbers?

Operations and Algebraic Thinking—2.OA.2 *Also 2.NBT.5*
MATHEMATICAL PRACTICES
MP.6, MP.8

Listen and Draw

Write the sum of each pair of addends.

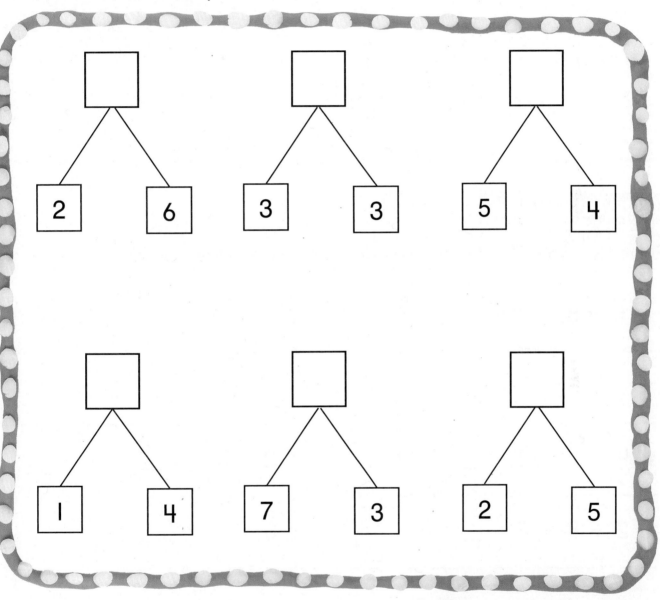

FOR THE TEACHER • After children have recorded the sum of each pair of addends, have them share their answers and discuss the strategies used.

Math Talk

Mathematical Practices

Describe how you found the sum of 5 and 4.

You can group numbers in different ways to add.

Choose two addends.
Look for facts you know.

Changing the way the numbers are grouped does not change the sum.

3 + 2 + 7 = ?

5 + 7 = __12__

3 + 2 + 7 = ?

3 + 9 = _____

3 + 2 + 7 = ?

10 + 2 = _____

MATH BOARD

Solve two ways. Circle the two addends you add first.

1. 1 + 8 + 2 = _____   1 + 8 + 2 = _____

2. 7 + 3 + 3 = _____   7 + 3 + 3 = _____

3. 4 + 2 + 4 = _____   4 + 2 + 4 = _____

✓ 4. 2 + 8 + 2 = _____   2 + 8 + 2 = _____

✓ 5.   3   3   6.   7   7
          2   2   0   0
        + 6   + 6   + 2   + 2
        ___   ___   ___   ___

134 one hundred thirty-four

On Your Own

Solve two ways. Circle the two addends you add first.

7. $4 + 1 + 6 =$ _____ $4 + 1 + 6 =$ _____

8. $4 + 3 + 3 =$ _____ $4 + 3 + 3 =$ _____

9. $1 + 5 + 3 =$ _____ $1 + 5 + 3 =$ _____

10. $6 + 4 + 4 =$ _____ $6 + 4 + 4 =$ _____

11. $5 + 5 + 5 =$ _____ $5 + 5 + 5 =$ _____

12. $7 + 0 + 6 =$ _____ $7 + 0 + 6 =$ _____

13.
```
    5          5
    3          3
  + 4        + 4
  ___        ___
```

14.
```
    4          4
    2          2
  + 5        + 5
  ___        ___
```

MATHEMATICAL PRACTICE ⑦ Look for Structure

Write the missing addend.

15.
```
    5
    5
  + ☐
  ___
   14
```

16.
```
    4
    ☐
  + 4
  ___
   12
```

17.
```
    3
    ☐
  + 7
  ___
   11
```

18.
```
    5
    3
  + ☐
  ___
   13
```

Problem Solving • Applications

Choose a way to solve.
Write or draw to explain.

19. *THINK SMARTER* Nick, Alex, and
Sophia eat 15 raisins in all.
Nick and Alex each eat
4 raisins. How many raisins
does Sophia eat?

_____ raisins

20. **MATHEMATICAL PRACTICE ①** Analyze
There are 5 green grapes
and 4 red grapes in a bowl.
Eli puts 4 more grapes in
the bowl. How many grapes
are in the bowl now?

_____ grapes

21. *THINK SMARTER* Mrs. Moore bought
4 small apples, 6 medium apples,
and 3 large apples. How many
apples did she buy?

_____ apples

 TAKE HOME ACTIVITY • Have your child describe
two ways to add 3, 6, and 2.

FOR MORE PRACTICE:
Standards Practice Book

Name _____

Algebra • Relate Addition and Subtraction

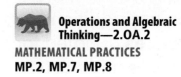

Operations and Algebraic Thinking—2.OA.2
MATHEMATICAL PRACTICES
MP.2, MP.7, MP.8

Essential Question How are addition and subtraction related?

Complete the bar model to show the problem.

8	7

_____

_____ soccer balls

_____	7

15

_____ soccer balls

FOR THE TEACHER • Read the following problems. Have children complete the bar model for each. The soccer team has 8 red balls and 7 yellow balls. How many soccer balls does the team have? The soccer team has 15 balls inside the locker room. The children took the 7 yellow balls outside. How many soccer balls were inside?

Math Talk

Mathematical Practices

Explain how the bar models for the problems are alike and how they are different.

Chapter 3

one hundred thirty-seven **137**

You can use addition facts to remember **differences**. Related facts have the same whole and parts.

Think of the addends in an addition fact to find the difference for a related subtraction fact.

6	7

$$\underline{13}$$

	7

13

$6 + 7 = \underline{13}$

$13 - 7 = \underline{}$

Share and Show

 MATH BOARD

Write the sum and the difference for the related facts.

1. $5 + 4 = \underline{}$

$9 - 4 = \underline{}$

2. $2 + 7 = \underline{}$

$9 - 2 = \underline{}$

3. $3 + 8 = \underline{}$

$11 - 8 = \underline{}$

4. $5 + 8 = \underline{}$

$13 - 5 = \underline{}$

5. $\underline{} = 1 + 8$

$\underline{} = 9 - 1$

6. $9 + 9 = \underline{}$

$18 - 9 = \underline{}$

7. $\underline{} = 8 + 7$

$\underline{} = 15 - 8$

8. $4 + 7 = \underline{}$

$11 - 7 = \underline{}$

9. $7 + 5 = \underline{}$

$12 - 7 = \underline{}$

138 one hundred thirty-eight

On Your Own

Write the sum and the difference for the related facts.

10. 4 + 3 = ____   11.   2 + 6 = ____   12.   6 + 4 = ____

7 − 3 = ____   8 − 6 = ____   10 − 6 = ____

13. 7 + 3 = ____   14.   8 + 6 = ____   15.   ____ = 3 + 9

10 − 7 = ____   14 − 6 = ____   ____ = 12 − 9

16. 6 + 5 = ____   17.   7 + 7 = ____   18.   9 + 6 = ____

11 − 5 = ____   14 − 7 = ____   15 − 9 = ____

19. 5 + 9 = ____   20.   ____ = 4 + 8   21.   9 + 7 = ____

14 − 9 = ____   ____ = 12 − 4   16 − 7 = ____

MATHEMATICAL PRACTICE 6 **Make Connections**

Write a related subtraction fact for each addition fact.

22. 7 + 8 = 15   23. 5 + 7 = 12

_____   _____

24. 6 + 7 = 13   25. 9 + 8 = 17

_____   _____

Problem Solving • Applications

WRITE ▸ Math

Solve. Write or draw to explain.

26. Trevor has 7 kites. Pam has 4 kites. How many more kites does Trevor have than Pam?

_____ more kites

---

27. **THINK SMARTER** Mr. Sims has a bag of 7 pears and a bag of 6 pears. His family eats 5 pears. How many pears does he have now?

_____ pears

---

28. **THINK SMARTER** Elin counts 7 geese in the water and some geese on the shore. There are 16 geese in all. Draw a picture to show the two groups of geese.

Write a number sentence that can help you find how many geese are on the shore.

_____

How many geese are on the shore? _____ geese

TAKE HOME ACTIVITY • Ask your child to name some subtraction facts that he or she knows well.

FOR MORE PRACTICE:
Standards Practice Book

Practice Subtraction Facts

Essential Question What are some ways to remember differences?

Operations and Algebraic Thinking—2.OA.2

MATHEMATICAL PRACTICES
MP.1

Listen and Draw *Real World*

Use Gina's model to answer the question.

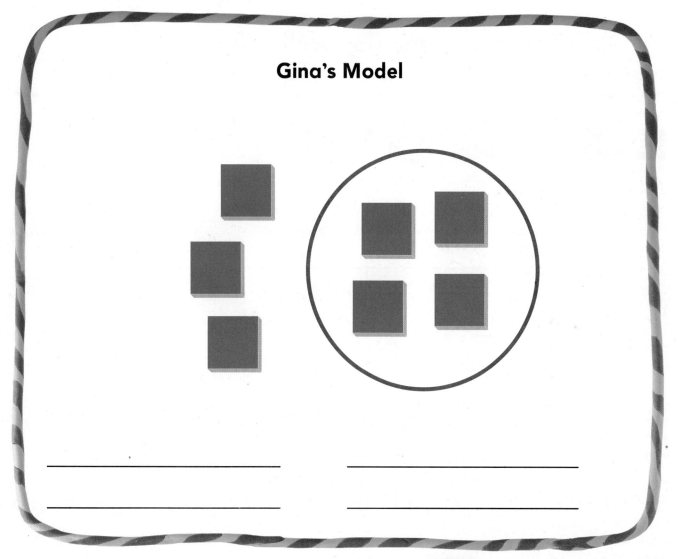

Gina's Model

_____   _____

_____   _____

FOR THE TEACHER • Tell children that Gina put 4 color tiles inside the circle and then put 3 color tiles outside the circle. Then ask: What addition fact could be written for Gina's model? Repeat with stories for the three facts that are related to this addition fact.

Math Talk

Mathematical Practices

Explain how the different facts for Gina's model are related.

Chapter 3   one hundred forty-one **141**

© Houghton Mifflin Harcourt Publishing Company

Model and Draw

These are some ways to find differences.

You can count back by 1, 2, or 3.

$7 - 2 =$ _____

> Start with 7.
> Say: 6, 5.

$9 - 3 =$ _____

> Start with 9.
> Say: 8, 7, 6.

You can think about a missing addend to subtract.

$8 - 5 =$ ▨

> $5 + 3 = 8$

So, $8 - 5 =$ _____.

Share and Show

Write the difference.

1. $6 - 4 =$ _____

2. $10 - 7 =$ _____

3. _____ $= 5 - 2$

4. $14 - 6 =$ _____

5. _____ $= 8 - 4$

6. $11 - 3 =$ _____

7. _____ $= 7 - 5$

8. $10 - 4 =$ _____

9. $5 - 0 =$ _____

10. $13 - 9 =$ _____

11. $9 - 3 =$ _____

12. _____ $= 7 - 6$

13. $12 - 3 =$ _____

14. $6 - 3 =$ _____

15. $9 - 5 =$ _____

16. $10 - 6 =$ _____

✓ 17. _____ $= 8 - 3$

✓ 18. $13 - 5 =$ _____

On Your Own

Write the difference.

19. $11 - 2 =$ ___

20. $9 - 7 =$ ___

21. ___ $= 7 - 4$

22. $12 - 5 =$ ___

23. $8 - 6 =$ ___

24. ___ $= 7 - 0$

25. ___ $= 10 - 5$

26. $15 - 8 =$ ___

27. $13 - 7 =$ ___

28. $10 - 8 =$ ___

29. $8 - 5 =$ ___

30. ___ $= 9 - 6$

31. ___ $= 9 - 4$

32. $11 - 8 =$ ___

33. $12 - 7 =$ ___

34. **THINK SMARTER**

Write the differences.
Then write the next fact
in the pattern.

$10 - 1 =$ ___

$8 - 1 =$ ___

$6 - 1 =$ ___

$4 - 1 =$ ___

_____

$12 - 9 =$ ___

$13 - 9 =$ ___

$14 - 9 =$ ___

$15 - 9 =$ ___

_____

$18 - 9 =$ ___

$17 - 8 =$ ___

$16 - 7 =$ ___

$15 - 6 =$ ___

_____

TAKE HOME ACTIVITY • With your child, practice
saying subtraction facts from this lesson.

FOR MORE PRACTICE:
Standards Practice Book

Mid-Chapter Checkpoint

Concepts and Skills

Write the sum. (2.0A.2)

1. $3 + 6 =$ _____   2. $8 + 0 =$ _____   3. $7 + 7 =$ _____

4. $9 + 4 =$ _____   5. _____ $= 5 + 6$ 6. $2 + 8 =$ _____

7. $3 + 7 + 2 =$ _____   8. $4 + 4 + 6 =$ _____

Show how you can make a ten to find the sum.
Write the sum. (2.0A.2)

9. $9 + 7 =$ _____   10. $6 + 8 =$ _____

        $10 +$ _____ $=$ _____ $10 +$ _____ $=$ _____

Write the sum and the difference for the related facts. (2.0A.2)

11. $5 + 4 =$ _____   12. $3 + 9 =$ _____   13. $8 + 7 =$ _____

   $9 - 4 =$ _____ $12 - 9 =$ _____ $15 - 8 =$ _____

14. **THINK SMARTER** Lily has 6 toys cars.
Yong has 5 toy cars. How many
toy cars do they have? (2.0A.2)

_____ toy cars

Name _____

Use Ten to Subtract

Essential Question How does getting to 10 in subtraction help when finding differences?

 Operations and Algebraic Thinking—2.OA.2 *Also 2.MD.6*
MATHEMATICAL PRACTICES
MP.5, MP.8

Circle to show the amount you subtract for each problem.

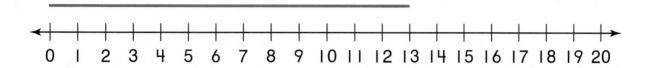

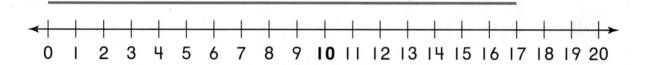

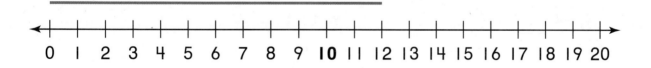

FOR THE TEACHER • Read the following problem. Deveron has 13 crayons. He gives 3 crayons to Tyler. How many crayons does Deveron have now? Have children circle the part of the blue line segment that shows what is subtracted from the total. Repeat for two more problems.

 Math Talk **Mathematical Practices**

Describe a pattern in the three problems and answers.

Model and Draw

You can subtract in steps to use a tens fact.

$$14 - 6 = ?$$

4   2

Subtract in steps:
14 − 4 = 10
10 − 2 = 8

−2   −4

0 1 2 3 4 5 6 7 8 9 **10** 11 12 13 14 15 16 17 18 19 20

So, $14 - 6 = \underline{8}$.

Share and Show

MATH BOARD

Show the tens fact you used. Write the difference.

0 1 2 3 4 5 6 7 8 9 **10** 11 12 13 14 15 16 17 18 19 20

1. $12 - 5 = \underline{}$

2 3

$10 - \underline{} = \underline{}$

2. $11 - 6 = \underline{}$

1 5

$10 - \underline{} = \underline{}$

3. $15 - 7 = \underline{}$

$10 - \underline{} = \underline{}$

4. $13 - 7 = \underline{}$

$10 - \underline{} = \underline{}$

Name _____

Show the tens fact you used. Write the difference.

```
  0  1  2  3  4  5  6  7  8  9  10  11  12  13  14  15  16  17  18  19  20
```

5. 13 − 5 = ____

    3   2

   10 − ____ = ____

6. 15 − 6 = ____

    5   1

   10 − ____ = ____

7. 12 − 8 = ____

   10 − ____ = ____

8. 14 − 8 = ____

   10 − ____ = ____

9. 12 − 6 = ____

   10 − ____ = ____

10. 16 − 7 = ____

   10 − ____ = ____

Solve. Write or draw to explain.

11. **THINK SMARTER** Beth has a box of 16 crayons. She gives 3 crayons to Jake and 7 crayons to Wendy. How many crayons does Beth have now?

____ crayons

Problem Solving • Applications

WRITE ▶ Math

Go DEEPER Write number sentences that use both addition and subtraction. Use each choice only once.

9 ✗ 2
3 ✗ 4
1 + 4
14 − 6
5 + 4
15 − 6
10 − 5
4 + 4

12. $$9 - 2 = 3 + 4$$
$$7 = 7$$

13. _____ = _____

14. _____ = _____

15. _____ = _____

16. **THINK SMARTER** Does the number sentence have the same difference as $15 - 7 = $ ▓ ? Choose Yes or No.

$10 - 6 = $ ▓   ○ Yes   ○ No

$10 - 2 = $ ▓   ○ Yes   ○ No

$10 - 4 = $ ▓   ○ Yes   ○ No

TAKE HOME ACTIVITY • Ask your child to name pairs of numbers that have a difference of 10. Then have him or her write the number sentences.

FOR MORE PRACTICE:
Standards Practice Book

© Houghton Mifflin Harcourt Publishing Company

Name _____

Algebra • Use Drawings to Represent Problems

Operations and Algebraic Thinking—2.OA.1
MATHEMATICAL PRACTICES
MP.1, MP.4

Essential Question How are bar models used to show addition and subtraction problems?

Listen and Draw Real World

Complete the bar model to show the problem.
Complete the number sentence to solve.

_____ + _____ = _____   _____ pennies

_____ − _____ = _____   _____ pennies

Math Talk
Mathematical Practices

Explain how the problems are alike and how they are different.

FOR THE TEACHER • Read each problem and have children complete the bar models. Hailey has 5 pennies in her pocket and 7 pennies in her wallet. How many pennies does she have? Blake has 12 pennies in his bank. He gives 5 pennies to his sister. How many pennies does he have now?

Chapter 3

You can use bar models to show problems.

Ben eats 14 crackers. Ron eats 6 crackers. How many more crackers does Ben eat than Ron?

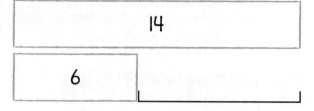

$$14 - 6 = 8$$

_____ more crackers

Suzy had 14 cookies. She gave 6 cookies to Grace. How many cookies does Suzy have now?

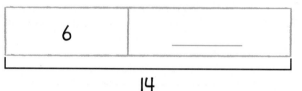

_____

_____ cookies

Share and Show

Complete the bar model. Then write a number sentence to solve.

✓1. Mr. James bought 15 plain bagels and 9 raisin bagels. How many more plain bagels than raisin bagels did he buy?

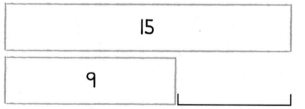

_____

 _____ more plain bagels

On Your Own

Complete the bar model. Then write
a number sentence to solve.

2. Cole has 5 books about dogs
   and 6 books about cats. How
   many books does Cole have?

| 5 | 6 |

_____

_____

_____ books

3. **THINK SMARTER** Anne has 16 blue
   clips and 9 red clips. How many
   more blue clips than red clips
   does she have?

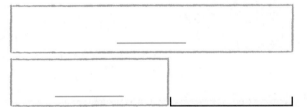

_____

 _____ more blue clips

4. **GO DEEPER** Fill in the blank. Then
   label the bar model and solve.

   Miss Gore had 18 pencils. She
   gave ____ pencils to Erin.
   How many pencils does
   Miss Gore have now?

   _____ pencils

Problem Solving • Applications (Real World)   WRITE ⟩ Math

Use the information in the table to solve. Write or draw to explain.

Jenna's Flowers	
Flowers	Number
roses	6
tulips	8
daisies	11

5. Jenna put all of the roses and all of the tulips into a vase. How many flowers did she put into the vase?

_____ flowers

6. THINK SMARTER Four of the daisies are white. The other daisies are yellow. How many daisies are yellow?

_____ yellow daisies

7. THINK SMARTER Rita counts 4 frogs in the grass and some other frogs in the water. There are 10 frogs in all. How many frogs are in the water? Draw a picture and write a number sentence to solve.

_____

_____ frogs are in the water.

 TAKE HOME ACTIVITY • Ask your child to describe what he or she learned in this lesson.

FOR MORE PRACTICE: Standards Practice Book

Name _____

Algebra • Use Equations to Represent Problems

Essential Question How are number sentences used to show addition and subtraction situations?

Operations and Algebraic Thinking—2.OA.1
MATHEMATICAL PRACTICES
MP.1, MP.2, MP.4

Listen and Draw Real World

Write a story problem that could be solved using this bar model.

	9

15

_____

_____

_____

_____

_____

FOR THE TEACHER • Discuss with children how this bar model can be used to represent an addition or a subtraction situation.

Math Talk **Mathematical Practices**

Would you add or subtract to solve your story problem? **Explain.**

Chapter 3

Model and Draw

A number sentence can be used to show a problem.

There were some girls and 4 boys at the park.
There were 9 children in all. How many girls were
at the park?

$$\blacksquare + 4 = 9$$

Think: $5 + 4 = 9$

So, there were ____5____ girls at the park.

> The ■ is a placeholder for the missing number.

Share and Show

MATH BOARD

Write a number sentence for the problem.
Use a ■ for the missing number. Then solve.

☑ 1. There were 14 ants on the
sidewalk. Then 6 ants went into
the grass. How many ants were
still on the sidewalk?

_____

_____ ants

☑ 2. There were 7 big dogs and
4 little dogs at the park. How
many dogs were at the park?

_____

_____ dogs

On Your Own

Write a number sentence for the problem.
Use a ▢ for the missing number. Then solve.

3. A group of children were flying
13 kites. Some kites were put
away. Then the children were
flying 7 kites. How many kites
were put away?

_____

_____ kites

4. There are 18 boys at the
field. 9 of the boys are playing
soccer. How many boys are not
playing soccer?

_____

_____ boys

5. **MATHEMATICAL PRACTICE ②** Use Reasoning
Matthew found 9 acorns.
Greg found 6 acorns. How
many acorns did the
two boys find?

_____

_____ acorns

6. *THINK SMARTER* There were some
ducks in a pond. Four more
ducks joined them. Then there
were 12 ducks in the pond.
How many ducks were
in the pond at first?

_____ ducks

Problem Solving • Applications (Real World)   WRITE ▸ Math

Read the story. Write or draw to show
how you solved the problems.

> At camp, 5 children are playing games
> and 4 children are making crafts.
> 5 other children are having a snack.

7. How many children are
   at camp?

   _____ children

8. **Go DEEPER** Suppose 7 more
   children arrive at camp and
   join the children playing games.
   How many more children are
   playing games than children
   not playing games?

   _____ more children

Personal Math Trainer

9. **THINK SMARTER +** Ashley had 9 crayons. She gave
   4 crayons to her brother. How many crayons
   does Ashley have now? Write a number
   sentence for the problem. Use ▨ for the
   missing number. Then solve.

   _____

   Ashley has _____ crayons now.

 TAKE HOME ACTIVITY • Ask your child to explain how
he or she solved one of the problems on this page.

FOR MORE PRACTICE:
Standards Practice Book

Name _____

Problem Solving • Equal Groups

Essential Question How can acting it out help when solving a problem about equal groups?

Number and Operations in Base Ten—2.NBT.2 Also 2.OA.4
MATHEMATICAL PRACTICES
MP.1, MP.5, MP.7

Theo puts his stickers in 5 rows.
There are 2 stickers in each row.
How many stickers does Theo have?

 Unlock the Problem Real World

Hands On

What do I need to find?	**What information do I need to use?**
how many stickers	5 rows of stickers
Theo has	2 stickers in each row

Show how to solve the problem.

HOME CONNECTION • Your child used counters to act out the problem. Counters are a concrete tool that helps children act out the problem.

Chapter 3

one hundred fifty-seven **157**

Act out the problem.
Draw to show what you did.

1. Maria puts all of her postcards in 6 rows. There are 2 postcards in each row. How many postcards does Maria have?

_____ postcards

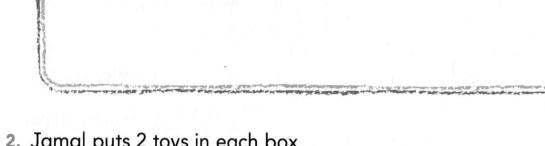

2. Jamal puts 2 toys in each box. How many toys will he put in 8 boxes?

_____ toys

Math Talk

Mathematical Practices

Explain how acting it out and skip counting helped you solve the second problem.

Name _____

Act out the problem.
Draw to show what you did.

3. Mr. Fulton puts 2 bananas on each tray. How many bananas are on 6 trays?

_____ bananas

---

4. There are 7 rows of apples. There are 2 apples in each row. How many apples are there?

_____ apples

---

5. **THINK SMARTER** There are 4 plates. Dexter puts 2 grapes on each plate. Then he puts 2 grapes on each of 6 more plates. How many grapes in all does he put on the plates?

_____ grapes

Problem Solving • Applications WRITE ❭ Math

6. **MATHEMATICAL PRACTICE 6** Make Connections

Angela used these counters to act out a problem.

Write a problem about equal groups that Angela could have modeled with these counters.

● ● ●
● ●
● ●
● ●
● ●

_____

_____

_____

7. **THINK SMARTER** Max and 8 friends get books from the library. Each person gets 2 books. Draw a picture to show the groups of books.

How many books did they get?

_____ books

 TAKE HOME ACTIVITY • Ask your child to explain how he or she solved one of the problems in this lesson.

FOR MORE PRACTICE: Standards Practice Book

© Houghton Mifflin Harcourt Publishing Company

160 one hundred sixty

Name _____

Algebra • Repeated Addition

Essential Question How can you write an addition sentence for problems with equal groups?

Operations and Algebraic Thinking—2.OA.4
MATHEMATICAL PRACTICES
MP.4, MP.6

Listen and Draw · Real World

Use counters to model the problem.
Then draw a picture of your model.

FOR THE TEACHER • Read the following problem and have children first model the problem with counters and then draw a picture of their models. Clayton has 3 rows of cards. There are 5 cards in each row. How many cards does Clayton have?

Math Talk · **Mathematical Practices**

Describe how you found the number of counters in your model.

Chapter 3

You can use addition to find the total amount when you have equal groups.

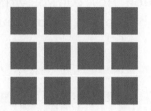

3 rows of 4

Write: ___4___ + ___4___ + ___4___ = _____

_____ in all

Share and Show

Find the number of shapes in each row.
Complete the addition sentence to find the total.

1.

3 rows of _____

___ + ___ + ___ = ____

2.

4 rows of _____

__ + __ + __ + __ = ___

3.

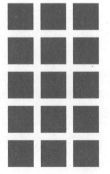

5 rows of _____

___ + ___ + ___ + ___ + ___ = ____

On Your Own

Find the number of shapes in each row.
Complete the addition sentence to find the total.

4.

2 rows of _____

____ + ____ = ____

5.

3 rows of _____

____ + ____ + ____ = ____

6.

4 rows of _____

__ + __ + __ + __ = ____

7.

4 rows of _____

__ + __ + __ + __ = ____

8.

5 rows of _____

____ + ____ + ____ + ____ + ____ = ____

Problem Solving • Applications 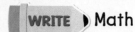 WRITE Math

Solve. Write or draw to explain.

9. **THINK SMARTER** There are
6 photos on the wall. There
are 2 photos in each row.
How many rows of photos
are there?

_____ rows

10. **GO DEEPER** Mrs. Chen makes
5 rows of 2 chairs and
2 rows of 3 chairs.
How many chairs does
Mrs. Chen use?

_____ chairs

11. **THINK SMARTER** Find the number of counters in
each row. Complete the number sentence
to find the total number of counters.

_____ + _____ + _____ = _____

_____ counters

 TAKE HOME ACTIVITY • Have your child use small objects to
make 2 rows with 4 objects in each row. Then have your child find
the total number of objects.

FOR MORE PRACTICE:
Standards Practice Book

✓ Chapter 3 Review/Test

1. Erin puts 3 small cans, 4 medium cans, and 5 large cans on a shelf. How many cans does she put on the shelf?

   _____ cans

2. Fill in the bubble next to all the doubles facts you could use to find the sum of 3 + 2?

   ○ 2 + 2

   ○ 5 + 5

   ○ 3 + 3

   ○ 1 + 1

3. Does the number sentence have the same difference as 14 − 6 = ▇?
   Choose Yes or No.

10 − 1 = ▇	○ Yes	○ No
10 − 2 = ▇	○ Yes	○ No
10 − 3 = ▇	○ Yes	○ No
10 − 4 = ▇	○ Yes	○ No

GO DIGITAL Assessment Options
Chapter Test

4. Mr. Brown sold 5 red backpacks and 8 blue backpacks.
   Write the number sentence. Show how you can make
   a ten to find the sum. Write the sum.

   $5 + 8 =$ _____

   $10 +$ _____ $=$ _____

---

5. Find the number of shapes in each row.

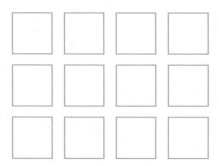

   3 rows of _____

   Complete the addition sentence to find the total.

   _____ $+$ _____ $+$ _____ $=$ _____

---

6. Tanya and 2 friends put rocks on the table.
   Each person put 2 rocks on the table. Draw a
   picture to show the groups of rocks.

   How many rocks did they put on the table?

   _____ rocks

166 one hundred sixty-six

7. Lily sees 15 tan puppies and 8 white puppies at the pet store. How many more tan puppies than white puppies does she see? Draw a picture and write a number sentence to solve.

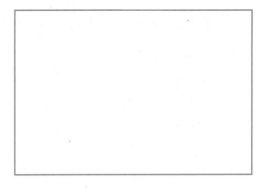

_____

_____ more tan puppies

8. Mark counts 6 ducks in a pond and some ducks on the grass. There are 14 ducks in all. Draw a picture to show the two groups of ducks.

Write a number sentence that can help you find how many ducks are on the grass.

_____ + _____ = _____

How many ducks are on the grass?   _____ ducks

9. There are 8 peaches in a basket. Mrs. Dalton puts 7 more peaches in the basket. Complete the addition sentence to find how many peaches are in the basket now.

_____ peaches

10. Use the numbers on the tiles to write the differences. Then write the next fact in the pattern.

| 4 | 5 | 6 | 7 |

$12 - 6 = $ _____

$12 - 7 = $ _____

$12 - 8 = $ _____

_____

$11 - 6 = $ _____

$12 - 6 = $ _____

$13 - 6 = $ _____

_____

11. Jose wanted to share 18 strawberries with his brother equally. Draw a picture to show how Jose can share the strawberries.

How many strawberries will Jose receive?

_____ strawberries

12. Hank has 13 grapes. He gives 5 grapes to his sister. How many grapes does Hank have now? Write a number sentence for the problem. Use ▧ for the missing number. Then solve.

_____

_____ grapes

Curious about Math

The keys of a modern piano are made from wood or plastic. A modern piano has 36 black keys and 52 white keys. How many keys is this in all?

Show What You Know

Addition Patterns

Add 2. Complete each addition sentence.

1. $1 + \underline{2} = \underline{3}$

2. $2 + \underline{} = \underline{}$

3. $3 + \underline{} = \underline{}$

4. $4 + \underline{} = \underline{}$

5. $5 + \underline{} = \underline{}$

6. $6 + \underline{} = \underline{}$

Addition Facts

Write the sum.

7. $\begin{array}{r} 7 \\ +3 \\ \hline \end{array}$
8. $\begin{array}{r} 8 \\ +8 \\ \hline \end{array}$
9. $\begin{array}{r} 6 \\ +7 \\ \hline \end{array}$
10. $\begin{array}{r} 4 \\ +4 \\ \hline \end{array}$
11. $\begin{array}{r} 9 \\ +5 \\ \hline \end{array}$
12. $\begin{array}{r} 8 \\ +7 \\ \hline \end{array}$

Tens and Ones

Write how many tens and ones for each number.

13. 43

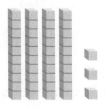

_____ tens _____ ones

14. 68

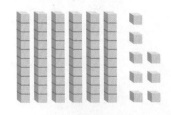

_____ tens _____ ones

This page checks understanding of important skills needed for success in Chapter 4.

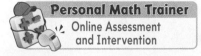

Personal Math Trainer
Online Assessment and Intervention

© Houghton Mifflin Harcourt Publishing Company

Vocabulary Builder

Review Words
sum
addend
digit
tens
ones

Visualize It

Use review words to fill in the graphic organizer.

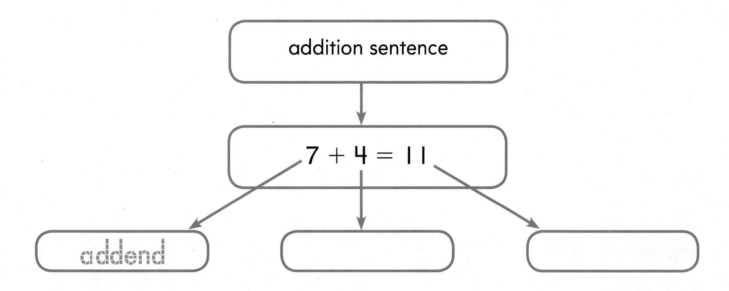

addition sentence

$7 + 4 = 11$

addend

Understand Vocabulary

1. Write a number with the **digit** 3 in
   the **tens** place.   _____

2. Write a number with the **digit** 5 in
   the **ones** place.   _____

3. Write a number that has the same **digit**
   in the **tens** place and in the **ones** place.   _____

4. Write a number with **digits** that have
   a **sum** of 8.   _____

GO DIGITAL
• Interactive Student Edition
• Multimedia eGlossary

Game

What is the Sum?

Materials

- 12 🔴
- 12 🟡
- 1 🎲

Play with a partner.

1 Put your 🔴 on START.

2 Toss the 🎲. Move that many spaces.

3 Say the sum. Your partner checks your answer.

4 If your answer is correct, find that number in the middle of the board. Put one of your on that number.

5 Take turns until both players reach FINISH. The player with more on the board wins.

START

FINISH

$$\begin{array}{r} 2 \\ +7 \\ \hline \end{array}$$

$$\begin{array}{r} 6 \\ +5 \\ \hline \end{array}$$

$$\begin{array}{r} 3 \\ +9 \\ \hline \end{array}$$

$$\begin{array}{r} 0 \\ +7 \\ \hline \end{array}$$

$$\begin{array}{r} 8 \\ +6 \\ \hline \end{array}$$

$$\begin{array}{r} 9 \\ +8 \\ \hline \end{array}$$

7	18	9	11	15
13	6	17	8	10
16	4	12	14	5

$$\begin{array}{r} 6 \\ +2 \\ \hline \end{array}$$

$$\begin{array}{r} 1 \\ +4 \\ \hline \end{array}$$

$$\begin{array}{r} 8 \\ +7 \\ \hline \end{array}$$

$$\begin{array}{r} 5 \\ +8 \\ \hline \end{array}$$

$$\begin{array}{r} 9 \\ +9 \\ \hline \end{array}$$

$$\begin{array}{r} 7 \\ +9 \\ \hline \end{array}$$

$$\begin{array}{r} 2 \\ +2 \\ \hline \end{array}$$

$$\begin{array}{r} 4 \\ +6 \\ \hline \end{array}$$

$$\begin{array}{r} 5 \\ +1 \\ \hline \end{array}$$

Name _____

Break Apart Ones to Add

Essential Question How does breaking apart a number make it easier to add?

Number and Operations
in Base Ten—2.NBT.5
MATHEMATICAL PRACTICES
MP.4, MP.6

Listen and Draw Real World   Hands On

Use . Draw to show what you did.

Math Talk **Mathematical Practices**

FOR THE TEACHER • Read the following problem. Have children use blocks to solve. Griffin read 27 books about animals and 6 books about space. How many books did he read?

Describe what you did with the blocks.

© Houghton Mifflin Harcourt Publishing Company

Chapter 4

one hundred seventy-three **173**

Model and Draw

Break apart ones to make a ten.
Use this as a way to add.

$27 + 8 =$ ___?___

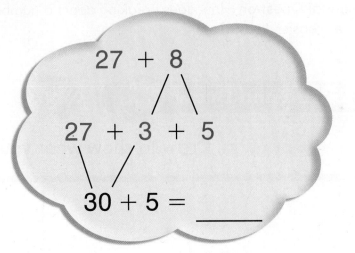

27 + 8

27 + 3 + 5

30 + 5 = _____

$27 + 8 =$ _____

Share and Show

Draw quick pictures. Break apart ones to
make a ten. Then add and write the sum.

1. $15 + 7 =$ _____

2. $26 + 5 =$ _____

✓ 3. $37 + 8 =$ _____

✓ 4. $28 + 6 =$ _____

On Your Own

Break apart ones to make a ten.
Then add and write the sum.

5. 23 + 9 = _____

6. 48 + 5 = _____

7. 18 + 5 = _____

8. 33 + 9 = _____

9. 27 + 6 = _____

10. 49 + 4 = _____

11. 24 + 8 = _____

12. 58 + 7 = _____

13. 36 + 8 = _____

14. 47 + 9 = _____

15. **THINK SMARTER** Bruce sees 29 oak trees and 4 maple trees at the park. Then he sees double the number of pine trees as maple trees. How many trees does Bruce see?

_____ trees

© Houghton Mifflin Harcourt Publishing Company • Image Credits: ©Digital Vision/Alamy

Problem Solving • Applications

WRITE ▶ Math

Solve. Write or draw to explain.

16. **GO DEEPER** Megan has 38 animal pictures, 5 people pictures, and 3 insect pictures. How many pictures does she have?

_____ pictures

17. **MATHEMATICAL PRACTICE ❶** Analyze

Jamal has a box with 22 toy cars in it. He puts 9 more toy cars into the box. Then he takes 3 toy cars out of the box. How many toy cars are in the box now?

_____ toy cars

18. **THINK SMARTER** Dan has 16 pencils. Quentin gives him 5 more pencils. Choose all the ways you can use to find how many pencils Dan has in all.

○ 16 + 5

○ 16 + 4 + 1

○ 16 − 5

 TAKE HOME ACTIVITY • Say a number from 0 to 9. Have your child name a number to add to yours to have a sum of 10.

FOR MORE PRACTICE: Standards Practice Book

Name _____

Use Compensation

Essential Question How can you make an addend a ten to help solve an addition problem?

Number and Operations in Base Ten—2.NBT.5
MATHEMATICAL PRACTICES
MP.4, MP.6

Listen and Draw

Draw quick pictures to show the problems.

FOR THE TEACHER • Have children draw quick pictures to solve this problem. Kara has 47 stickers. She buys 20 more stickers. How many stickers does she have now? Repeat for this problem. Tyrone has 30 stickers and buys 52 more stickers. How many stickers does he have now?

Math Talk

Mathematical Practices

Describe how you found how many stickers Tyrone has.

Chapter 4

Take ones from an addend to make the other addend the next tens number.

Adding can be easier when one of the addends is a tens number.

$$25 + 48 = ?$$

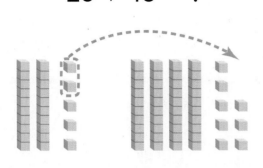

$$\underline{23} + \underline{50} = \underline{}$$

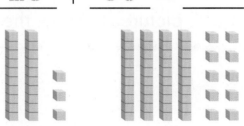

Share and Show

MATH BOARD

Show how to make one addend the next tens number. Complete the new addition sentence.

1. $37 + 25 = ?$

$$\underline{40} + \underline{} = \underline{}$$

2. $27 + 46 = ?$

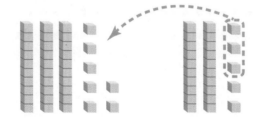

$$\underline{} + \underline{} = \underline{}$$

3. $14 + 29 = ?$

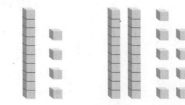

$$\underline{} + \underline{} = \underline{}$$

On Your Own

Show how to make one addend the next tens number.
Complete the new addition sentence.

4. $18 + 13 = ?$

_____ + _____ = _____

5. $24 + 18 = ?$

_____ + _____ = _____

6. $39 + 19 = ?$

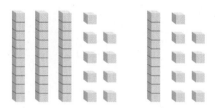

_____ + _____ = _____

Solve. Write or draw to explain.

7. **THINK SMARTER** Zach finds
38 sticks. Kelly finds 27 sticks.
How many more sticks do the
two children still need if they
want 70 sticks in all?

Math
on the
Spot

_____ more sticks

© Houghton Mifflin Harcourt Publishing Company

Problem Solving • Applications (Real World) WRITE ▶ Math

Solve. Write or draw to explain.

8. **MATHEMATICAL PRACTICE 6** Make Connections
The chart shows the leaves that Philip collected. He wants a collection of 52 leaves, using only two colors. Which two colors of leaves should he use?

_____ and _____

Leaves Collected	
Color	**Number**
green	27
brown	29
yellow	25

9. **THINK SMARTER** Ava has 39 sheets of white paper. She has 22 sheets of green paper. Draw a picture and write to explain how to find the number of sheets of paper Ava has.

Ava has _____ sheets of paper.

TAKE HOME ACTIVITY • Have your child choose one problem on this page and explain how to solve it in another way.

FOR MORE PRACTICE:
Standards Practice Book

Name _____

Break Apart Addends as Tens and Ones

Number and Operations in Base Ten—2.NBT.5
MATHEMATICAL PRACTICES
MP.6, MP.8

Essential Question How do you break apart addends to add tens and then add ones?

Listen and Draw

Write the number. Then write the number as tens plus ones.

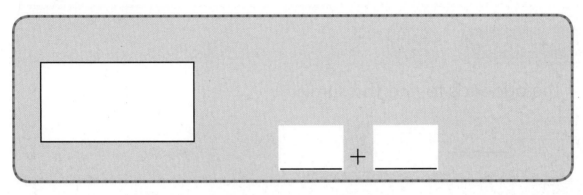

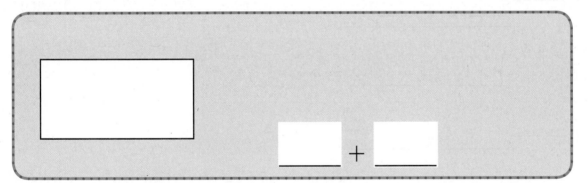

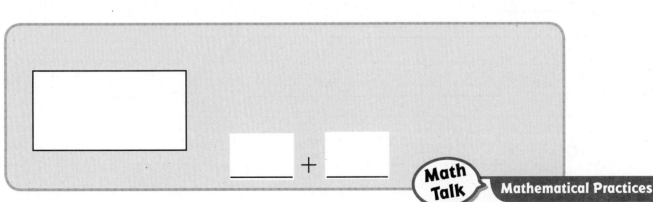

FOR THE TEACHER • Direct children's attention to the orange box. Have children write 25 inside the large rectangle. Then ask children to write 25 as tens plus ones. Repeat the activity for 36 and 42.

Math Talk | **Mathematical Practices**

What is the value of the 6 in the number 63? **Explain** how you know.

Chapter 4

one hundred eighty-one **181**

Model and Draw

Break apart the addends into tens and ones.
Add the tens and add the ones.
Then find the total sum.

27 $\longrightarrow$ 20 + 7
+48 $\longrightarrow$ 40 + 8

60 + 15 = ___

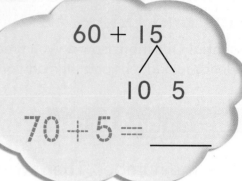

$60 + 15$

$10 \quad 5$

$70 + 5 =$ ___

Break apart the addends to find the sum.

1. 35 $\longrightarrow$ ___ + ___

    +54 $\longrightarrow$ ___ + ___

    ___ + ___ = ___

2. 43 $\longrightarrow$ ___ + ___

    +29 $\longrightarrow$ ___ + ___

    ___ + ___ = ___

3. 56 $\longrightarrow$ ___ + ___

    +38 $\longrightarrow$ ___ + ___

    ___ + ___ = ___

On Your Own

Break apart the addends to find the sum.

4.   14 $\longrightarrow$ _____ + _____

   +23 $\longrightarrow$ _____ + _____
   _____

   _____ + _____ = _____

---

5.   37 $\longrightarrow$ _____ + _____

   +45 $\longrightarrow$ _____ + _____
   _____

   _____ + _____ = _____

---

6.   54 $\longrightarrow$ _____ + _____

   +16 $\longrightarrow$ _____ + _____
   _____

   _____ + _____ = _____

---

7.   **THINK SMARTER** Julie read 18 pages of her book in the morning. She read the same number of pages in the afternoon. How many pages did she read?

_____ pages

Problem Solving • Applications | WRITE ▸ Math

Write or draw to explain.

8. **MATHEMATICAL PRACTICE ①** **Make Sense of Problems** Len has 35 baseball cards. The rest of his cards are basketball cards. He has 58 cards in all. How many basketball cards does he have?

_____ basketball cards

9. **MATHEMATICAL PRACTICE ①** **Evaluate** Tomás has 17 pencils. He buys 26 more pencils. How many pencils does Tomás have now?

_____ pencils

Personal Math Trainer

10. **THINK SMARTER ✚** Sasha used 38 red stickers and 22 blue stickers. Show how you can break apart the addends to find how many stickers Sasha used.

$$38 \longrightarrow \underline{\hspace{1cm}} + \underline{\hspace{1cm}}$$

$$+22 \longrightarrow \underline{\hspace{1cm}} + \underline{\hspace{1cm}}$$

$$\underline{\hspace{1cm}} + \underline{\hspace{1cm}} = \underline{\hspace{1cm}}$$

 TAKE HOME ACTIVITY • Write 32 + 48 on a sheet of paper. Have your child break apart the numbers and find the sum.

FOR MORE PRACTICE: Standards Practice Book

Name _____

Model Regrouping for Addition

Essential Question When do you regroup in addition?

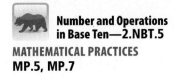

Number and Operations in Base Ten—2.NBT.5

MATHEMATICAL PRACTICES
MP.5, MP.7

Listen and Draw *Real World* **Hands On**

Use ▭▭▭▭ ▪ to model the problem.
Draw quick pictures to show what you did.

Tens	Ones

FOR THE TEACHER • Read the following problem. Brandon has 24 books. His friend Mario has 8 books. How many books do they have?

Math Talk **Mathematical Practices**

Describe how you made a ten in your model.

Chapter 4

one hundred eighty-five **185**

Add 37 and 25.

Step 1 Look at the ones. Can you make a ten?

Tens	Ones

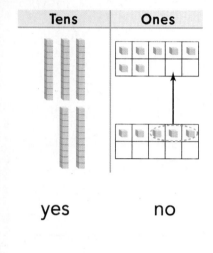

yes   no

Step 2 If you can make a ten, **regroup**.

Tens	Ones

Trade 10 ones for 1 ten to regroup.

Step 3 Write how many tens and ones. Write the sum.

Tens	Ones

_____ tens _____ ones

_____

Share and Show MATH BOARD

Draw to show the regrouping. Write how many tens and ones in the sum. Write the sum.

1. Add 47 and 15.

Tens	Ones

_____ tens _____ ones

_____

✓ 2. Add 48 and 8.

Tens	Ones

_____ tens _____ ones

_____

✓ 3. Add 26 and 38.

Tens	Ones

_____ tens _____ ones

_____

Name _____

On Your Own

Draw to show if you regroup. Write how many tens and ones in the sum. Write the sum.

4. Add 79 and 6.

Tens	Ones

_____ tens _____ ones

_____

5. Add 18 and 64.

Tens	Ones

_____ tens _____ ones

_____

6. Add 23 and 39.

Tens	Ones

_____ tens _____ ones

_____

7. Add 54 and 25.

Tens	Ones

_____ tens _____ ones

_____

8. Add 33 and 7.

Tens	Ones

_____ tens _____ ones

_____

9. Add 27 and 68.

Tens	Ones

_____ tens _____ ones

_____

10. **THINK SMARTER** Kara has 25 toy animals and 12 books. Jorge has 8 more toy animals than Kara has. How many toy animals does Jorge have?

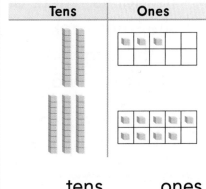

Math on the Spot

_____ toy animals

Problem Solving • Applications

WRITE ▶ Math

Write or draw to explain.

11. **MATHEMATICAL PRACTICE ①** **Make Sense of Problems** Mrs. Sanders has two fish tanks. There are 14 fish in the small tank. There are 27 fish in the large tank. How many fish are in the two tanks?

_____ fish

12. **THINK SMARTER** Charlie climbed 69 steps. Then he climbed 18 more steps. Show two different ways to find how many steps Charlie climbed.

Charlie climbed _____ steps.

 TAKE HOME ACTIVITY • Ask your child to write a word problem with 2-digit numbers about adding two groups of stamps.

FOR MORE PRACTICE: Standards Practice Book

Name _____

Model and Record 2-Digit Addition

Essential Question How do you record 2-digit addition?

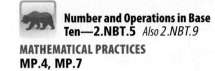

Number and Operations in Base Ten—2.NBT.5 *Also 2.NBT.9*
MATHEMATICAL PRACTICES
MP.4, MP.7

Use ▭▭▭▭▭ ▭ to model the problem.
Draw quick pictures to show what you did.

Tens	Ones

Math Talk
Mathematical Practices

Did you trade blocks in your model? **Explain** why or why not.

FOR THE TEACHER • Read the following problem. Mr. Riley's class collected 54 cans for the food drive. Miss Bright's class collected 35 cans. How many cans did the two classes collect?

Trace over the quick pictures in the steps.

Step 1 Model 37 + 26. Are there 10 ones to regroup?

Tens	Ones

Tens	Ones
	3	7
+	2	6

Step 2 Write the regrouped ten. Write how many ones are in the ones place now.

Tens	Ones

Tens	Ones
	3	7
+	2	6
		3

Step 3 How many tens are there? Write how many tens are in the tens place.

Tens	Ones

Tens	Ones
1	3	7
+	2	6
	6	3

Share and Show

Draw quick pictures to help you solve. Write the sum.

✓ 1.

Tens	Ones
	2	6
+	3	2

Tens	Ones

✓ 2.

Tens	Ones
	5	8
+	2	4

Tens	Ones

Name _____

Draw quick pictures to help you solve. Write the sum.

3.

Tens	Ones
□	
3	4
+	9

Tens	Ones

4.

Tens	Ones
□	
2	7
+ 2	4

Tens	Ones

5.

Tens	Ones
□	
3	5
+ 2	3

Tens	Ones

6.

Tens	Ones
□	
5	9
+	6

Tens	Ones

7. **THINK SMARTER** Tim has 36 stickers. Margo has 44 stickers. How many more stickers would they need to have 100 stickers altogether?

_____ more stickers

Problem Solving • Applications  WRITE Math

Write or draw to explain.

8. **MATHEMATICAL PRACTICE ①** **Make Sense of Problems**
Chris and Bianca got 80 points in all in the spelling contest. Each child got more than 20 points. How many points could each child have gotten?

Chris: _____ points

Bianca: _____ points

Personal Math Trainer

9. **THINK SMARTER +** Don built a tower with 24 blocks. He built another tower with 18 blocks. How many blocks did Don use for both towers? Draw quick pictures to solve. Write the sum.

Tens	Ones

_____ blocks

Did you regroup to find the answer? Explain.

_____

_____

_____

 TAKE HOME ACTIVITY • Write two 2-digit numbers and ask your child if he or she would regroup to find the sum.

FOR MORE PRACTICE: Standards Practice Book

Name _____

2-Digit Addition

Essential Question How do you record the steps when adding 2-digit numbers?

Number and Operations in Base Ten—2.NBT.5, 2.NBT.9
MATHEMATICAL PRACTICES
MP.3, MP.6, MP.8

Listen and Draw Real World

Draw quick pictures to model each problem.

Tens	Ones

Tens	Ones

FOR THE TEACHER • Read the following problem and have children draw quick pictures to solve. Jason scored 35 points in one game and 47 points in another game. How many points did Jason score? Repeat the activity with this problem. Patty scored 18 points. Then she scored 21 points. How many points did she score in all?

Math Talk **Mathematical Practices**

Explain when you need to regroup ones.

Chapter 4

one hundred ninety-three **193**

Add 59 and 24.

Step 1 Add the ones.

$9 + 4 = 13$

Tens	Ones

Tens	Ones
5	9
+ 2	4

Step 2 Regroup.
13 ones is the same as 1 ten 3 ones.

Tens	Ones

Tens	Ones
5	9
+ 2	4
	3

Step 3 Add the tens.

$1 + 5 + 2 = 8$

Tens	Ones

Tens	Ones
1	
5	9
+ 2	4
8	3

Share and Show

Regroup if you need to. Write the sum.

1.

Tens	Ones
4	2
+ 2	9

 2.

Tens	Ones
3	1
+ 1	4

3.

Tens	Ones
2	7
+ 4	5

Name _____

On Your Own

Regroup if you need to. Write the sum.

4.

Tens	Ones
☐	
4	8
+	7

5.

Tens	Ones
☐	
3	5
+ 4	2

6.

Tens	Ones
☐	
7	3
+ 2	0

7.

3	3
+ 2	7

8.

5	2
+	5

9.

3	6
+ 5	8

10.

6	4
+ 2	5

11.

3	5
+ 3	8

12.

3	8
+ 5	2

Solve. Write or draw to explain.

13. **THINK SMARTER** Jin has 31 books about cats and 19 books about dogs. He gives 5 books to his sister. How many books does Jin have now?

_____ books

Problem Solving • Applications Real World   WRITE ▸ Math

14. **GO DEEPER** Abby used a different way to add.
Find the sum, using Abby's way.

$$
\begin{array}{r}
35 \\
+\ 48 \\
\hline
13 \\
+\ 70 \\
\hline
83
\end{array}
$$

$$
\begin{array}{r}
5\ 7 \\
+\ 2\ 9 \\
\hline

\end{array}
$$

15. **MATHEMATICAL PRACTICE ③ Verify the Reasoning of Others**
Describe Abby's way of adding 2-digit numbers.

_____

_____

_____

16. **THINK SMARTER** Melissa saw 14 sea lions and
29 seals. How many animals did she see?
Write a number sentence to find the total
number of animals that she saw.

_____

Explain how the number sentence shows the problem.

_____

 TAKE HOME ACTIVITY • Ask your child to show you two ways
to add 45 and 38.

FOR MORE PRACTICE:
Standards Practice Book

Name _____

Practice 2-Digit Addition

Essential Question How do you record the steps when adding 2-digit numbers?

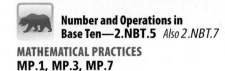

Number and Operations in Base Ten—2.NBT.5 *Also 2.NBT.7*
MATHEMATICAL PRACTICES
MP.1, MP.3, MP.7

Choose one way to solve the problem.
Draw or write to show what you did.

Math Talk

Mathematical Practices

Explain why you chose your way of solving the problem.

FOR THE TEACHER • Read the following problem. There were 45 boys and 63 girls who ran in the race. How many children ran in the race?

Chapter 4

Mrs. Meyers sold 47 snacks before the game. Then she sold 85 snacks during the game. How many snacks did she sell?

Step 1 Add the ones.

$7 + 5 = 12$

Regroup 12 ones as 1 ten 2 ones.

```
  1
  4 7
+ 8 5
─────
    2
```

Step 2 Add the tens.

$1 + 4 + 8 = 13$

```
  1
  4 7
+ 8 5
─────
    2
```

Step 3 13 tens can be regrouped as 1 hundred 3 tens. Write the hundreds digit and the tens digit in the sum.

```
  1
  4 7
+ 8 5
─────
13 2
```

Share and Show

Write the sum.

1.
```
  3 8
+ 9 4
```

2.
```
  4 5
+ 5 2
```

3.
```
  8 3
+ 7 6
```

4.
```
  5 6
+ 3 5
```

5.
```
  6 3
+ 5 1
```

6.
```
  7 4
+ 4 9
```

Name _____

On Your Own

Write the sum.

7.
$$\begin{array}{r} 5\ 2 \\ +\ \ 3\ 7 \\ \hline \end{array}$$

8.
$$\begin{array}{r} 8\ 8 \\ +\ \ 2\ 1 \\ \hline \end{array}$$

9.
$$\begin{array}{r} 7\ 4 \\ +\ \ 6\ 7 \\ \hline \end{array}$$

10.
$$\begin{array}{r} 9\ 3 \\ +\ \ 5\ 4 \\ \hline \end{array}$$

11.
$$\begin{array}{r} 9\ 2 \\ +\ \ 7\ 8 \\ \hline \end{array}$$

12.
$$\begin{array}{r} 5\ 6 \\ +\ \ 1\ 6 \\ \hline \end{array}$$

13.
$$\begin{array}{r} 3\ 1 \\ +\ \ 4\ 5 \\ \hline \end{array}$$

14.
$$\begin{array}{r} 4\ 3 \\ +\ \ 7\ 2 \\ \hline \end{array}$$

15. **THINK SMARTER** Without finding the sums, circle the pairs of addends for which the sum will be greater than 100.

Explain how you decided which pairs to circle.

73
18

54
71

47
62

36
59

_____

_____

_____

_____

TAKE HOME ACTIVITY • Tell your child two 2-digit numbers. Have him or her write the numbers and find the sum.

FOR MORE PRACTICE:
Standards Practice Book

Name _____

Concepts and Skills

Break apart ones to make a ten.
Then add and write the sum. (2.NBT.6)

1. $37 + 8 =$ _____

2. $55 + 7 =$ _____

Break apart the addends to find the sum. (2.NBT.6)

3. $27 \longrightarrow$ _____ + _____

   $+36 \longrightarrow$ _____ + _____

   _____ + _____ = _____

Write the sum. (2.NBT.5)

4.
$$\begin{array}{r} 2\ 8 \\ +\ \ 5\ 7 \\ \hline \end{array}$$

5.
$$\begin{array}{r} 6\ 7 \\ +\ \ 3\ 1 \\ \hline \end{array}$$

6.
$$\begin{array}{r} 7\ 1 \\ +\ \ 1\ 9 \\ \hline \end{array}$$

7. **THINK SMARTER** Julia collected 25 cans to recycle. Dan collected 14 cans. How many cans did they collect? (2.NBT.5)

_____ cans

Name _____

Rewrite 2-Digit Addition

Essential Question What are two different ways to write addition problems?

Number and Operations in Base Ten—2.NBT.5
MATHEMATICAL PRACTICES
MP.6, MP.7

Listen and Draw · Real World

Write the numbers for each addition problem.

+
_____

+
_____

+
_____

+
_____

FOR THE TEACHER • Read the following problem and have children write the addends in vertical format. Juan's family drove 32 miles to his grandmother's house. Then they drove 14 miles to his aunt's house. How many miles did they drive? Repeat for three more problems.

Math Talk **Mathematical Practices**

Explain why it is important to line up the digits of these addends in columns.

Chapter 4

two hundred one **201**

Add. 28 + 45 = ?

Step 1 For 28, write the tens digit in the tens column.

Write the ones digit in the ones column.

Repeat for 45.

```
  2 8
+ 4 5
```

Step 2 Add the ones. Regroup if you need to. Add the tens.

```
  2 8
+ 4 5
```

Share and Show

Rewrite the addition problem. Then add.

1. 25 + 8

   $+$ _____

2. 37 + 10

   $+$ _____

3. 25 + 45

   $+$ _____

4. 38 + 29

   $+$ _____

5. 20 + 45

   $+$ _____

6. 63 + 9

   $+$ _____

7. 15 + 36

   $+$ _____

8. 74 + 18

   $+$ _____

Name _____

On Your Own

Rewrite the addition problem. Then add.

9. 27 + 54   10. 34 + 30   11. 26 + 17   12. 48 + 38

+_____   +_____   +_____   +_____

13. 50 + 32   14. 61 + 38   15. 37 + 43   16. 79 + 17

+_____   +_____   +_____   +_____

17. 45 + 40   18. 21 + 52   19. 17 + 76   20. 68 + 29

+_____   +_____   +_____   +_____

21. **THINK SMARTER** For which of the problems above could you find the sum without rewriting it? Explain.

_____

_____

_____

Problem Solving • Applications

WRITE) Math

Use the table.
Write or draw to
show how you
solved the problem.

Points Scored This Season	
Player	Number of Points
Anna	26
Lou	37
Becky	23
Kevin	19

22. **MATHEMATICAL PRACTICE ①** Analyze Relationships
Which two players scored 56 points
in all? Add to check your answer.

_____ and_____

23. **THINK SMARTER** Shawn says he can find the sum
of 20 + 63 without rewriting it. Explain how
to find the sum using mental math.

_____

_____

_____

_____

TAKE HOME ACTIVITY • Have your child write and
solve another problem, using the table above.

FOR MORE PRACTICE:
Standards Practice Book

Name _____

Problem Solving • Addition

Essential Question How can drawing a diagram help when solving addition problems?

Operations and Algebraic Thinking—2.OA.1 *Also 2.NBT.5*
MATHEMATICAL PRACTICES
MP.1, MP.2, MP.4

Kendra had 13 crayons. Her dad gave her some more crayons. Then she had 19 crayons. How many crayons did Kendra's dad give her?

🔑 Unlock the Problem

What do I need to find?

how many crayons
_____
Kendra's dad gave her

What information do I need to use?

She had _____ crayons. After he gave her some more crayons, she had _____ crayons.

Show how to solve the problem.

13	_____

19

There are 19 crayons in all.

13 + ⬛ = 19
_____

_____ crayons

HOME CONNECTION • Your child used a bar model and a number sentence to represent the problem. These help show what the missing amount is in order to solve the problem.

Chapter 4

two hundred five **205**

Label the bar model. Write a number sentence with a ▇ for the missing number. Solve.

1. Mr. Kane has 24 red pens. He buys 19 blue pens. How many pens does he have now?

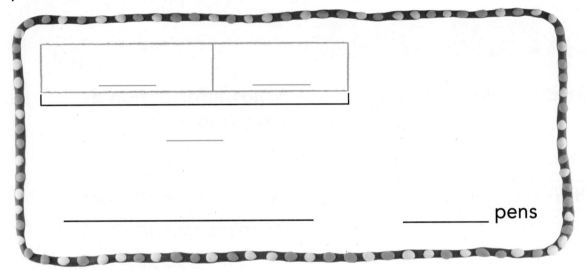

_____ _____ pens

2. Hannah has 10 pencils. Jim and Hannah have 17 pencils altogether. How many pencils does Jim have?

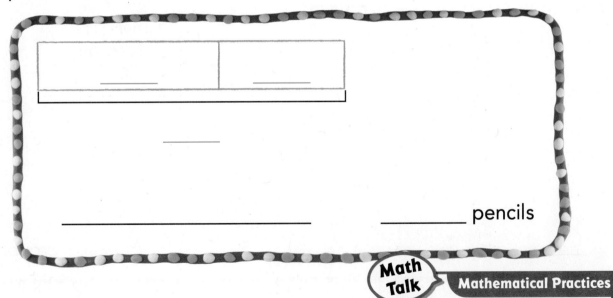

_____ _____ pencils

Math Talk **Mathematical Practices**

Explain how you know if an amount is a part or the whole in a problem.

Name _____

Label the bar model. Write a number sentence with a ▨ for the missing number. Solve.

3. Aimee and Matthew catch 17 crickets in all. Aimee catches 9 crickets. How many crickets does Matthew catch?

_____ crickets

_____

4. Percy counts 16 grasshoppers at the park. He counts 15 grasshoppers at home. How many grasshoppers does Percy count?

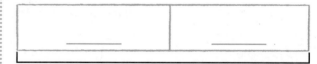

_____ grasshoppers

_____

5. **THINK SMARTER** There are three groups of owls. There are 17 owls in each of the first two groups. There are 47 owls in all. How many owls are in the third group?

_____ owls

  **WRITE** Math

Write or draw to explain.

6. There are 37 paper clips in the box and 24 paper clips on the table. How many paper clips in all are there?

_____ paper clips

---

7. **MATHEMATICAL PRACTICE ①** **Make Sense of Problems**
Jeff has 19 postcards and 2 pens. He buys 20 more postcards. How many postcards does he have now?

_____ postcards

---

8. **GO DEEPER** Alicia drew 15 flowers. Marie drew 4 more flowers than Alicia drew. How many flowers did they draw?

_____ flowers

---

9. **THINK SMARTER** There are 23 books in a box. There are 29 books on a shelf. How many books are there?

_____ books

 TAKE HOME ACTIVITY • Ask your child to explain how to solve one of the problems above.

FOR MORE PRACTICE: Standards Practice Book

© Houghton Mifflin Harcourt Publishing Company

Name _____

Algebra • Write Equations to Represent Addition

Essential Question How do you write a number sentence to represent a problem?

Operations and Algebraic Thinking—2.OA.1 *Also 2.NBT.5*
MATHEMATICAL PRACTICES
MP.1, MP.2, MP.4

Listen and Draw *Real World*

Draw to show how you found the answer.

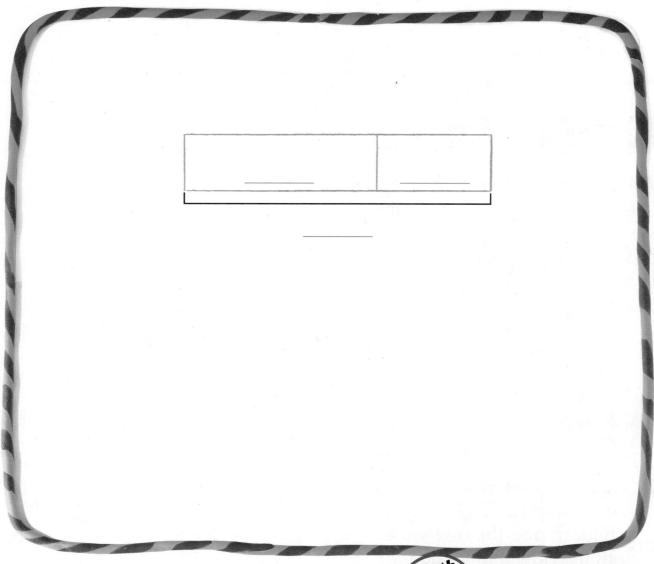

FOR THE TEACHER • Read the following problem and have children choose their own methods for solving. There are 15 children on the bus. Then 9 more children get on the bus. How many children are on the bus now?

Math Talk **Mathematical Practices**

Explain how you found the number of children on the bus.

You can write a number sentence to show a problem.

Sandy has 16 pencils. Nancy has 13 pencils. How many pencils do the two girls have?

$$16 + 13 = \blacksquare$$

THINK:
$$
\begin{array}{r}
16 \text{ pencils} \\
+\ 13 \text{ pencils} \\
\hline
29 \text{ pencils}
\end{array}
$$

The two girls have _____ pencils.

Share and Show

Write a number sentence for the problem.
Use a ▇ for the missing number. Then solve.

☑1. Carl sees 25 melons at the store. 15 are small and the rest are large. How many melons are large?

_____

_____ melons

☑2. 83 people went to a movie on Thursday. 53 of them were children and the rest were adults. How many adults were at the movie?

_____

_____ adults

On Your Own

Write a number sentence for the problem.
Use a ▢ for the missing number. Then solve.

3. Jake had some stamps. Then
he bought 20 more stamps.
Now he has 56 stamps. How
many stamps did Jake have
to start?

_____   _____ stamps

---

4. THINK SMARTER Braden's class went to the
park. They saw 26 oak trees and
14 maple trees. They also saw 13 cardinals
and 35 blue jays. Compare the number of
trees and the number of birds that
the class saw.

_____ ◯ _____

---

5. MATHEMATICAL PRACTICE 6 Explain Amy needs about
70 paper clips. Without adding,
circle 2 boxes that would be close
to the amount that she needs.

| 70 clips | 81 clips | 54 clips |
| 19 clips | 35 clips | 32 clips |

Explain how you made your choices.

_____

_____

_____

Problem Solving • Applications   WRITE ⟩ Math

6. **MATHEMATICAL PRACTICE ①** Make Sense of Problems
Mr. Walton baked 24 breads last week.
He baked 28 breads this week. How many
breads did he bake in the two weeks?   _____ breads

---

7. **THINK SMARTER** Denise saw these bags of
oranges at the store.

10 oranges   14 oranges   12 oranges   11 oranges

Denise bought 26 oranges. Which two
bags of oranges did she buy?
Draw or write to show how you solved the problem.

Explain how you found the numbers that have a sum of 26.

_____

_____

_____

TAKE HOME ACTIVITY • Have your child explain how he or she
writes a number sentence to stand for a problem.

FOR MORE PRACTICE:
Standards Practice Book

Name _____

Algebra • Find Sums for 3 Addends

Essential Question What are some ways to add 3 numbers?

Number and Operations in Base Ten—2.NBT.6
MATHEMATICAL PRACTICES
MP.6, MP.8

Listen and Draw Real World

Draw to show each problem.

Math Talk

Mathematical Practices

Which numbers did you add first in the first problem? **Explain** why.

FOR THE TEACHER • Read the following problem and have children draw to show it. Mr. Kim bought 5 blue balloons, 4 red balloons, and 5 yellow balloons. How many balloons did Mr. Kim buy? Repeat for another problem.

Chapter 4

two hundred thirteen **213**

Model and Draw

There are different ways to add three numbers.

How can you add 23, 41, and 17?

Think of different ways to choose digits in the ones column to add first.

> You can make a ten first. Then add the other ones digit. Then add the tens.

> Add from top to bottom. First add the top two digits in the ones column, then add the next digit. Then add the tens.

```
  2 3
  4 1
+ 1 7
-----
```

$3 + 7 = 10$
$10 + 1 = 11$

```
  2 3
  4 1
+ 1 7
-----
```

$3 + 1 = 4$
$4 + 7 = 11$

Share and Show

Add.

1.
```
    33
    34
 + 32
-----
```

2.
```
    47
    21
 +  7
-----
```

3.
```
    65
    13
 + 15
-----
```

4.
```
    58
    27
 + 22
-----
```

5.
```
    12
    22
 + 36
-----
```

6.
```
    10
    42
 + 36
-----
```

✓7.
```
    31
    21
 + 16
-----
```

✓8.
```
    30
    29
 + 48
-----
```

Name _____

On Your Own

Add.

9.
```
   22
   27
 +18
```

10.
```
   26
   31
 +19
```

11.
```
   24
   11
 +53
```

12.
```
   33
   43
 +  4
```

13.
```
   40
   17
 +32
```

14.
```
   25
   25
 +25
```

15.
```
   19
   65
 +24
```

16.
```
   73
    4
 + 16
```

17.
```
   35
   24
 +58
```

18.
```
   32
   18
 + 28
```

19.
```
   42
   31
 +12
```

20.
```
   70
   18
 +17
```

21. **THINK SMARTER** Sophia had 44 marbles. She bought 24 more marbles. Then John gave her 35 marbles. How many marbles does Sophia have now?

Math on the Spot

_____ marbles

Problem Solving • Applications (Real World)   WRITE ▸ Math

Solve. Write or draw to explain.

22. **MATHEMATICAL PRACTICE ①** Evaluate Mrs. Shaw has 23 red notebooks, 15 blue notebooks, and 27 green notebooks. How many notebooks does she have?

_____ notebooks

23. **MATHEMATICAL PRACTICE ④** Model Mathematics Write a story problem that could be solved using this number sentence.

$$12 + 28 + \blacksquare = 53$$

_____

_____

_____

_____

24. **THINK SMARTER** Mr. Samson gave his students 31 yellow pencils, 27 red pencils, and 25 blue pencils. How many pencils did he give to his students?

_____ pencils

 TAKE HOME ACTIVITY • Ask your child to show you two ways to add 17, 13, and 24.

FOR MORE PRACTICE: Standards Practice Book

Name _____

Algebra • Find Sums for 4 Addends

Essential Question What are some ways to add 4 numbers?

Number and Operations in Base Ten—2.NBT.6
MATHEMATICAL PRACTICES
MP.6, MP.8

Show how you solved each problem.

Math Talk Mathematical Practices

Describe how you found the answer to the first problem.

FOR THE TEACHER • Read this problem and have children choose a way to solve it. Shelly counts 16 ants in her ant farm. Pedro counts 22 ants in his farm. Tara counts 14 ants in her farm. How many ants do the 3 children count? Repeat for another problem.

Model and Draw

You can add digits in a column in more than one way. Add the ones first. Then add the tens.

Find a sum that you know.
Then add to it.

$$\begin{array}{r} 3\;1 \\ 1\;4 \\ 2\;7 \\ +2\;4 \end{array}$$

THINK:
8 + 1 = 9, then add on 7 more. The sum of the ones is 16 ones.

Add pairs of digits first.
Then add these sums.

$$\begin{array}{r} 3\;1 \\ 1\;4 \\ 2\;7 \\ +2\;4 \end{array}$$

THINK:
5 + 11 = 16, so there are 16 ones in all.

Share and Show

Add.

1.
$$\begin{array}{r} 23 \\ 11 \\ 22 \\ +31 \end{array}$$

2.
$$\begin{array}{r} 30 \\ 15 \\ 3 \\ +25 \end{array}$$

3.
$$\begin{array}{r} 13 \\ 26 \\ 54 \\ +12 \end{array}$$

4.
$$\begin{array}{r} 27 \\ 2 \\ 23 \\ +13 \end{array}$$

☑5.
$$\begin{array}{r} 45 \\ 14 \\ 35 \\ +51 \end{array}$$

☑6.
$$\begin{array}{r} 32 \\ 21 \\ 15 \\ +30 \end{array}$$

On Your Own

Add.

7.	8.	9.
36	14	22
12	23	13
21	20	15
+ 26	+ 11	+ 27

10.	11.	12.
45	59	34
12	31	10
41	51	31
+ 22	+ 73	+ 22

13.	14.	15.
14	21	16
40	12	61
51	32	25
+ 32	+ 24	+ 44

Solve. Write or draw to explain.

16. **THINK SMARTER** Laney added four numbers which have a total of 128. She spilled some juice over one number. What is that number?

$$22 + 43 + + 30 = 128$$

_____

Problem Solving • Applications  WRITE Math

Use the table.
Write or draw to show how
you solved the problems.

Shells Collected at the Beach	
Child	Number of Shells
Katie	34
Paul	15
Noah	26
Laura	21

17. **MATHEMATICAL PRACTICE ①** **Evaluate** How many shells did the four children collect at the beach?

_____ shells

18. **GO DEEPER** Which two children collected more shells at the beach, Katie and Paul, or Noah and Laura?

19. **THINK SMARTER** There were 24 red beads, 31 blue beads, and 8 green beads in a jar. Then Emma put 16 beads into the jar. Write a number sentence to show the number of beads in the jar.

_____

 TAKE HOME ACTIVITY • Have your child explain what he or she learned in this lesson.

FOR MORE PRACTICE:
Standards Practice Book

✓ Chapter 4 Review/Test

1. Beth baked 24 carrot muffins. She baked 18 apple muffins. How many muffins did Beth bake?

   Label the bar model. Write a number sentence with a ▇ for the missing number. Solve.

   ┌──────────────────────┬──────────────────┐
   │   _____   │   _____   │
   └──────────────────────┴──────────────────┘

   _____

   _____   _____ muffins

2. Carlos has 23 red keys, 36 blue keys, and 44 green keys. How many keys does he have?

   Carlos has │ 67 │ keys.
              │ 80 │
              │ 103 │

3. Mike sees 17 blue cars and 25 green cars at the toy store. How many cars does he see?

   ○ 17   ○ 25   ○ 25   ○ 17
     + 25   − 17   + 17   + 17
     ____   ____   ____   ____

   Mike sees _____ cars.

   Describe how you solved the problem.

   _____

   _____

4. Jerry has 53 pencils in one drawer. He has 27 pencils in another drawer.

   Draw a picture or write to explain how to find the number of pencils in both drawers.

   Jerry has _____ pencils.

---

5. Lauren sees 14 birds. Her friend sees 7 birds. How many birds do Lauren and her friend see? Draw quick pictures to solve. Write the sum.

Tens	Ones

   _____ birds

   Did you regroup to find the answer? Explain.

   _____

   _____

---

6. Matt says he can find the sum of 45 + 50 without rewriting it. Explain how you can solve this problem using mental math.

   _____

   _____

7. Ling sees the three signs at the theater.

Section A	Section B	Section C
35 seats	43 seats	17 seats

Which two sections have 78 seats?

Explain how you made your choices.

_____

_____

---

8. Leah put 21 white marbles, 31 black marbles, and 7 blue marbles in a bag. Then her sister added 19 yellow marbles.

Write a number sentence to show the number of marbles in the bag.

_____

---

9. Nicole made a necklace. She used 13 red beads and 26 blue beads. Show how you can break apart the addends to find how many beads Nicole used.

$$13 \longrightarrow \underline{\quad\quad} + \underline{\quad\quad}$$

$$+\ 26 \longrightarrow \underline{\quad\quad} + \underline{\quad\quad}$$

$$\underline{\quad\quad} + \underline{\quad\quad} = \underline{\quad\quad}$$

10. Without finding the sums, does the pair of addends have a sum greater than 100? Choose Yes or No.

51 + 92	○ Yes	○ No
42 + 27	○ Yes	○ No
82 + 33	○ Yes	○ No
62 + 14	○ Yes	○ No

Explain how you decided which pairs have a sum greater than 100.

_____

_____

_____

11. Leslie finds 24 paper clips in her desk. She finds 8 more paper clips in her pencil box. Choose all the ways you can use to find how many paper clips Leslie has in all.

- ○ 24 + 8
- ○ 24 − 8
- ○ 24 + 6 + 2

12. Mr. O'Brien visited a lighthouse. He climbed 26 stairs. Then he climbed 64 more stairs to the top. How many stairs did he climb at the lighthouse?

_____ stairs

© Houghton Mifflin Harcourt Publishing Company

2-Digit Subtraction

There are hundreds of different kinds of dragonflies. If 52 dragonflies are in a garden and 10 fly away, how many dragonflies are left? How many are left if 10 more fly away?

Show What You Know

Subtraction Patterns

Subtract 2. Complete each subtraction sentence.

1. 7 − __2__ = __5__   4. 4 − ____ = ____

2. 6 − ____ = ____   5. 3 − ____ = ____

3. 5 − ____ = ____   6. 2 − ____ = ____

Subtraction Facts

Write the difference.

7. 8   8. 14   9. 9   10. 16   11. 12   12. 10
  − 5   − 6   − 6   − 7   − 6   − 8

Tens and Ones

Write how many tens and ones are in each model.

13. 54   14. 45

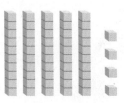   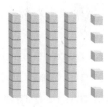

____ tens ____ ones   ____ tens ____ ones

This page checks understanding of important
skills needed for success in Chapter 5.

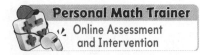

Personal Math Trainer
Online Assessment
and Intervention

Name _____

Vocabulary Builder

Review Words
difference
regroup
tens
ones
digit

Visualize It

Fill in the boxes of the graphic organizer.

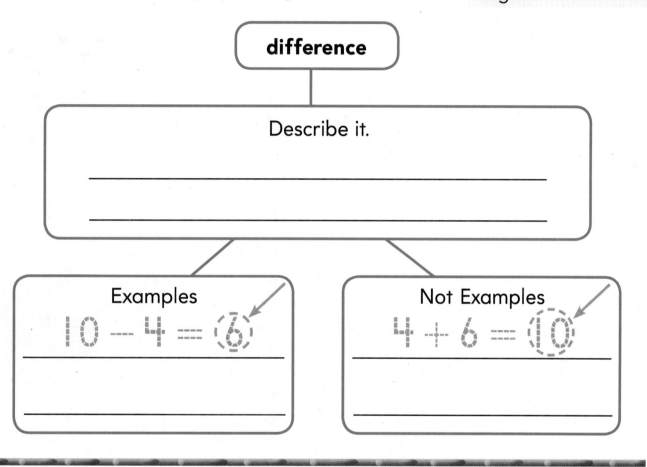

difference

Describe it.

_____

_____

Examples	Not Examples
10 − 4 = 6	4 + 6 = 10

Understand Vocabulary

Draw a line to complete the sentence.

1. A **digit** can be •   • as 2 **tens**.

2. You can **regroup** •   • 0, 1, 2, 3, 4, 5, 6, 7, 8, or 9.

3. 20 **ones** are the same •   • to trade 10 ones for 1 ten.

© Houghton Mifflin Harcourt Publishing Company

GO DIGITAL
• Interactive Student Edition
• Multimedia eGlossary

Game Subtraction Search

Materials

• 3 sets of number cards 4–9   • 18 ⬤

Play with a partner.

1. Shuffle all the cards. Place them face down in one stack.

2. Take one card. Find a square with a subtraction problem with this number as the difference. Your partner checks your answer.

3. If you are correct, place a ⬤ on that square. If there is no match, skip your turn.

4. Take turns. The first player to have ⬤ on all the squares wins.

Player 1

12 − 5	9 − 2	10 − 5
16 − 7	13 − 7	17 − 9
7 − 3	11 − 5	18 − 9

Player 2

8 − 3	15 − 7	11 − 6
17 − 8	9 − 3	16 − 8
13 − 9	6 − 2	14 − 7

Name _____

Algebra • Break Apart Ones to Subtract

Essential Question How does breaking apart a number make subtracting easier?

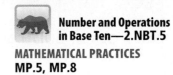

Number and Operations in Base Ten—2.NBT.5

MATHEMATICAL PRACTICES
MP.5, MP.8

Listen and Draw

Write two addends for each sum.

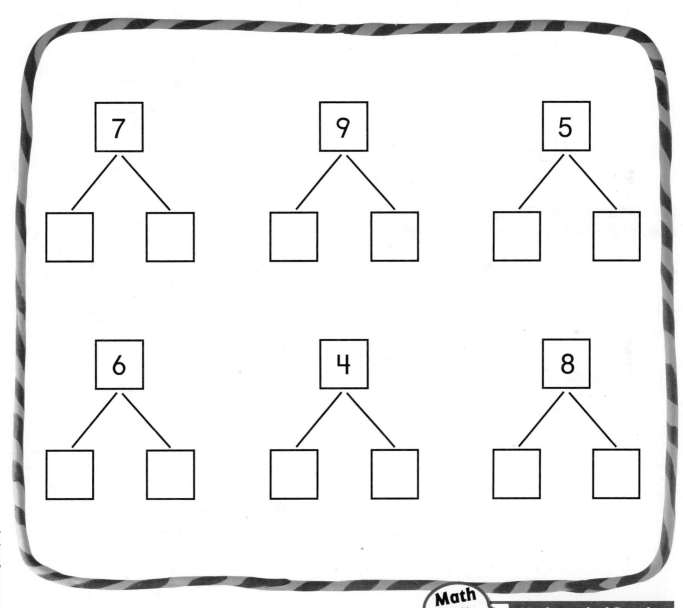

FOR THE TEACHER • After children have recorded addends for each sum, have a class discussion about the different facts that children represented on their papers.

Math Talk

Mathematical Practices

Describe how you chose addends for each sum.

Chapter 5

two hundred twenty-nine **229**

Break apart ones. Subtract in two steps.

$63 - 7 = \blacksquare$

3 4

Start at 63.
Subtract 3 to get
to 60. Then subtract
4 more.

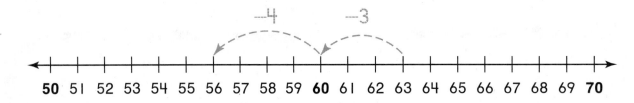

So, $63 - 7 = $ _____.

Share and Show

MATH BOARD

Break apart ones to subtract. Write the difference.

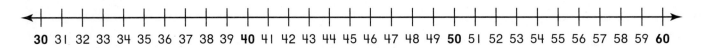

1. $55 - 8 = $ _____

5 3

2. $42 - 5 = $ _____

2 3

3. $41 - 9 = $ _____

4. $53 - 6 = $ _____

5. $44 - 7 = $ _____

6. $52 - 8 = $ _____

Name _____

On Your Own

Break apart ones to subtract. Write the difference.

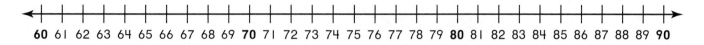

60 61 62 63 64 65 66 67 68 69 **70** 71 72 73 74 75 76 77 78 79 **80** 81 82 83 84 85 86 87 88 89 **90**

7. $75 - 7 =$ _____

8. $86 - 8 =$ _____

9. $82 - 5 =$ _____

10. $83 - 7 =$ _____

11. $72 - 7 =$ _____

12. $76 - 9 =$ _____

13. $85 - 8 =$ _____

14. $71 - 6 =$ _____

15. **THINK SMARTER** Cheryl brought 27 bagels for the bake sale. Mike brought 24 bagels. They sold all but 9 of them. How many bagels did they sell?

_____ bagels

16. **MATHEMATICAL PRACTICE ❶** Analyze Lexi has 8 fewer crayons than Ken. Ken has 45 crayons. How many crayons does Lexi have?

_____ crayons

Problem Solving • Applications  WRITE ▸ Math

Write or draw to explain.

17. Cheryl built a toy train with 27 train cars. Then she added 18 more train cars. How many train cars are on the toy train now?

_____ train cars

18.  **Analyze**

Samuel had 46 marbles. He gave some marbles to a friend and has 9 marbles left. How many marbles did Samuel give to his friend?

_____ marbles

19. *THINK SMARTER* Matthew had 73 blocks. He gave 8 blocks to his sister. How many blocks does Matthew have now?

Draw or write to show how to solve the problem.

Matthew has _____ blocks now.

 TAKE HOME ACTIVITY • Ask your child to describe how to find 34 − 6.

Name _____

Algebra • Break Apart Numbers to Subtract

Essential Question How does breaking apart a number make subtracting easier?

Number and Operations in Base Ten—2.NBT.5
MATHEMATICAL PRACTICES
MP.5, MP.8

Listen and Draw · Real World

Draw jumps on the number line to show how to break apart the number to subtract.

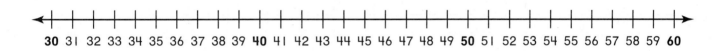

30 31 32 33 34 35 36 37 38 39 **40** 41 42 43 44 45 46 47 48 49 **50** 51 52 53 54 55 56 57 58 59 **60**

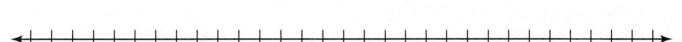

50 51 52 53 54 55 56 57 58 59 **60** 61 62 63 64 65 66 67 68 69 **70** 71 72 73 74 75 76 77 78 79 **80**

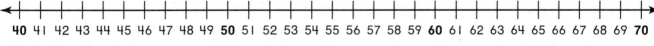

40 41 42 43 44 45 46 47 48 49 **50** 51 52 53 54 55 56 57 58 59 **60** 61 62 63 64 65 66 67 68 69 **70**

FOR THE TEACHER • Read the following problem. Have children draw jumps on the number line to solve. Mrs. Hill had 45 paintbrushes. She gave 9 paintbrushes to students in her art class. How many paintbrushes does Mrs. Hill have now? Repeat the same problem situation for 72 − 7 and 53 − 6.

Math Talk **Mathematical Practices**

For one of the problems, **describe** what you did.

Chapter 5

two hundred thirty-three **233**

Model and Draw

Break apart the number you are subtracting
into tens and ones.

Subtract 10.
Next, subtract 2 to get to 60.
Then subtract 5 more.

$$72 - 17 = \blacksquare$$

10 7

2 5

10 + 2 + 5 = 17

−5   −2   −10

50 51 52 53 54 55 56 57 58 59 **60** 61 62 63 64 65 66 67 68 69 **70** 71 72 73 74 75 76 77 78 79 **80**

So, $72 - 17 =$ _____ .

Share and Show

Break apart the number you are subtracting.
Write the difference.

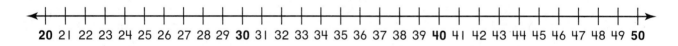

20 21 22 23 24 25 26 27 28 29 **30** 31 32 33 34 35 36 37 38 39 **40** 41 42 43 44 45 46 47 48 49 **50**

1. $43 - 18 =$ _____

10 8

3 5

2. $45 - 14 =$ _____

10 4

✓ 3. $46 - 17 =$ _____

✓ 4. $44 - 16 =$ _____

On Your Own

Break apart the number you are subtracting.
Write the difference.

40 41 42 43 44 45 46 47 48 49 **50** 51 52 53 54 55 56 57 58 59 **60** 61 62 63 64 65 66 67 68 69 **70**

5. $57 - 15 =$ _____

6. $63 - 17 =$ _____

7. $68 - 19 =$ _____

8. $61 - 18 =$ _____

9. **THINK SMARTER** Jane has 53 toys in a box. She takes some toys out. Now there are 36 toys in the box. How many toys did Jane take out of the box?

_____ toys

10. **GO DEEPER** Look at Tom's steps to solve a problem. Solve this problem in the same way.

$$42 - 15 = ?$$

Tom
$35 - 18 = ?$
$35 - 10 = 25$
$25 - 5 = 20$
$20 - 3 = \boxed{17}$

Problem Solving • Applications (Real World)

11. 38 people are in the library. Then 33 more people go into the library. How many people are in the library now?

_____ people

12. **MATHEMATICAL PRACTICE ①** **Analyze** Alex has 24 toys in a chest. He takes some toys out of the chest. Then there are 16 toys in the chest. How many toys did he take out of the chest?

_____ toys

13. **THINK SMARTER** Gail has two piles of newspapers. There are 32 papers in the first pile. There are 19 papers in the second pile. How many more papers are in the first pile than in the second pile?

_____ more papers

Write or draw to explain how you solved the problem.

 TAKE HOME ACTIVITY • Ask your child to write a subtraction story that uses 2-digit numbers.

FOR MORE PRACTICE: Standards Practice Book

© Houghton Mifflin Harcourt Publishing Company

236 two hundred thirty-six

Model Regrouping for Subtraction

Essential Question When do you regroup in subtraction?

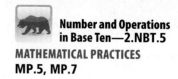

Number and Operations in Base Ten—2.NBT.5
MATHEMATICAL PRACTICES
MP.5, MP.7

Listen and Draw *Real World* Hands On

Use  to model the problem.
Draw quick pictures to show your model.

Tens	Ones

Math Talk

Mathematical Practices

Describe why you traded a tens block for 10 ones blocks.

FOR THE TEACHER • Read the following problem. Michelle counted 21 butterflies in her garden. Then 7 butterflies flew away. How many butterflies were still in the garden?

Chapter 5

Model and Draw

How do you subtract 26 from 53?

Step 1 Show 53. Are there enough ones to subtract 6?

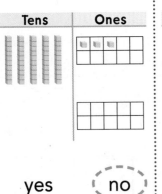

Tens	Ones

yes   (no)

Step 2 If there are not enough ones, regroup 1 ten as 10 ones.

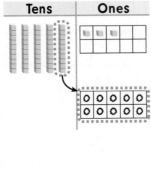

Tens	Ones

Step 3 Subtract 6 ones from 13 ones.

Tens	Ones

Step 4 Subtract the tens. Write the tens and ones. Write the difference.

Tens	Ones

____ tens ____ ones

_____

Share and Show

MATH BOARD

Draw to show the regrouping. Write the difference two ways. Write the tens and ones. Write the number.

1. Subtract 13 from 41.

Tens	Ones

____ tens ____ ones

_____

✓2. Subtract 9 from 48.

Tens	Ones

____ tens ____ ones

_____

✓3. Subtract 28 from 52.

Tens	Ones

____ tens ____ ones

_____

Name _____

On Your Own

Draw to show the regrouping. Write the difference two ways. Write the tens and ones. Write the number.

4. Subtract 8 from 23.

Tens	Ones

_____ ten _____ ones

_____

5. Subtract 36 from 45.

Tens	Ones

_____ tens _____ ones

_____

6. Subtract 6 from 43.

Tens	Ones

_____ tens _____ ones

_____

7. Subtract 39 from 67.

Tens	Ones

_____ tens _____ ones

_____

8. Subtract 21 from 50.

Tens	Ones

_____ tens _____ ones

_____

9. Subtract 29 from 56.

Tens	Ones

_____ tens _____ ones

_____

10. **GO DEEPER** Draw to find what number was subtracted from 53.

Subtract _____ from 53.

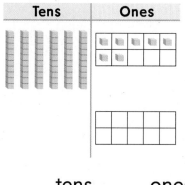
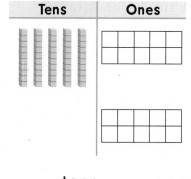

__3__ tens __4__ ones

__34__

Tens	Ones

Problem Solving • Applications WRITE ▸ Math

Write or draw to explain.

11. **THINK SMARTER** Billy has 18 fewer marbles than Sara. Sara has 34 marbles. How many marbles does Billy have?

_____ marbles

Personal Math Trainer

12. **THINK SMARTER +** There are 67 toy animals in the store. Then the clerk sells 19 toy animals. How many toy animals are in the store now?

Draw to show how to find the answer.

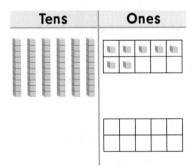

Tens	Ones

_____ toy animals

Describe how you solved the problem.

_____

_____

_____

 TAKE HOME ACTIVITY • Ask your child to write a subtraction story and then explain how to solve it.

FOR MORE PRACTICE:
Standards Practice Book

Name _____

Model and Record 2-Digit Subtraction

Essential Question How do you record 2-digit subtraction?

Number and Operations in Base Ten—2.NBT.5 *Also 2.NBT.9*
MATHEMATICAL PRACTICES
MP.4, MP.7

Listen and Draw *Real World* | *Hands On*

Use ▭▭▭▭ ▪ to model the problem.
Draw quick pictures to show your model.

Tens	Ones

Math Talk **Mathematical Practices**

Did you trade blocks in your model? **Explain** why or why not.

FOR THE TEACHER • Read the following problem. Mr. Kelly made 47 muffins. His students ate 23 of the muffins. How many muffins were not eaten?

Model and Draw

Trace over the quick pictures in the steps.

Subtract.   56
            −19

Step 1 Show 56. Are there enough ones to subtract 9?

Tens	Ones
5	6
− 1	9

Step 2 If there are not enough ones, regroup 1 ten as 10 ones.

Tens	Ones
4	16
5	6
− 1	9

Step 3 Subtract the ones.

$16 − 9 = 7$

Tens	Ones
4	16
5	6
− 1	9
	7

Step 4 Subtract the tens.

$4 − 1 = 3$

Tens	Ones
4	16
5	6
− 1	9
3	7

Share and Show

Draw a quick picture to solve. Write the difference.

1.

Tens	Ones
4	7
− 1	5

Tens	Ones

2.

Tens	Ones
3	2
− 1	8

Tens	Ones

On Your Own

Draw a quick picture to solve. Write the difference.

3.

Tens	Ones
□	□
3	5
2	9

Tens	Ones

4.

Tens	Ones
□	□
2	8
	5

Tens	Ones

5.

Tens	Ones
□	□
5	3
2	6

Tens	Ones

6.

Tens	Ones
□	□
3	2
1	3

Tens	Ones

7.

Tens	Ones
□	□
4	4
1	7

Tens	Ones

8.

Tens	Ones
□	□
3	8
1	8

Tens	Ones

Problem Solving • Applications

9. **THINK SMARTER** Claire's puzzle has 85 pieces. She has used 46 pieces so far. How many puzzle pieces have not been used yet?

_____ puzzle pieces

---

10. **MATHEMATICAL PRACTICE ①** **Analyze** There were some people at the park. 24 people went home. Then there were 19 people at the park. How many people were at the park before?

_____ people

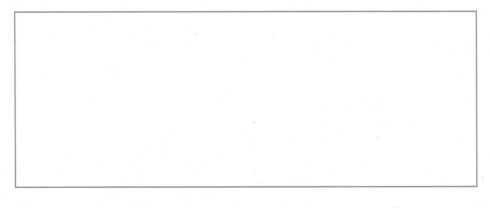

11. **THINK SMARTER** Mr. Sims has a box of 44 erasers. He gives 28 erasers to his students. How many erasers does Mr. Sims have now?

Show how you solved the problem.

_____ erasers

 TAKE HOME ACTIVITY • Write 73 − 28 on a sheet of paper. Ask your child if he or she would regroup to find the difference.

FOR MORE PRACTICE: Standards Practice Book

Name _____

2-Digit Subtraction

Essential Question How do you record the steps when subtracting 2-digit numbers?

Number and Operations in Base Ten—2.NBT.5
Also 2.NBT.9
MATHEMATICAL PRACTICES
MP.3, MP.6, MP.8

Listen and Draw (Real World)

Draw a quick picture to model each problem.

Tens	Ones

Tens	Ones

Math Talk · **Mathematical Practices**

Explain how you know when to regroup.

FOR THE TEACHER • Read the following problem. Devin had 36 toy robots on his shelf. He moved 12 of the robots to his closet. How many robots are on the shelf now? Repeat the activity with this problem: Devin had 54 toy cars. He gave 9 of them to his brother. How many cars does Devin have now?

Subtract. 42
        − 1 5

Step 1 Are there enough ones to subtract 5?

Step 2 Regroup 1 ten as 10 ones.

Step 3 Subtract the ones.
$$12 - 5 = 7$$

Step 4 Subtract the tens.
$$3 - 1 = 2$$

Tens	Ones
IIII	°°

Tens	Ones
4	2
− 1	5

Tens	Ones
3	12
4	2
− 1	5

Tens	Ones
3	12
4	2
− 1	5
	7

Tens	Ones
3	12
4	2
− 1	5
2	7

Share and Show

Regroup if you need to. Write the difference.

1.

Tens	Ones
3	1
− 1	4

✓2.

Tens	Ones
5	6
− 2	1

✓3.

Tens	Ones
7	2
− 3	5

Name _____

On Your Own

Regroup if you need to. Write the difference.

4.
Tens	Ones
☐	☐
2	3
− 1	4

5.
Tens	Ones
☐	☐
8	7
− 5	7

6.
Tens	Ones
☐	☐
3	4
− 1	8

7.
Tens	Ones
☐	☐
6	1
− 1	3

8.

4	5
− 1	8

9.

5	2
− 3	6

10.

3	2
− 1	3

11.

7	5
− 4	3

12.

5	6
− 2	7

13.

9	4
− 2	9

14.

8	7
− 3	9

15.

8	3
− 4	6

16. *THINK SMARTER* Spencer wrote 5 fewer stories than Katie. Spencer wrote 18 stories. How many stories did Katie write?

_____ stories

Problem Solving • Applications  WRITE ▸ Math

17. **MATHEMATICAL PRACTICE 6** **Explain a Method**
    Circle the problems below that you could use mental math to solve.

$54 - 10 =$ _____ $63 - 27 =$ _____ $93 - 20 =$ _____

$39 - 2 =$ _____ $41 - 18 =$ _____ $82 - 26 =$ _____

Explain your choices.

_____

_____

_____

Personal Math Trainer

18. **THINK SMARTER +** There are 34 chickens in the barn. If 16 chickens go outside into the yard, how many chickens will still be in the barn?

Circle the number from the box to make the sentence true.

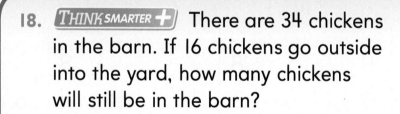

There are | 8 / 18 / 28 | chickens still in the barn.

 TAKE HOME ACTIVITY • Ask your child to write a 2-digit subtraction problem with no regrouping needed. Have your child explain why he or she chose those numbers.

FOR MORE PRACTICE: Standards Practice Book

Practice 2-Digit Subtraction

Essential Question How do you record the steps when subtracting 2-digit numbers?

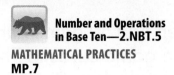

Number and Operations in Base Ten—2.NBT.5

MATHEMATICAL PRACTICES
MP.7

 **Listen and Draw** Real World

Choose one way to solve the problem.
Draw or write to show what you did.

> **Math Talk** **Mathematical Practices**
>
> **Describe** a different way that you could have solved the problem.

FOR THE TEACHER • Read the following problem and have children choose their own methods for solving it. There are 74 books in Mr. Barron's classroom. 19 of the books are about computers. How many of the books are not about computers?

Carmen had 50 game cards. Then she gave 16 game cards to Theo. How many game cards does Carmen have now?

Step 1 Look at the ones. There are not enough ones to subtract 6 from 0. So, regroup.

$$
\begin{array}{r}
^4\!\!\!\not{5}\;^{10}\!\!\!\not{0} \\
-\;1\;6 \\
\hline
\end{array}
$$

Step 2 Subtract the ones.

$10 - 6 = 4$

$$
\begin{array}{r}
^4\!\!\!\not{5}\;^{10}\!\!\!\not{0} \\
-\;1\;6 \\
\hline
4
\end{array}
$$

Step 3 Subtract the tens.

$4 - 1 = 3$

$$
\begin{array}{r}
^4\!\!\!\not{5}\;^{10}\!\!\!\not{0} \\
-\;1\;6 \\
\hline
3\;4
\end{array}
$$

Share and Show

Write the difference.

1.
$$
\begin{array}{r}
3\;8 \\
-\;1\;9 \\
\hline
\end{array}
$$

2.
$$
\begin{array}{r}
6\;5 \\
-\;3\;2 \\
\hline
\end{array}
$$

3.
$$
\begin{array}{r}
5\;0 \\
-\;1\;2 \\
\hline
\end{array}
$$

4.
$$
\begin{array}{r}
2\;3 \\
-\;\;\;4 \\
\hline
\end{array}
$$

✓5.
$$
\begin{array}{r}
7\;0 \\
-\;3\;8 \\
\hline
\end{array}
$$

✓6.
$$
\begin{array}{r}
5\;2 \\
-\;1\;7 \\
\hline
\end{array}
$$

Name _____

Write the difference.

7.	8.	9.	10.
4 1 − 2 4	5 8 − 1 6	6 0 − 1 3	5 2 − 4 7

11.	12.	13.	14.
7 2 − 4 6	3 7 − 6	7 4 − 4 6	9 0 − 1 8

15. **GO DEEPER** Write the missing numbers in the subtraction problems. The regrouping for each problem is shown.

```
  6 15        7 13

−  _ _      −  _ _
   4 7         2 5
```

16. **THINK SMARTER** Adam takes 38 rocks out of a box. There are 23 rocks left in the box. How many rocks were in the box to start?

_____ rocks

 TAKE HOME ACTIVITY • Ask your child to show you one way to find 80 − 34.

Chapter 5 • Lesson 6

FOR MORE PRACTICE:
Standards Practice Book

Name _____

Concepts and Skills

Break apart the number you are subtracting. Use the number line to help. Write the difference. (2.NBT.5)

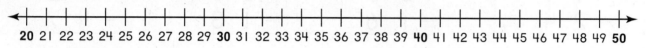

20 21 22 23 24 25 26 27 28 29 **30** 31 32 33 34 35 36 37 38 39 **40** 41 42 43 44 45 46 47 48 49 **50**

1. $34 - 8 =$ _____

2. $45 - 17 =$ _____

Draw a quick picture to solve. Write the difference. (2.NBT.5)

3.

Tens	Ones
☐	☐
4	2
− 2	9

Tens	Ones

4.

Tens	Ones
☐	☐
5	4
− 2	3

Tens	Ones

Write the difference. (2.NBT.5)

5.
```
  7 8
− 4 3
```

6.
```
  6 0
− 2 6
```

7.
```
  8 5
− 3 7
```

8. **THINK SMARTER** Marissa had 51 toy dinosaurs.
She gave 14 toy dinosaurs to her brother.
How many toy dinosaurs does she have now? (2.NBT.5)

_____ toy dinosaurs

Name _____

Rewrite 2-Digit Subtraction

Essential Question What are two different ways to write subtraction problems?

Number and Operations in Base Ten—2.NBT.5
MATHEMATICAL PRACTICES
MP.6, MP.7

 **Listen and Draw** Real World

Write the numbers for each subtraction problem.

− _____	− _____
− _____	− _____

Math Talk
Mathematical Practices

Explain why it is important to line up the digits of the numbers in columns.

FOR THE TEACHER • Read the following problem. Have children write the numbers in vertical format. There were 45 children at a party. Then 23 children went home. How many children were still at the party? Repeat for three more problems.

Chapter 5

What is 81 − 36?
Rewrite the subtraction problem.
Then find the difference.

Step 1 For 81, write the tens
digit in the tens column.

Write the ones digit
in the ones column.

Repeat for 36.

Step 2 Look at the ones.
Regroup if you need to.

Subtract the ones.
Subtract the tens.

$$\begin{array}{r} \overset{7}{\cancel{8}} \ \overset{11}{\cancel{1}} \\ -\ 3 \quad 6 \end{array}$$

Share and Show

MATH BOARD

Rewrite the subtraction problem. Then find the difference.

1. 37 − 4

2. 48 − 24

3. 85 − 37

4. 63 − 19

_____ _____ _____ _____

5. 62 − 37

6. 51 − 27

☑7. 76 − 3

☑8. 95 − 48

_____ _____ _____ _____

On Your Own

Rewrite the subtraction problem. Then find the difference.

9. $49 - 8$

$-$ _____

10. $85 - 47$

$-$ _____

11. $63 - 23$

$-$ _____

12. $51 - 23$

$-$ _____

13. $60 - 15$

$-$ _____

14. $94 - 58$

$-$ _____

15. $47 - 20$

$-$ _____

16. $35 - 9$

$-$ _____

17. $78 - 10$

$-$ _____

18. $54 - 38$

$-$ _____

19. $92 - 39$

$-$ _____

20. $87 - 28$

$-$ _____

21. **THINK SMARTER** For which of the problems above could you find the difference without rewriting it? Explain.

_____

_____

_____

Problem Solving • Applications

WRITE Math

Read about the class trip. Then answer the questions.

> Pablo's class went to the art museum. They saw 26 paintings done by children. They saw 53 paintings done by adults. They also saw 18 sculptures and 31 photographs.

22. How many more paintings were done by adults than by children?

_____ more paintings

23. GO DEEPER How many more paintings than sculptures did they see?

_____ more paintings

24. THINK SMARTER Tom drew 23 pictures last year. Beth drew 14 pictures. How many more pictures did Tom draw than Beth?

Fill in the bubble next to all the ways to show the problem.

○ 23
  − 14   ○ 23
           + 14   ○ 23 − 14   ○ 23 + 14

_____ more pictures

 TAKE HOME ACTIVITY • Ask your child to write and solve a subtraction problem about a family trip.

FOR MORE PRACTICE: Standards Practice Book

Name _____

Add to Find Differences

Essential Question How can you use addition to solve subtraction problems?

Number and Operations in Base Ten—2.NBT.5
MATHEMATICAL PRACTICES
MP.5, MP.8

Listen and Draw Real World

Draw pictures to show the problem.
Then write a number sentence for your drawing.

_____   _____ markers

Now draw pictures to show the next part of the problem. Write a number sentence for your drawing.

_____   _____ markers

FOR THE TEACHER • Have children draw pictures to represent this problem. Sophie had 25 markers. She gave 3 markers to Josh. How many markers does Sophie have now? Then ask children: How many markers will Sophie have if Josh gives the 3 markers back to her?

Math Talk

Mathematical Practices

Describe what happens when you add back the number that you had subtracted.

Model and Draw

Count up from the number you are
subtracting to find the difference.

$$45 - 38 = \blacksquare$$

Start at 38. Count up to 40.

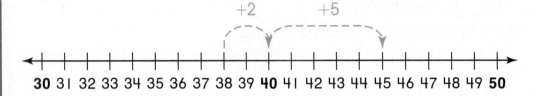

+2   +5

30 31 32 33 34 35 36 37 38 39 **40** 41 42 43 44 45 46 47 48 49 **50**

Then count up 5 more to 45.

2 + 5 = 7

So, $45 - 38 =$ _____.

Share and Show

 MATH BOARD

Use the number line. Count up to find the difference.

1. $36 - 27 =$ _____

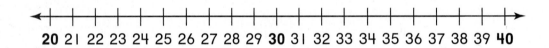

20 21 22 23 24 25 26 27 28 29 **30** 31 32 33 34 35 36 37 38 39 **40**

2. $56 - 49 =$ _____

40 41 42 43 44 45 46 47 48 49 **50** 51 52 53 54 55 56 57 58 59 **60**

3. $64 - 58 =$ _____

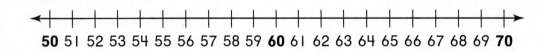

50 51 52 53 54 55 56 57 58 59 **60** 61 62 63 64 65 66 67 68 69 **70**

Name _____

Use the number line. Count up to find the difference.

4. 33 − 28 = _____

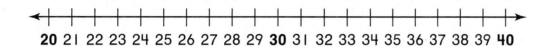

20 21 22 23 24 25 26 27 28 29 **30** 31 32 33 34 35 36 37 38 39 **40**

5. 45 − 37 = _____

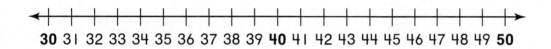

30 31 32 33 34 35 36 37 38 39 **40** 41 42 43 44 45 46 47 48 49 **50**

6. 58 − 49 = _____

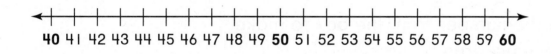

40 41 42 43 44 45 46 47 48 49 **50** 51 52 53 54 55 56 57 58 59 **60**

7. **THINK SMARTER** There were 55 books on the table. Sandra picked up some of the books. Now there are 49 books on the table. How many books did Sandra pick up?

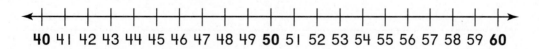

40 41 42 43 44 45 46 47 48 49 **50** 51 52 53 54 55 56 57 58 59 **60**

_____ books

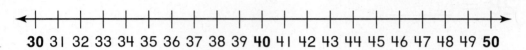

Problem Solving • Applications 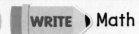 WRITE ▸ Math

Solve. You may wish to use the number line to help.

```
←——+—+—+—+—+—+—+—+—+—+—+—+—+—+—+—+—+—+—+—+—+—→
  30 31 32 33 34 35 36 37 38 39 40 41 42 43 44 45 46 47 48 49 50
```

8. There are 46 game pieces in a box. Adam takes 38 game pieces out of the box. How many game pieces are still in the box?

_____ game pieces

9. **THINK SMARTER** Rachel had 27 craft sticks.
Then she gave 19 craft sticks to Theo.
How many craft sticks does Rachel have now?

Circle the number from the box to make the sentence true.

Rachel has
6
7
8
craft sticks now.

Explain how you can use addition to solve the problem.

_____

_____

TAKE HOME ACTIVITY • Have your child describe how he or she used a number line to solve one problem in this lesson.

FOR MORE PRACTICE:
Standards Practice Book

Name _____

Problem Solving • Subtraction

Essential Question How can drawing a diagram help when solving subtraction problems?

Operations and Algebraic Thinking—2.OA.1; *Also 2.NBT.5*
MATHEMATICAL PRACTICES
MP.1, MP.2, MP.4

Jane and her mom made 33 puppets for the craft fair. They sold 14 puppets. How many puppets do they still have?

🔑 Unlock the Problem

What do I need to find?

how many puppets
_____
they still have

What information do I need to use?

They made _____ puppets.

They sold _____ puppets.

Show how to solve the problem.

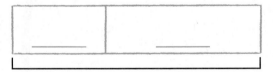

$$33 - 14 = \blacksquare$$
_____

_____ puppets

HOME CONNECTION • Your child used a bar model and a number sentence to represent the problem. Using a bar model helps show what is known and what is needed to solve the problem.

Label the bar model. Write a number sentence with a ▇ for the missing number. Solve.

> • What do I need to find?
> • What information do I need to use?

1. Carlette had a box of 46 craft sticks. She used 28 craft sticks to make a sailboat. How many craft sticks were not used?

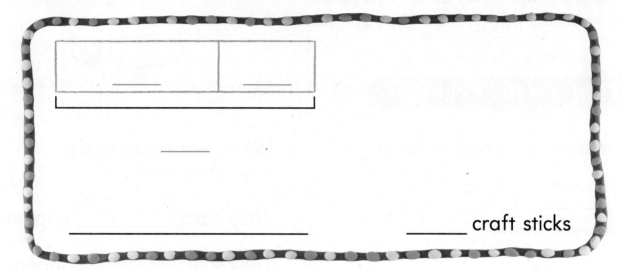

_____   _____ craft sticks

2. Rob's class made 31 clay bowls. Sarah's class made 15 clay bowls. How many more clay bowls did Rob's class make than Sarah's class?

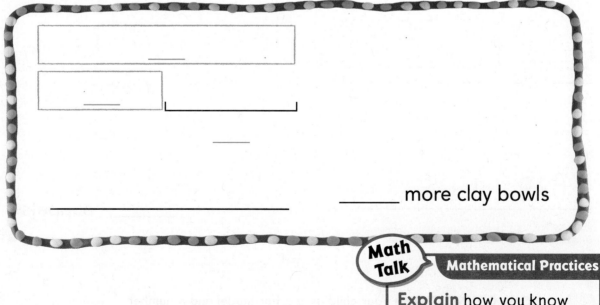

_____   _____ more clay bowls

Math Talk

Mathematical Practices

Explain how you know that Exercise 1 is a take-away problem.

Name _____

Label the bar model. Write a number sentence
with a ▨ for the missing number. Solve.

---

3. Mr. Hayes makes 32 wooden
frames. He gives away
15 frames as gifts. How many
frames does he still have?

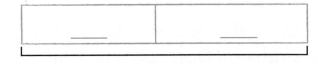

_____ frames

_____

---

4. Wesley has 21 ribbons in a
box. He has 15 ribbons on
the wall. How many more
ribbons does he have in
the box than on the wall?

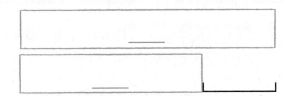

_____ more ribbons

_____

---

5. THINK SMARTER Jennifer wrote
9 poems at school and
11 poems at home. She wrote
5 more poems than Nell. How
many poems did Nell write?

_____ poems

On Your Own   WRITE ▸ Math

6. **GO DEEPER** There are 70 children. 28 children are hiking and 16 are at a picnic. The rest of the children are playing soccer. How many children are playing soccer?

Draw a model with bars for the problem. Describe how your drawing shows the problem. Then solve the problem.

_____

_____

_____

7. **THINK SMARTER** There are 48 crackers in a bag. The children eat 25 crackers. How many crackers are still in the bag?

Circle the bar model that can be used to solve the problem.

25	23

48

48	25

73

73	48

25

Write a number sentence with a ▇ for the missing number. Solve.

_____

_____ crackers

TAKE HOME ACTIVITY • Ask your child to explain how he or she solved one of the problems on this page.

FOR MORE PRACTICE: Standards Practice Book

Algebra • Write Equations to Represent Subtraction

Essential Question How do you write a number sentence to represent a problem?

Operations and Algebraic Thinking—2.OA.1 *Also 2.NBT.5*
MATHEMATICAL PRACTICES
MP.1, MP.2, MP.3, MP.4

Listen and Draw *Real World*

Draw to show the problem. Write a number sentence. Then solve.

_____

Math Talk **Mathematical Practices**

Describe how your drawing shows the problem.

FOR THE TEACHER • Read this problem to children. Franco has 53 crayons. He gives some crayons to Courtney. Now Franco has 38 crayons. How many crayons did Franco give to Courtney?

You can write a number sentence to show a problem.

Liza has 65 postcards. She gives 24 postcards to Wesley. How many postcards does Liza have now?

$$65 - 24 = \boxed{}$$

THINK:

65 postcards
−24 postcards
41 postcards

Liza has _____ postcards now.

Share and Show

Write a number sentence for the problem.
Use a ▢ for the missing number. Then solve.

◯1. There were 32 birds in the trees. Then 18 birds flew away. How many birds are in the trees now?

_____

_____ birds

◯2. Carla read 43 pages in her book. Joe read 32 pages in his book. How many more pages did Carla read than Joe?

_____

_____ more pages

On Your Own

Write a number sentence for the problem.
Use a ▮ for the missing number. Then solve.

3. There were 40 ants on a rock.
Some ants moved to the
grass. Now there are 26 ants
on the rock. How many ants
moved to the grass?

_____   _____ ants

4. **THINK SMARTER** Keisha had a bag
of ribbons. She took 29 ribbons
out of the bag. Then there
were 17 ribbons still in the bag.
How many ribbons were in the
bag to start?

_____   _____ ribbons

5. **GO DEEPER** There are 50 bees in
a hive. Some bees fly out.
If fewer than 20 bees are still
in the hive, how many bees
could have flown out?

Use subtraction to prove your
answer.

_____ bees

Problem Solving • Applications WRITE ▸ Math

6. **MATHEMATICAL PRACTICE 6** **Make Connections**
Brendan made this number line to find a difference. What was he subtracting from 100? Explain your answer.

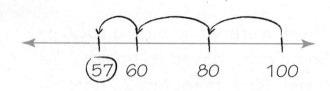

_____

_____

_____

_____

7. **THINK SMARTER** There are 52 pictures on the wall.
37 are wild cats and the rest are birds.
How many of the pictures are birds?

Use the numbers and symbols on the tiles to complete the number sentence for the problem.

| 15 | 25 | 37 | 52 | − | + | = |

_____

_____ birds

 TAKE HOME ACTIVITY • Have your child explain how he or she solved one problem in this lesson.

FOR MORE PRACTICE:
Standards Practice Book

Name _____

Solve Multistep Problems

Essential Question How do you decide what steps to do to solve a problem?

Operations and Algebraic
Thinking—2.OA.1 *Also 2.NBT.5*
MATHEMATICAL PRACTICES
MP.1, MP.2, MP.4

Listen and Draw (Real World)

Label the bar model to show each problem. Then solve.

_____   _____

_____

_____   _____

_____

FOR THE TEACHER • Read this 1st problem for children. Cassie has 32 sheets of paper. She gives Jeff 9 sheets of paper. How many sheets of paper does Cassie have now? After children solve, read this 2nd problem. Cassie draws 18 pictures. Jeff draws 16 pictures. How many pictures do they draw?

Math Talk

Mathematical Practices

Describe how the two bar models are different.

Bar models help you know what to do to solve a problem.

Ali has 27 stamps. Matt has 38 stamps. How many more stamps are needed so they will have 91 stamps?

27	38

First, find how many stamps they have now.

_____

They have _____ stamps now.

Next, find how many more stamps they need.

91

They need _____ more stamps.

Share and Show

Complete the bar models for the steps you do to solve the problem.

THINK: What do you need to find first?

✓ 1. Jen has 93 beads. Ana has 46 red beads and 29 blue beads. How many more beads does Ana need to have 93 beads also?

_____

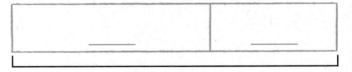

_____ more beads

On Your Own

Complete the bar models for the steps you do to solve the problem.

2. Max has 35 trading cards. He buys 22 more cards. Then he gives 14 cards to Rudy. How many cards does Max have now?

_____ cards

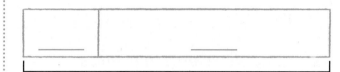

3. Drew has 32 toy cars. He trades 7 of those cars for 11 other toy cars. How many toy cars does Drew have now?

_____ toy cars

4. Marta and Debbie each have 17 ribbons. They buy 1 package with 8 ribbons in it. How many ribbons do they have now?

_____ ribbons

Problem Solving • Applications

WRITE ▶ Math

5. **THINK SMARTER** Shelby had 32 rocks. She finds 33 more rocks at the park and gives 28 rocks to George. How many rocks does she have now?

_____ rocks

6. **GO DEEPER** Benjamin finds 31 pinecones at the park. Together, Jenna and Ellen find the same number of pinecones as Benjamin. How many pinecones could each girl have found?

Jenna: _____ pinecones

Ellen: _____ pinecones

7. **THINK SMARTER** Tanya finds 22 leaves. Maurice finds 5 more leaves than Tanya finds. How many leaves do the children find? Draw to show how you solve the problem.

_____ leaves

TAKE HOME ACTIVITY • Have your child explain how he or she would solve Exercise 6 if the number 31 was changed to 42.

FOR MORE PRACTICE: Standards Practice Book

 ## ✓ Chapter 5 Review/Test

1. Do you need to regroup to subtract? Choose Yes or No.

65 – 23	○ Yes	○ No
50 – 14	○ Yes	○ No
37 – 19	○ Yes	○ No
77 – 60	○ Yes	○ No

2. Use the number line. Count up to find the difference.

52 – 48 = _____

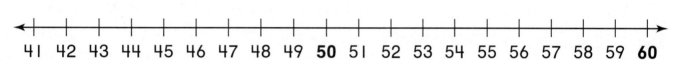

41 42 43 44 45 46 47 48 49 **50** 51 52 53 54 55 56 57 58 59 **60**

3. Ed has 28 blocks. Sue has 34 blocks. Who has more blocks? How many more? Label the bar model. Solve.

Circle the word and number from each box to make the sentence true.

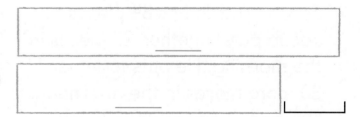

Ed		6	
Sue	has	16	more blocks.
		52	

Break apart the number you are subtracting.
Write the difference?

4. 42 − 8 = _____

5. 53 − 16 = _____

6. What is 33 − 19? Use the numbers on the tiles to rewrite the subtraction problem. Then find the difference.

| 14 | 19 | 33 | 52 |

_____
− _____
_____

_____

7. Jacob's puzzle has 84 pieces. Jacob puts together 27 pieces in the morning. He puts together 38 more pieces in the afternoon. How many pieces does Jacob need to put together to finish the puzzle?

Complete the bar models for the steps you do to solve the problem.

_____ more pieces

Name _____

Regroup if you need to. Write the difference.

8.

Tens	Ones
□	□
5	5
− 2	8

9.

Tens	Ones
□	□
3	2
− 1	2

10. Find the difference.

$$\begin{array}{r} 90 \\ -\ 62 \\ \hline \end{array}$$

Fill in the bubble next to one number from each column to show the difference.

Tens	Ones
○ 2	○ 1
○ 3	○ 2
○ 5	○ 8

11. There are 22 children at the park. 5 children are on the swings. The rest of the children are playing ball. How many children are playing ball?

  ○ 13   ○ 23   ○ 17   ○ 27

12. Subtract 27 from 43. Draw to show the regrouping. Fill in the bubble next to all the ways to write the difference.

○ 1 ten 6 ones

○ 66

○ 6 tens 1 one

○ 16

---

13. Jill collects stamps. Her stamp book has space for 64 stamps. She needs 18 more stamps to fill the book. How many stamps does Jill have now?

Write a number sentence for the problem.

Use a ▮ for the missing number. Then solve.

_____

Jill has _____ stamps.

---

14. Draw a quick picture to solve. Write the difference.

Tens	Ones
☐	☐
6	2
− 2	5

Tens	Ones

Explain what you did to find the difference.

_____

_____

3-Digit Addition and Subtraction

Curious about Math

Monarch butterflies roost together during migration.

If you count 83 butterflies on one tree and 72 on another, how many butterflies have you counted altogether?

Name _____

Show What You Know ✓

Model Subtracting Tens

Write the difference.

1.

5 tens — 3 tens = _____ tens

50 — 30 = _____

2.

7 tens — 2 tens = _____ tens

70 — 20 = _____

2-Digit Addition

Write the sum.

3.
$$
\begin{array}{r} 54 \\ + 25 \\ \hline \end{array}
$$

4.
$$
\begin{array}{r} 35 \\ + 18 \\ \hline \end{array}
$$

5.
$$
\begin{array}{r} 82 \\ + 67 \\ \hline \end{array}
$$

6.
$$
\begin{array}{r} 29 \\ + 81 \\ \hline \end{array}
$$

Hundreds, Tens, and Ones

Write the hundreds, tens, and ones shown. Write the number.

7.

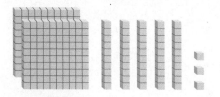

Hundreds	Tens	Ones

_____

8.

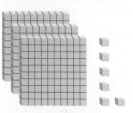

Hundreds	Tens	Ones

_____

This page checks understanding of important skills needed for success in Chapter 6.

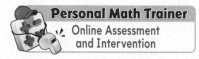

Personal Math Trainer

Online Assessment and Intervention

Vocabulary Builder

Review Words
regroup
sum
difference
hundreds

Visualize It

Fill in the graphic organizer by writing examples of ways to **regroup**.

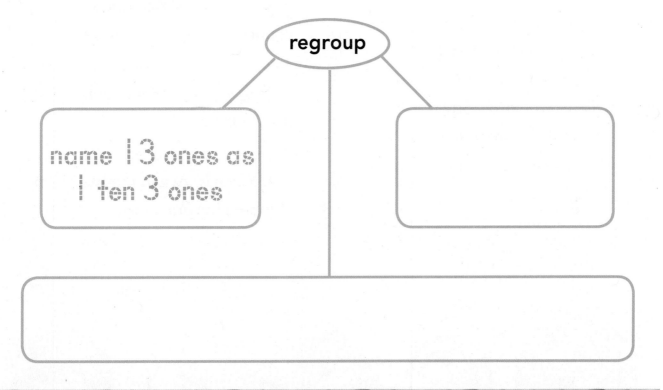

regroup

name 13 ones as
1 ten 3 ones

Understand Vocabulary

1. Write a number that has a **hundreds** digit that is greater than its tens digit. _____

2. Write an addition sentence that has a **sum** of 20. _____

3. Write a subtraction sentence that has a **difference** of 10. _____

GO DIGITAL
• Interactive Student Edition
• Multimedia eGlossary

 # Game 2-Digit Shuffle

Materials
- number cards 10–50
- 15 • 15 ◯

Play with a partner.

1 Shuffle the number cards. Place them face down in a pile.

2 Take two cards. Say the sum of the two numbers.

3 Your partner checks your sum.

4 If your sum is correct, place a counter on a button. If you regrouped to solve, place a counter on another button.

5 Take turns. Cover all the buttons. The player with more counters on the board wins.

6 Repeat the game, saying the difference between the two numbers for each turn.

Name _____

Draw to Represent 3-Digit Addition

Essential Question How do you draw quick pictures to show adding 3-digit numbers?

Number and Operations in Base Ten—2.NBT.7
MATHEMATICAL PRACTICES
MP.5, MP.6

 **Listen and Draw** Real World

Draw quick pictures to model the problem.
Then solve.

Tens	Ones

_____ pages

Math Talk **Mathematical Practices**

Explain how your quick pictures show the problem.

 FOR THE TEACHER • Read this problem to children. Manuel read 45 pages in a book. Then he read 31 more pages. How many pages did Manuel read? Have children draw quick pictures to solve the problem.

Chapter 6

two hundred eighty-one **281**

Model and Draw

Add 234 and 141.

Hundreds	Tens	Ones

___3___ hundreds ___7___ tens ___5___ ones

_375_

Share and Show

Draw quick pictures. Write how many hundreds, tens, and ones in all. Write the number.

1. Add 125 and 344.

Hundreds	Tens	Ones

_____ hundreds _____ tens _____ ones

_____

2. Add 307 and 251.

Hundreds	Tens	Ones

_____ hundreds _____ tens _____ ones

_____

On Your Own

Draw quick pictures. Write how many hundreds, tens, and ones in all. Write the number.

3. Add 231 and 218.

Hundreds	Tens	Ones

_____ hundreds _____ tens _____ ones

_____

4. Add 232 and 150.

Hundreds	Tens	Ones

_____ hundreds _____ tens _____ ones

_____

5. **THINK SMARTER** Use the quick pictures to find the two numbers being added. Then write how many hundreds, tens, and ones in all. Write the number.

Hundreds	Tens	Ones

Add _____ and _____.

_____ hundreds _____ tens _____ ones

_____

Problem Solving • Applications

 WRITE ▶ Math

6. **MATHEMATICAL PRACTICE ②** **Represent a Problem**

There are 125 poems in Carrie's book and 143 poems in Angie's book. How many poems are in these two books?

Draw a quick picture to solve.

_____ poems

Personal Math Trainer

7. **THINK SMARTER +** Rhys wants to add 456 and 131.

Help Rhys solve this problem. Draw quick pictures. Write how many hundreds, tens, and ones in all. Write the number.

Hundreds	Tens	Ones

_____ hundreds _____ tens _____ ones

_____

 TAKE HOME ACTIVITY • Write 145 + 122. Have your child explain how he or she can draw quick pictures to find the sum.

FOR MORE PRACTICE: Standards Practice Book

Name _____

Break Apart 3-Digit Addends

Essential Question How do you break apart
addends to add hundreds, tens, and then ones?

**Number and Operations
in Base Ten—2.NBT.7**
MATHEMATICAL PRACTICES
MP.6, MP.8

Listen and Draw

Write the number. Draw a quick picture for the
number. Then write the number in different ways.

_____

____ hundreds ____ tens ____ ones

_____ + _____ + _____

_____

____ hundreds ____ tens ____ ones

_____ + _____ + _____

Math Talk — **Mathematical Practices**

What number can be
written as 400 + 20 + 9?

FOR THE TEACHER • Have children write 258
on the blank in the left corner of the first box.
Have children draw a quick picture for this
number and then complete the other two forms
for the number. Repeat the activity for 325.

Chapter 6

Break apart the addends into hundreds, tens, and ones. Add the hundreds, the tens, and the ones. Then find the total sum.

$$538 \longrightarrow 500 + 30 + 8$$
$$+216 \longrightarrow 200 + 10 + 6$$
$$700 + \underline{} + \underline{} = \underline{}$$

Share and Show

Break apart the addends to find the sum.

1. $321 \longrightarrow$ _____ + _____ + _____
   $+457 \longrightarrow$ _____ + _____ + _____

   _____ + _____ + _____ = _____

2. $744 \longrightarrow$ _____ + _____ + _____
   $+162 \longrightarrow$ _____ + _____ + _____

   _____ + _____ + _____ = _____

3. $254 \longrightarrow$ _____ + _____ + _____
   $+536 \longrightarrow$ _____ + _____ + _____

   _____ + _____ + _____ = _____

On Your Own

Break apart the addends to find the sum.

4. 374 ⟶ _____ + _____ + _____

    +518 ⟶ _____ + _____ + _____

    _____ + _____ + _____ = _____

5. 425 ⟶ _____ + _____ + _____

    +232 ⟶ _____ + _____ + _____

    _____ + _____ + _____ = _____

6. 849 ⟶ _____ + _____ + _____

    +123 ⟶ _____ + _____ + _____

    _____ + _____ + _____ = _____

7. **THINK SMARTER** Mr. Jones has many sheets of paper. He has 158 sheets of blue paper, 100 sheets of red paper, and 231 sheets of green paper. How many sheets of paper does he have?

_____ sheets of paper

Problem Solving • Applications  WRITE Math

8. **GO DEEPER** Wesley added in a different way.

```
  327
+ 468
```
```
  700      7 hundreds
   80      8 tens
+  15      15 ones
  795
```

Use Wesley's way to find the sum.

```
  539
+ 247
```

9. **THINK SMARTER** There are 376 children at one school.
There are 316 children at another school.
How many children are at the two schools?

```
  376  ⟶  300 + 70 + 6
+ 316  ⟶  300 + 10 + 6
```

Select one number from each column to solve the problem.

Hundreds	Tens	Ones
○ 2	○ 4	○ 2
○ 4	○ 8	○ 3
○ 6	○ 9	○ 6

TAKE HOME ACTIVITY • Write 347 + 215. Have your child break apart the numbers and then find the sum.

FOR MORE PRACTICE:
Standards Practice Book

© Houghton Mifflin Harcourt Publishing Company

Name _____

3-Digit Addition: Regroup Ones

Essential Question When do you regroup ones in addition?

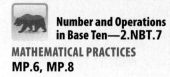

Number and Operations
in Base Ten—2.NBT.7
MATHEMATICAL PRACTICES
MP.6, MP.8

Use ▦ ▭ to model the problem.
Draw quick pictures to show what you did.

Hundreds	Tens	Ones

Math Talk **Mathematical Practices**

Describe how you modeled the problem.

FOR THE TEACHER • Read the following problem and have children model it with blocks. There were 213 people at the show on Friday and 156 people at the show on Saturday. How many people were at the show on the two nights? Have children draw quick pictures to show how they solved the problem.

© Houghton Mifflin Harcourt Publishing Company

Add the ones.

$6 + 7 = 13$

Regroup 13 ones
as 1 ten 3 ones.

Hundreds	Tens	Ones
	[1]	
2	4	6
+ 1	1	7
		3

Hundreds	Tens	Ones

Add the tens.

$1 + 4 + 1 = 6$

Hundreds	Tens	Ones
	1	
2	4	6
+ 1	1	7
	6	3

Hundreds	Tens	Ones

Add the hundreds.

$2 + 1 = 3$

Hundreds	Tens	Ones
	1	
2	4	6
+ 1	1	7
3	6	3

Hundreds	Tens	Ones

Write the sum.

1.

Hundreds	Tens	Ones
3	2	8
+ 1	3	4

2.

Hundreds	Tens	Ones
4	4	5
+	2	3

On Your Own

Write the sum.

3.

Hundreds	Tens	Ones
	☐	
5	2	6
+ 1	0	3

4.

Hundreds	Tens	Ones
	☐	
3	4	8
+	1	9

5.

Hundreds	Tens	Ones
	☐	
6	2	8
+ 3	4	7

6.

Hundreds	Tens	Ones
	☐	
2	3	5
+ 2	5	7

7.

Hundreds	Tens	Ones
	☐	
5	6	2
+ 3	2	9

8.

Hundreds	Tens	Ones
	☐	
1	4	7
+ 1	2	5

9. THINK SMARTER On Thursday, there were 326 visitors at the zoo. There were 200 more visitors at the zoo on Friday than on Thursday. How many visitors were at the zoo on both days?

Math on the Spot

_____ visitors

Problem Solving • Applications  WRITE ▸ Math

Solve. Write or draw to explain.

10.  **Model with Mathematics** The gift shop is 140 steps away from the zoo entrance. The train stop is 235 steps away from the gift shop. How many total steps is this?

_____ steps

11. **THINK SMARTER** Katina's class used 249 noodles to decorate their bulletin board. Gunter's class used 318 noodles. How many noodles did the two classes use?

_____ noodles

Did you have to regroup to solve? Explain.

 TAKE HOME ACTIVITY • Ask your child to explain why he or she regrouped in only some of the problems in this lesson.

FOR MORE PRACTICE:
Standards Practice Book

3-Digit Addition: Regroup Tens

Essential Question When do you regroup tens in addition?

Number and Operations in Base Ten—2.NBT.7
MATHEMATICAL PRACTICES
MP.6, MP.8

Listen and Draw Real World · Hands On

Use  to model the problem.
Draw quick pictures to show what you did.

Hundreds	Tens	Ones

Math Talk · Mathematical Practices

Explain how your quick pictures show what happened in the problem.

FOR THE TEACHER • Read the following problem and have children model it with blocks. On Monday, 253 children visited the zoo. On Tuesday, 324 children visited the zoo. How many children visited the zoo those two days? Have children draw quick pictures to show how they solved the problem.

Add the ones.

$2 + 5 = 7$

Hundreds	Tens	Ones
☐	☐	
1	4	2
+ 2	8	5
		7

Hundreds	Tens	Ones
☐	||||	° °
☐ ☐	||||||||	° ° ° ° °

Add the tens.

$4 + 8 = 12$

Regroup 12 tens as
1 hundred 2 tens.

Hundreds	Tens	Ones
1	☐	
1	4	2
+ 2	8	5
	2	7

Hundreds	Tens	Ones
☐ ☐	||||	° °
☐ ☐	||||||||	° ° ° ° °

Add the hundreds.

$1 + 1 + 2 = 4$

Hundreds	Tens	Ones
1	☐	
1	4	2
+ 2	8	5
4	2	7

Hundreds	Tens	Ones
☐ ☐		° °
☐ ☐	||	° ° ° ° °

MATH BOARD

Write the sum.

1.
Hundreds	Tens	Ones
☐	☐	
3	4	7
+ 2	9	1

2.
Hundreds	Tens	Ones
☐	☐	
1	6	5
+ 3	5	4

3.
Hundreds	Tens	Ones
☐	☐	
5	3	8
+ 1	4	0

On Your Own

Write the sum.

4.

Hundreds	Tens	Ones
☐	☐	
1	5	6
+	4	2

5.

Hundreds	Tens	Ones
☐	☐	
7	6	4
+ 1	5	3

6.

Hundreds	Tens	Ones
☐	☐	
3	7	2
+ 1	8	5

7.

$$\begin{array}{r} 2\ \ 2\ \ 4 \\ +\ 1\ \ 5\ \ 7 \\ \hline \end{array}$$

8.

$$\begin{array}{r} 2\ \ 5\ \ 4 \\ +\ 4\ \ 0\ \ 5 \\ \hline \end{array}$$

9.

$$\begin{array}{r} 6\ \ 4\ \ 4 \\ +\ \ \ \ 9\ \ 2 \\ \hline \end{array}$$

10.

$$\begin{array}{r} 1\ 3\ 2 \\ +\ 2\ 5\ 8 \\ \hline \end{array}$$

11.

$$\begin{array}{r} 3\ 1\ 4 \\ +\ 4\ 3\ 5 \\ \hline \end{array}$$

12.

$$\begin{array}{r} 7\ 5\ 3 \\ +\ 1\ 5\ 2 \\ \hline \end{array}$$

MATHEMATICAL PRACTICE 6 Attend to Precision

Rewrite the numbers. Then add.

13. $760 + 178$

$$\begin{array}{r} + \\ \hline \end{array}$$

14. $216 + 346$

$$\begin{array}{r} + \\ \hline \end{array}$$

15. $423 + 285$

$$\begin{array}{r} + \\ \hline \end{array}$$

Problem Solving • Applications WRITE ▸ Math

16. *THINK SMARTER* These lists show the pieces of fruit sold. How many pieces of fruit did Mr. Olson sell?

Mr. Olson	Mr. Lee
257 apples	314 pears
281 plums	229 peaches

_____ pieces of fruit

---

17. *GO DEEPER* Who sold more pieces of fruit?

_____

How many more?

_____ more pieces of fruit

18. *THINK SMARTER* At the city park theater, 152 people watched the morning play. Another 167 watched the afternoon play.

How many people watched the two plays?   _____ people

Fill in the bubble next to each true sentence about how to solve the problem.

○ You need to regroup the tens as 1 ten and 9 ones.

○ You need to regroup the tens as 1 hundred and 1 ten.

○ You need to add 2 ones + 7 ones.

○ You need to add 1 hundred + 1 hundred + 1 hundred.

 TAKE HOME ACTIVITY • Have your child choose a new combination of two fruits on this page and find the total number of pieces of the two types of fruit.

FOR MORE PRACTICE: Standards Practice Book

Name _____

Addition: Regroup Ones and Tens

Essential Question How do you know when to regroup in addition?

Number and Operations in Base Ten—2.NBT.7
MATHEMATICAL PRACTICES
MP.6, MP.8

Listen and Draw (Real World)

Use mental math. Write the sum for each problem.

$$
\begin{array}{r} 40 \\ +\ 20 \\ \hline \end{array}
\qquad
\begin{array}{r} 200 \\ +\ 700 \\ \hline \end{array}
\qquad
\begin{array}{r} 70 \\ +\ 30 \\ \hline \end{array}
\qquad
\begin{array}{r} 500 \\ +\ 300 \\ \hline \end{array}
$$

$10 + 30 + 40 =$ _____

$100 + 400 + 200 =$ _____

$10 + 50 + 40 =$ _____

$600 + 300 =$ _____

Math Talk

Mathematical Practices

Were some problems easier to solve than other problems? **Explain.**

FOR THE TEACHER • Encourage children to do these addition problems quickly. You may wish to first discuss the problems with children, noting that each problem is limited to just adding tens or just adding hundreds.

Sometimes you will regroup more than once
in addition problems.

$$
\begin{array}{r}
\overset{1\ \ 1}{2\ 5\ 9} \\
+\ 4\ 7\ 6 \\
\hline
7\ 3\ 5
\end{array}
$$

9 ones + 6 ones = 15 ones,
or 1 ten 5 ones

1 ten + 5 tens + 7 tens = 13 tens,
or 1 hundred 3 tens

1 hundred + 2 hundreds + 4 hundreds =
7 hundreds

THINK:
Are there 10 or more ones?
Are there 10 or more tens?

Share and Show

MATH
BOARD

Write the sum.

1.

$$
\begin{array}{r}
1\ 8\ 4 \\
+\ 3\ 2\ 9 \\
\hline
\end{array}
$$

2.

$$
\begin{array}{r}
5\ 4\ 6 \\
+\ 2\ 7\ 8 \\
\hline
\end{array}
$$

3.

$$
\begin{array}{r}
3\ 2\ 7 \\
+\ 3\ 5\ 3 \\
\hline
\end{array}
$$

4.

$$
\begin{array}{r}
2\ 3\ 4 \\
+\ 1\ 5\ 2 \\
\hline
\end{array}
$$

✔ 5.

$$
\begin{array}{r}
3\ 7\ 5 \\
+\ 2\ 7\ 2 \\
\hline
\end{array}
$$

✔ 6.

$$
\begin{array}{r}
1\ 8\ 9 \\
+\ 6\ 2\ 3 \\
\hline
\end{array}
$$

Name _____

On Your Own

Write the sum.

7.
```
  5 7 4
+ 2 8 1
-------
```

8.
```
  4 1 6
+ 4 8 3
-------
```

9.
```
  3 4 6
+ 5 9 7
-------
```

10.
```
  3 6 5
+ 2 8 3
-------
```

11.
```
  6 4 7
+ 1 0 9
-------
```

12.
```
  5 4 6
+ 3 5 6
-------
```

13.
```
  3 4 8
+ 6 3 1
-------
```

14.
```
  4 5 5
+ 1 3 9
-------
```

15.
```
  5 6 3
+ 2 4 5
-------
```

16. THINK SMARTER Miko wrote these problems.
What are the missing digits?

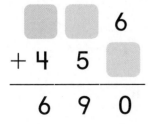

TAKE HOME ACTIVITY • Have your child explain how to solve 236 + 484.

FOR MORE PRACTICE:
Standards Practice Book

 **Mid-Chapter Checkpoint**

Concepts and Skills

Break apart the addends to find the sum. (2.NBT.7)

1.   567 → _____ + _____ + _____

   +324 → _____ + _____ + _____
                 _____

         _____ + _____ + _____ = _____

Write the sum. (2.NBT.7)

2.
```
  2 4 8
+ 3 4 6
-------
```

3.
```
  6 1 0
+ 2 6 4
-------
```

4.
```
  3 9 1
+ 5 3 7
-------
```

5. **THINK SMARTER** There are 148 small sand dollars and 119 large sand dollars on the beach. How many sand dollars are on the beach? (2.NBT.7)

_____ sand dollars

Estimation in 3-Digit Addition

Essential Question How do you make reasonable estimates when solving problems?

Number and Operations in Base Ten—2.NBT.7.1
MATHEMATICAL PRACTICES
MP.8

Listen and Draw

How many hundreds does each number have?

427 has _____ hundreds.

651 has _____ hundreds.

348 has _____ hundreds.

What is each sum?

$$\begin{array}{r} 500 \\ + 100 \\ \hline \end{array} \qquad \begin{array}{r} 300 \\ + 400 \\ \hline \end{array} \qquad \begin{array}{r} 600 \\ + 200 \\ \hline \end{array} \qquad \begin{array}{r} 100 \\ + 800 \\ \hline \end{array}$$

FOR THE TEACHER • The activity in the first box is a review of identifying the hundreds digit and describing its value in a 3-digit number. The activity in the second box is for practicing the mental math skill of adding multiples of hundreds.

Math Talk **Mathematical Practices**

Describe how you found the sum for each addition problem.

An **estimate** tells about how many.

Look at the hundreds digits.

Use an estimate when an exact answer is not needed.

$$
\begin{array}{r}
518 \\
+\ 336 \\
\hline
\end{array}
\longrightarrow
\begin{array}{r}
500 \\
+\ 300 \\
\hline
800
\end{array}
$$

An estimate for the sum is _____.

Share and Show

Use the values of the hundreds digits to estimate the sum.

1.
$$
\begin{array}{r}
257 \\
+\ 320 \\
\hline
\end{array}
\longrightarrow
\quad +\ \rule{2cm}{0.4pt}
$$

An estimate for the sum is _____.

2.
$$
\begin{array}{r}
719 \\
+\ 138 \\
\hline
\end{array}
\longrightarrow
\quad +\ \rule{2cm}{0.4pt}
$$

An estimate for the sum is _____.

3.
$$
\begin{array}{r}
231 \\
+\ 525 \\
\hline
\end{array}
\longrightarrow
\quad +\ \rule{2cm}{0.4pt}
$$

An estimate for the sum is _____.

Name _____

Use the values of the hundreds digits to estimate the sum.

4.

$$\begin{array}{r} 625 \\ + 309 \\ \hline \end{array}$$ $\longrightarrow$ $\begin{array}{r} \\ + \underline{} \\ \end{array}$

An estimate for the sum is _____.

5. **THINK SMARTER** There are 246 children at Debbie's school. There are 328 children at Jacob's school. Without adding, explain how you could estimate the number of children at the two schools.

_____

_____

_____

6. **MATHEMATICAL PRACTICE 3** Verify the Reasoning of Others
There are two boxes of crayons. There are 138 crayons in the first box and 309 crayons in the second box. Manuel estimates that there are about 700 crayons altogether.

Do you agree? Explain why.

_____

_____

_____

Problem Solving • Applications (Real World)

Solve. Write or draw to explain.

7. **GO DEEPER** Daniel has two boxes of trading cards. There are 327 cards in one box and 418 cards in the other box.

   If he buys a pack of 225 cards, estimate the number of cards that he will have then.

   Write or draw to show how you made your estimate.

   about _____ cards

8. **THINK SMARTER** Andy's family drove 318 miles on Saturday and 553 miles on Sunday. About how far did Andy's family drive in all?

   Fill in the bubble next to all the sentences that describe what you would do to estimate the distance.

   ○ I would add 300 + 500.

   ○ I would regroup the tens.

   ○ I would add the hundreds digits.

   ○ I would add 100 to the hundreds digits.

TAKE HOME ACTIVITY • Have your child describe what he or she learned in this lesson.

FOR MORE PRACTICE: Standards Practice Book

Problem Solving • 3-Digit Subtraction

Essential Question How can making a model help when solving subtraction problems?

Number and Operations
in Base Ten—2.NBT.7
MATHEMATICAL PRACTICES
MP.1, MP.4

There were 436 people at the art show. 219 people went home. How many people stayed at the art show?

♀ Unlock the Problem *Real World*   *Hands On*

What do I need to find?

how many people
_____
stayed at the art show

What information do I need to use?

_____ people were at the art show.

Then, _____ people went home.

Show how to solve the problem.

Make a model. Then draw a quick picture of your model.

_____ people

 HOME CONNECTION • Your child used a model and a quick picture to represent and solve a subtraction problem.

Make a model to solve. Then draw a quick picture of your model.

- What do I need to find?
- What information do I need to use?

1. There are 532 pieces of art at the show. 319 pieces of art are paintings. How many pieces of art are not paintings?

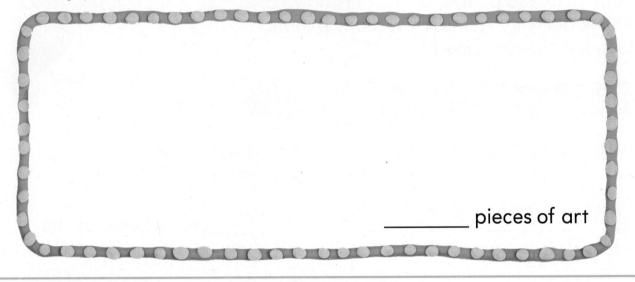

_____ pieces of art

2. 245 children go to the face-painting event. 114 of the children are boys. How many of the children are girls?

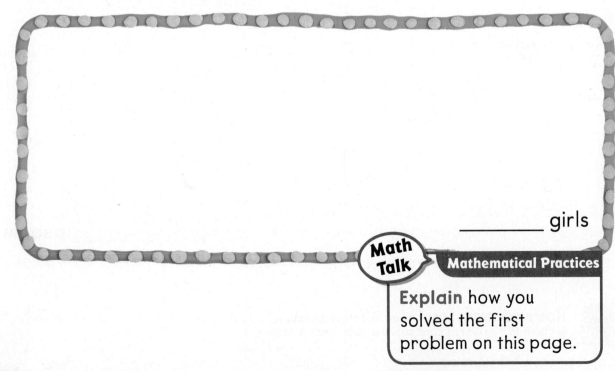

_____ girls

Math Talk

Mathematical Practices

Explain how you solved the first problem on this page.

© Houghton Mifflin Harcourt Publishing Company

Name _____

Make a model to solve. Then draw
a quick picture of your model.

3. There were 237 books on the
table. Miss Jackson took
126 books off the table.
How many books were still
on the table?

_____ books

4. There were 232 postcards on
the table. The children used
118 postcards. How many
postcards were not used?

_____ postcards

5. **THINK SMARTER** 164 children and
31 adults saw the movie in the
morning. 125 children saw the
movie in the afternoon. How
many fewer children saw the
movie in the afternoon than
in the morning?

_____ fewer children

On Your Own

MATHEMATICAL PRACTICE ① **Make Sense of Problems**

6. There were some grapes in a bowl. Clancy's friends ate 24 of the grapes. Then there were 175 grapes in the bowl. How many grapes were in the bowl before?

_____ grapes

7. THINK SMARTER At Gregory's school, there are 547 boys and girls. There are 246 boys. How many girls are there?

Draw a quick picture to solve.

Circle the number that makes the sentence true.

There are
| 201 |
| 301 |
| 793 |
girls.

TAKE HOME ACTIVITY • Ask your child to choose one of the problems in this lesson and solve it in a different way.

FOR MORE PRACTICE:
Standards Practice Book

© Houghton Mifflin Harcourt Publishing Company

Name _____

3-Digit Subtraction: Regroup Tens

Essential Question When do you regroup tens in subtraction?

Number and Operations in Base Ten—2.NBT.7
MATHEMATICAL PRACTICES
MP.6, MP.8

Listen and Draw Real World  Hands On

Use ▦ ▭ ▪ to model the problem.
Draw a quick picture to show what you did.

Hundreds	Tens	Ones

Math Talk Mathematical Practices

Describe what to do when there are not enough ones to subtract from.

FOR THE TEACHER • Read the following problem and have children model it with blocks. 473 people went to the football game. 146 people were still there at the end of the game. How many people left before the end of the game? Have children draw quick pictures of their models.

Model and Draw

$354 - 137 = ?$

Are there enough ones to subtract 7?

yes   (no)

Regroup 1 ten as 10 ones.

Hundreds	Tens	Ones
	4	14
3	5	4
− 1	3	7

Hundreds	Tens	Ones

Now there are enough ones.

Subtract the ones.

$14 - 7 = 7$

Hundreds	Tens	Ones
	4	14
3	5	4
− 1	3	7
		7

Hundreds	Tens	Ones

Subtract the tens.

$4 - 3 = 1$

Subtract the hundreds.

$3 - 1 = 2$

Hundreds	Tens	Ones
	4	14
3	5	4
− 1	3	7
2	1	7

Hundreds	Tens	Ones

Share and Show

Solve. Write the difference.

1.

Hundreds	Tens	Ones
	□	□
4	3	1
− 3	2	6

2.

Hundreds	Tens	Ones
	□	□
6	5	8
− 2	3	7

On Your Own

Solve. Write the difference.

3.

Hundreds	Tens	Ones
	☐	☐
7	2	8
− 1	0	7

4.

Hundreds	Tens	Ones
	☐	☐
4	5	2
− 2	1	6

5.

Hundreds	Tens	Ones
	☐	☐
9	6	5
− 2	3	8

6.

Hundreds	Tens	Ones
	☐	☐
4	8	9
− 1	4	9

7.

Hundreds	Tens	Ones
	☐	☐
6	4	5
− 2	2	7

8.

Hundreds	Tens	Ones
	☐	☐
6	7	0
− 1	3	8

9. **THINK SMARTER** There were
287 music books and
134 science books in the store.
After some books were sold,
there are 159 books left.
How many books were sold?

_____ books

Problem Solving • Applications

 **① Make Sense of Problems**

Solve. Write or draw to explain.

10. There are 235 whistles and 42 bells in the store. Ryan counts 128 whistles on the shelf. How many whistles are not on the shelf?

_____ whistles

Personal Math Trainer

11. **THINK SMARTER ╋** Dr. Jackson had 326 stamps.

He sells 107 stamps. How many stamps does he have now?

_____ stamps

Would you do these things to solve the problem?
Choose Yes or No.

Subtract 107 from 326.	○ Yes	○ No
Regroup 1 ten as 10 ones.	○ Yes	○ No
Regroup the hundreds.	○ Yes	○ No
Subtract 7 ones from 16 ones.	○ Yes	○ No
Add 26 + 10.	○ Yes	○ No

 TAKE HOME ACTIVITY • Ask your child to explain why he or she regrouped in only some of the problems in this lesson.

FOR MORE PRACTICE:
Standards Practice Book

Name _____

3-Digit Subtraction: Regroup Hundreds

Essential Question When do you regroup hundreds in subtraction?

Number and Operations in Base Ten—2.NBT.7, 2.NBT.9

MATHEMATICAL PRACTICES
MP.6, MP.8

Listen and Draw

Draw quick pictures to show the problem.

Hundreds	Tens	Ones

Math Talk

Mathematical Practices

Describe what to do when there are not enough tens to subtract from.

FOR THE TEACHER • Read the following problem and have children model it with quick pictures. The Reading Club has 349 books. 173 of the books are about animals. How many books are not about animals?

Model and Draw

$428 - 153 = ?$

Subtract the ones.

$8 - 3 = 5$

Hundreds	Tens	Ones
[ ] 4	[ ] 2	[ ] 8
− 1	5	3
		5

Hundreds	Tens	Ones

There are not enough tens to subtract from.

Regroup 1 hundred. 4 hundreds 2 tens is now 3 hundreds 12 tens.

Hundreds	Tens	Ones
[3] 4	[12] 2	[ ] 8
− 1	5	3
		5

Hundreds	Tens	Ones

Subtract the tens.

$12 - 5 = 7$

Subtract the hundreds.

$3 - 1 = 2$

Hundreds	Tens	Ones
[3] 4̸	[12] 2	[ ] 8
− 1	5	3
2	7	5

Hundreds	Tens	Ones

Share and Show

Solve. Write the difference.

☑ 1.

Hundreds	Tens	Ones
[ ]	[ ]	[ ]
4	7	8
− 3	5	6

☑ 2.

Hundreds	Tens	Ones
[ ]	[ ]	[ ]
8	1	4
− 2	6	3

314 three hundred fourteen

Name _____

On Your Own

Solve. Write the difference.

3.

Hundreds	Tens	Ones
☐	☐	☐
6	2	9
− 4	8	2

4.

Hundreds	Tens	Ones
☐	☐	☐
9	3	6
− 1	7	3

5.

4	3	5
− 1	9	2

6.

3	8	7
−	4	7

7.

```
  5 8 8
− 4 5 0
```

8.

```
  3 4 5
− 2 6 3
```

MATHEMATICAL PRACTICE ③ Make Arguments

9. Choose one exercise above. Describe the subtraction that you did. Be sure to tell about the values of the digits in the numbers.

_____

_____

_____

_____

Problem Solving • Applications

 **WRITE** ▸ Math

10. **THINK SMARTER** Sam made two towers. He used 139 blocks for the first tower. He used 276 blocks in all. For which tower did he use more blocks? _____

Explain how you solved the problem.

_____

_____

11. **THINK SMARTER** This is how many points each class scored in a math game.

| **Mrs. Rose** 444 points | **Mr. Chang** 429 points | **Mr. Pagano** 293 points |

How many more points did Mr. Chang's class score than Mr. Pagano's class? Draw a picture and explain how you found your answer.

_____ more points

 TAKE HOME ACTIVITY • Have your child explain how to find the difference for 745 − 341.

FOR MORE PRACTICE: Standards Practice Book

Name _____

Subtraction: Regroup Hundreds and Tens

Number and Operations in Base Ten—2.NBT.7
MATHEMATICAL PRACTICES
MP.6, MP.8

Essential Question How do you know when to regroup in subtraction?

Listen and Draw Real World

Use mental math. Write the difference for each problem.

50	600	80	900
− 20	− 400	− 30	− 300

90 − 40 = _____

700 − 500 = _____

70 − 60 = _____

800 − 300 = _____

Math Talk **Mathematical Practices**

Were some problems easier to solve than other problems? **Explain.**

FOR THE TEACHER • Encourage children to do these subtraction problems quickly. You may wish to first discuss the problems with children, noting that each problem is limited to just subtracting tens or just subtracting hundreds.

Model and Draw

Sometimes you will regroup more than once in subtraction problems.

$$\begin{array}{r} \overset{\overset{11}{\cancel{6}}}{7} \;\; \overset{\cancel{1}}{2} \;\; \overset{15}{\cancel{5}} \\ - \; 3 \;\; 4 \;\; 9 \\ \hline 3 \;\; 7 \;\; 6 \end{array}$$

Regroup 2 tens 5 ones as 1 ten 15 ones. Subtract the ones.

Regroup 7 hundreds 1 ten as 6 hundreds 11 tens. Subtract the tens.

Subtract the hundreds.

Share and Show

Solve. Write the difference.

1.

$$\begin{array}{r} 4 \;\; 2 \;\; 1 \\ - \; 1 \;\; 3 \;\; 8 \\ \hline \end{array}$$

2.

$$\begin{array}{r} 2 \;\; 7 \;\; 4 \\ - \; 1 \;\; 8 \;\; 2 \\ \hline \end{array}$$

3.

$$\begin{array}{r} 5 \;\; 4 \;\; 6 \\ - \; 2 \;\; 6 \;\; 7 \\ \hline \end{array}$$

4.

$$\begin{array}{r} 8 \;\; 5 \;\; 9 \\ - \;\;\;\;\; 5 \;\; 7 \\ \hline \end{array}$$

✓5.

$$\begin{array}{r} 7 \;\; 4 \;\; 7 \\ - \; 1 \;\; 5 \;\; 9 \\ \hline \end{array}$$

✓6.

$$\begin{array}{r} 9 \;\; 3 \;\; 8 \\ - \; 3 \;\; 7 \;\; 0 \\ \hline \end{array}$$

On Your Own

Solve. Write the difference.

7.

```
    3   4   2
 -  1   3   8
_____
```

8.

```
    4   6   3
 -  2   8   1
_____
```

9.

```
    8   5   5
 -  4   9   7
_____
```

10.

```
    6   5   7
 -  3   8   4
_____
```

11.

```
    5   2   1
 -  1   4   6
_____
```

12.

```
    7   5   8
 -  5   3   7
_____
```

13.

```
    5   4   2
 -  1   6   8
_____
```

14.

```
    8   2   3
 -  6   7   3
_____
```

15.

```
    9   4   7
 -  5   7   9
_____
```

16. _THINK SMARTER_ Alex wrote these problems.
What are the missing digits?

```
          4    15
    9     ▢    ▢
 -  6     2    8
_____
    3     2    7
```

```
          7    13
    ▢     ▢    7
 -  1     5    ▢
_____
    6     8    1
```

Problem Solving • Applications  WRITE Math

17. **GO DEEPER** This is how Walter found the difference for 617 − 350.

Find the difference for 843 − 270 using Walter's way.

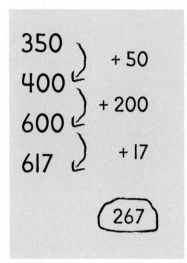

350 ⎱ + 50
400 ⎰
400 ⎱ + 200
600 ⎰
600 ⎱ + 17
617 ⎰

267

18. **MATHEMATICAL PRACTICE ①** **Analyze** There are 471 children at Caleb's school. 256 children ride buses to get to school.

How many children do not ride buses to get to school?

_____ children

19. **THINK SMARTER** Mrs. Herrell had 427 pinecones. She gave 249 pinecones to her children.

How many pinecones does she still have?

_____ pinecones

 TAKE HOME ACTIVITY • Ask your child to find the difference when subtracting 182 from 477.

FOR MORE PRACTICE: Standards Practice Book

Name _____

Regrouping with Zeros

Essential Question How do you regroup when there are zeros in the number you start with?

Number and Operations in Base Ten—2.NBT.7
MATHEMATICAL PRACTICES
MP.6, MP.8

Listen and Draw

Draw or write to show how you solved the problem.

 FOR THE TEACHER • Read the following problem and have children solve. Mr. Sanchez made 403 cookies. He sold 159 cookies. How many cookies does Mr. Sanchez have now? Encourage children to discuss and show different ways to solve the problem.

Math Talk **Mathematical Practices**

Describe another way that you could solve the problem.

Chapter 6

three hundred twenty-one **321**

Model and Draw

Ms. Dean has a book with 504 pages in it. She has read 178 pages so far. How many more pages does she still have to read?

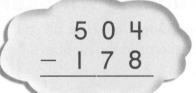
$$\begin{array}{r} 5\ 0\ 4 \\ -\ 1\ 7\ 8 \\ \hline \end{array}$$

Step 1 There are not enough ones to subtract from.

Since there are 0 tens, regroup 5 hundreds as 4 hundreds 10 tens.

$$\begin{array}{r} \overset{4}{\cancel{5}}\ \overset{10}{\cancel{0}}\ 4 \\ -\ 1\ 7\ 8 \\ \hline \end{array}$$

Step 2 Next, regroup 10 tens 4 ones as 9 tens 14 ones.

Now there are enough ones to subtract from.

$$14 - 8 = 6$$

$$\begin{array}{r} \overset{4}{\cancel{5}}\ \overset{9}{\cancel{10}}\overset{14}{\cancel{4}} \\ -\ 1\ 7\ 8 \\ \hline 6 \end{array}$$

Step 3 Subtract the tens.

$$9 - 7 = 2$$

Subtract the hundreds.

$$4 - 1 = 3$$

$$\begin{array}{r} \overset{4}{\cancel{5}}\ \overset{9}{\cancel{10}}\overset{14}{\cancel{4}} \\ -\ 1\ 7\ 8 \\ \hline 3\ 2\ 6 \end{array}$$

Share and Show

Solve. Write the difference.

1.
$$\begin{array}{r} 3\ 0\ 8 \\ -\ 2\ 5\ 9 \\ \hline \end{array}$$

✓ 2.
$$\begin{array}{r} 7\ 5\ 5 \\ -\ 4\ 3\ 8 \\ \hline \end{array}$$

✓ 3.
$$\begin{array}{r} 8\ 0\ 1 \\ -\ 3\ 7\ 5 \\ \hline \end{array}$$

322 three hundred twenty-two

Name _____

On Your Own

Solve. Write the difference.

4.
```
    5  6  3
 -  1  8  2
_____
```

5.
```
    9  0  4
 -  5  6  8
_____
```

6.
```
    7  0  5
 -  2  3  1
_____
```

7.
```
    6  0  3
 -  3  2  8
_____
```

8.
```
    4  4  2
 -  2  3  8
_____
```

9.
```
    9  0  1
 -  6  7  5
_____
```

10.
```
    7  0  2
 -  4  2  6
_____
```

11.
```
    6  8  4
 -  2  1  9
_____
```

12.
```
    4  7  9
 -  1  3  7
_____
```

13. **THINK SMARTER** Miguel has 125 more baseball cards than Chad. Miguel has 405 baseball cards. How many baseball cards does Chad have?

Math on the Spot

_____ baseball cards

Problem Solving • Applications (Real World)   WRITE ▸ Math

14. **MATHEMATICAL PRACTICE ①** **Analyze** Claire has 250 pennies. Some are in a box and some are in her bank. There are more than 100 pennies in each place. How many pennies could be in each place?

Explain how you solved the problem.

_____ pennies in a box

_____ pennies in her bank

_____

_____

_____

_____

15. **THINK SMARTER** There are 404 people at the baseball game. 273 people are fans of the blue team. The rest are fans of the red team. How many people are fans of the red team?

Does the sentence describe how to find the answer? Choose Yes or No.

Regroup 1 ten as 14 ones.   ○ Yes   ○ No

Regroup 1 hundred as 10 tens.   ○ Yes   ○ No

Subtract 3 ones from 4 ones.   ○ Yes   ○ No

Subtract 2 hundreds from 4 hundreds.   ○ Yes   ○ No

There are _____ fans of the red team.

 TAKE HOME ACTIVITY • Ask your child to explain how he or she solved one of the problems in this lesson.

FOR MORE PRACTICE: Standards Practice Book

Name _____

Estimation in 3-Digit Subtraction

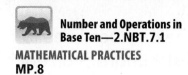

Number and Operations in Base Ten—2.NBT.7.1
MATHEMATICAL PRACTICES
MP.8

Essential Question How do you make reasonable estimates when solving problems?

Listen and Draw

Which is the nearest hundred to the number?

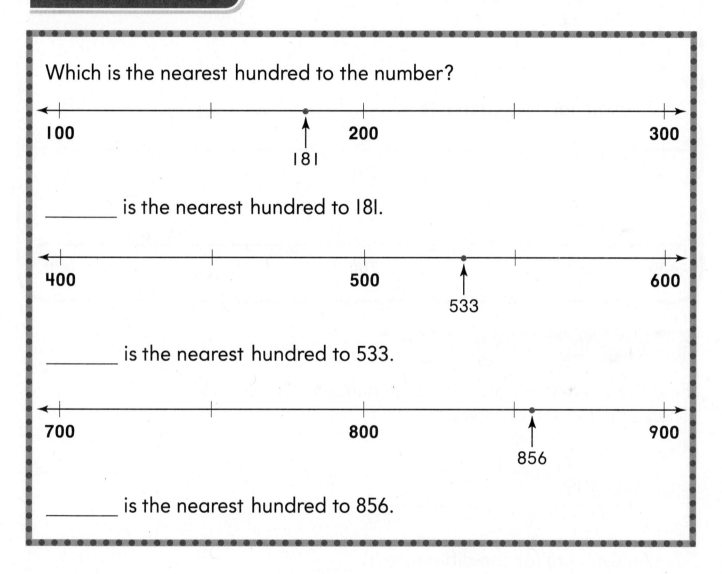

100   200   300

↑
181

_____ is the nearest hundred to 181.

400   500   600

↑
533

_____ is the nearest hundred to 533.

700   800   900

↑
856

_____ is the nearest hundred to 856.

FOR THE TEACHER • For each number line, direct children's attention to the point on the number line with the arrow and number label below it. Have children then determine which hundreds number is closest to that point

Math Talk **Mathematical Practices**

How can the halfway marks between the hundreds numbers help? **Explain.**

Model and Draw

Use the number lines to find the nearest hundred for each number.

> Use the nearest hundreds numbers to estimate the difference.

$$
\begin{array}{r}
725 \\
-\ 287 \\
\end{array}
\longrightarrow
\begin{array}{r}
700 \\
-\ 300 \\
\hline
400 \\
\end{array}
$$

An estimate for the difference is _____.

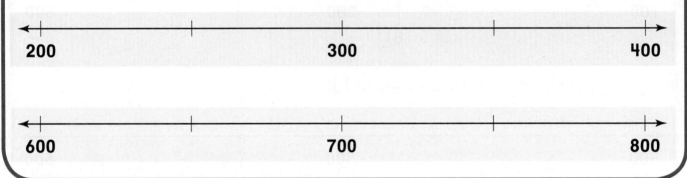

Share and Show

 MATH BOARD

Find the nearest hundred for each number.
Then estimate the difference.

☑ 1.

$$
\begin{array}{r}
672 \\
-\ 309 \\
\end{array}
\longrightarrow
\begin{array}{r}
- \\
\hline
 \\
\end{array}
$$

An estimate for the difference is _____.

☑ 2.

$$
\begin{array}{r}
765 \\
-\ 288 \\
\end{array}
\longrightarrow
\begin{array}{r}
- \\
\hline
 \\
\end{array}
$$

An estimate for the difference is _____.

On Your Own

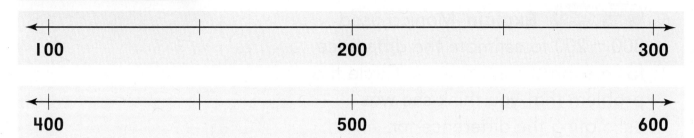

Find the nearest hundred for each number.
Then estimate the difference.

3. $\begin{array}{r} 518 \\ -\ 173 \\ \hline \end{array}$ $\longrightarrow$ $\begin{array}{r} - \\ \hline \end{array}$

An estimate for the difference is _____.

4. **THINK SMARTER** There are 574 people at the game. There are 119 people at the park. Describe how you could estimate how many more people are at the game than the park.

_____

_____

_____

5. **MATHEMATICAL PRACTICE ②** Use Reasoning
   At the store, there are 388 apples and 124 plums. Estimate how many more apples than plums are at the store.

about _____ more apples

Problem Solving • Applications

WRITE ▶ Math

6. **MATHEMATICAL PRACTICE 6** **Explain** Monica used $800 - 200$ to estimate the difference for a subtraction problem. Circle the problem that you think she was estimating the difference for.

$$951 - 126 \qquad 814 - 227 \qquad 735 - 104$$

Explain your choice.

_____

_____

_____

7. **THINK SMARTER** Lin has more beads than Ben. Lin uses $600 - 500$ to estimate how many more beads.

Fill in the bubble next to all the problems she may have been estimating for.

○ $698 - 530$ ○ $602 - 495$ ○ $590 - 511$ ○ $630 - 599$

TAKE HOME ACTIVITY • Have your child describe how he or she used estimation in this lesson.

FOR MORE PRACTICE:
Standards Practice Book

✓ Chapter 6 Review/Test

1. Mr. Kent's art class used 234 craft sticks. Ms. Reed's art class used 358 craft sticks. How many craft sticks did the two classes use?

   _____ craft sticks

2. At the library, there are 668 books and magazines. There are 565 books at the library. How many magazines are there?

   Circle the number that makes the sentence true.

   There are
   | 13 |
   | 103 |
   | 1,233 |
   magazines.

3. There are 176 girls and 241 boys at school. How many children are at school?

   $176 \longrightarrow 100 + 70 + 6$
   $+ 241 \longrightarrow 200 + 40 + 1$

   Select one number from each column to solve the problem.

Hundreds	Tens	Ones
○ 2	○ 1	○ 3
○ 3	○ 3	○ 5
○ 4	○ 4	○ 7

© Houghton Mifflin Harcourt Publishing Company • Image Credits: (c) PhotoDisc/Getty Images

4. Anna wants to add 246 and 132.

Help Anna solve this problem. Draw quick pictures. Write how many hundreds, tens, and ones in all. Write the number.

Hundreds	Tens	Ones

_____ hundreds _____ tens _____ ones

_____

5. Mrs. Preston had 513 leaves. She gave 274 leaves to her students. Draw to show how you found your answer.

How many leaves does she still have?

_____ leaves

6. A farmer has 218 pecan trees and 435 walnut trees. About how many trees does he have in all?

How would you estimate the number of trees? Fill in the bubble next to all the sentences that describe what you would do.

○ I would add the hundreds digits.

○ I would add 18 + 35.

○ I would regroup the ones.

○ I would add 200 + 400.

7. Amy has 408 beads. She gives 322 beads to her sister. How many beads does Amy have now?

Does the sentence describe how to find the answer? Choose Yes or No.

Regroup 1 ten as 18 ones.	○ Yes	○ No
Regroup 1 hundred as 10 tens.	○ Yes	○ No
Subtract 2 tens from 10 tens.	○ Yes	○ No

Amy has _____ beads.

8. Raul used this method to find the sum 427 + 316.

```
   427
 + 316
   700

    30
 +  13
   743
```

Use Raul's method to find this sum.

```
   229
 + 313


```

Describe how Raul solves addition problems.

_____

_____

9. Sally scores 802 points in a game. If Ty scores 364 points, how many more points does Sally score than Ty?

Fill in the bubble next to all the sentences that describe what you would do.

○ I would regroup 8 hundreds as 7 hundreds 10 tens.

○ I would start by subtracting ones without regrouping.

○ I would regroup 10 tens 2 ones as 9 tens 12 ones.

○ I would subtract 6 tens from 10 tens.

---

10. Use the numbers on the tiles to solve the problem.

```
  0        3        6
```

```
    2  5  7
  + ▨  4  ▨
  ─────────
    6  ▨  3
```

Describe how you solved the problem.

_____

_____

_____

_____

Making a Kite

by Kathryn Krieger and Christine Ruiz

CRITICAL AREA Using standard units of measure

Ellie and Mike get the materials to make a kite. Then they make the body of the kite.

Materials

paper kite pattern
tape
straw
10 small paper clips
scissors
hole punch
string
3 sheets of paper
streamer paper

1 Fold the pattern in half.

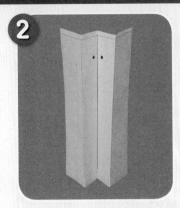

2 Fold along both dashed lines.

3 Tape on each end.

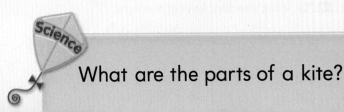

What are the parts of a kite?

Mike does not want the front of the kite to bend too much. He uses a straw to make the kite stronger.

Measure 3 paper clips long. Cut.

Tape the straw on the line.

Science

Why is a straw used as part of the kite?

335

The kite must have a string for Ellie or Mike to hold. If the kite does not have a string, it will blow away. Ellie will tie the string onto the kite.

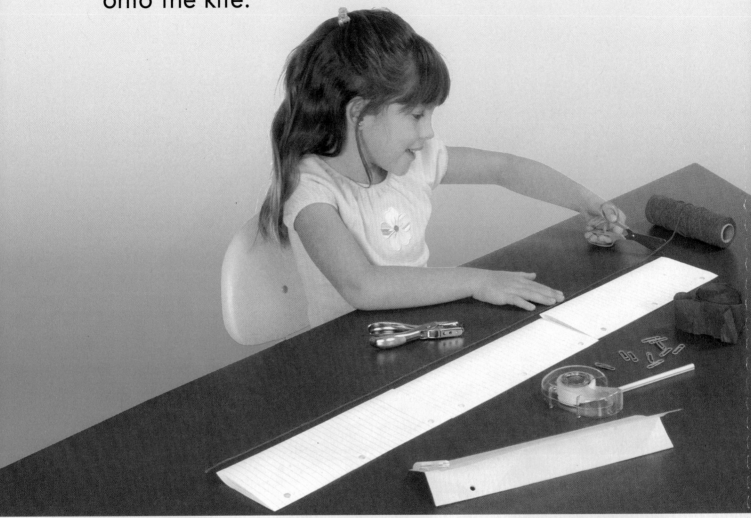

6 Punch one hole.

7 Measure 3 paper-lengths of string. Cut.

8 Put the string through the hole and tie it.

336 Why is a string needed on a kite?

A tail will help the kite fly straight. Mike measures streamer paper and will tape it to the kite. Then the kite will be finished!

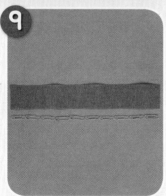

Measure 10 paper-clip-lengths of streamer paper. Cut.

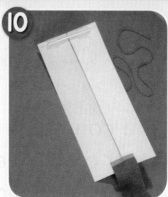

Tape the streamer to the kite as a tail.

Why is a tail needed on a kite?

You can make a kite too. Start at the beginning of this story. Follow the steps.

Science

How do all of the parts help the kite fly?

Write About the Story

Draw and write a story about making a kite. Explain how to measure the parts of the kite in your story.

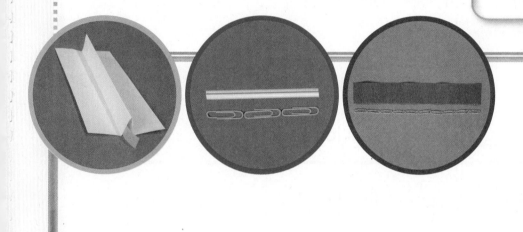

WRITE ▶ Math

_____
_____
_____
_____
_____

What is the length?

Estimate the length of each straw.
Then measure the length of each
straw using small paper clips.

1. Estimate: about _____ paper clips long

   Measure: about _____ paper clips long

2. Estimate: about _____ paper clips long

   Measure: about _____ paper clips long

3. Estimate: about _____ paper clips long

   Measure: about _____ paper clips long

 Look around the classroom. Find other
objects to measure. Measure the length
of each object using small paper clips.

Money and Time

A sundial shows the time using the position of the sun. It has numbers around it, like a clock face. What numbers are on a clock face?

Name _____

Order Numbers to 100 on a Number Line

Write the number that is just before, between, or just after.

1.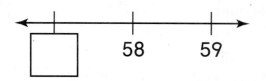

2.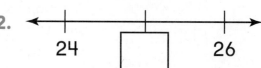

Skip Count by Fives and Tens

3. Count by fives. Write how many in all.

_____   _____ paints in all

4. Count by tens. Write how many in all.

_____   _____ paints in all

Time to the Hour

Write the time shown on the clock.

5.

6.

This page checks understanding of important skills needed for success in Chapter 7.

Personal Math Trainer
Online Assessment and Intervention

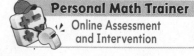

Name _____

Vocabulary Builder

Review Words
count
pattern
count on

Visualize It

Fill in the graphic organizer.
Show ways to **count on**.

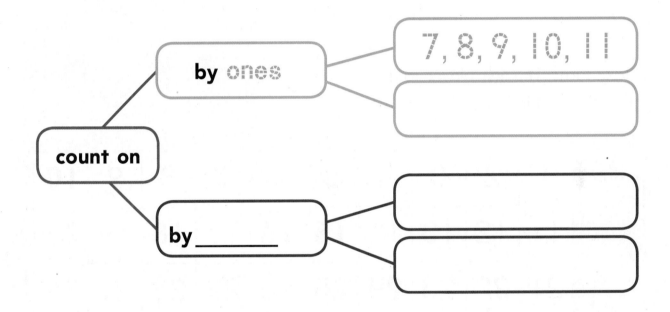

count on
by ones
7, 8, 9, 10, 11
by _____

Understand Vocabulary

Write the missing numbers in each counting **pattern.**

1. **Count** by ones.   40, ____, ____, ____, 44, ____, 46, ____

_____

2. **Count** by fives.   10, 15, ____, ____, ____, 35, ____, ____

_____

3. **Count** by tens.   20, ____, ____, 50, ____, ____, 80, ____

© Houghton Mifflin Harcourt Publishing Company

GO DIGITAL • Interactive Student Edition • Multimedia eGlossary

Chapter 7   three hundred forty-three **343**

Game

5 and 10 Count

Materials • 1 ▢ • 1 ▢ • 🔵

Play with a partner.

1 Spin the pointer on 🔵 for your starting number. Put your cube on that number.

2 Spin the pointer. Count on by that number two times.

3 Take turns. The first player to get to 100 wins. Play again.

10	5
5	10

1	2	3	4	**5**	6	7	8	9	**10**
11	12	13	14	**15**	16	17	18	19	**20**
21	22	23	24	**25**	26	27	28	29	**30**
31	32	33	34	**35**	36	37	38	39	**40**
41	42	43	44	**45**	46	47	48	49	**50**
51	52	53	54	**55**	56	57	58	59	**60**
61	62	63	64	**65**	66	67	68	69	**70**
71	72	73	74	**75**	76	77	78	79	**80**
81	82	83	84	**85**	86	87	88	89	**90**
91	92	93	94	**95**	96	97	98	99	**100**

Name _____

Dimes, Nickels, and Pennies

Essential Question How do you find the total value of a group of dimes, nickels, and pennies?

Measurement and Data—2.MD.8

MATHEMATICAL PRACTICES
MP.6, MP.7

Listen and Draw Real World   Hands On

Sort the coins. Then draw the coins.

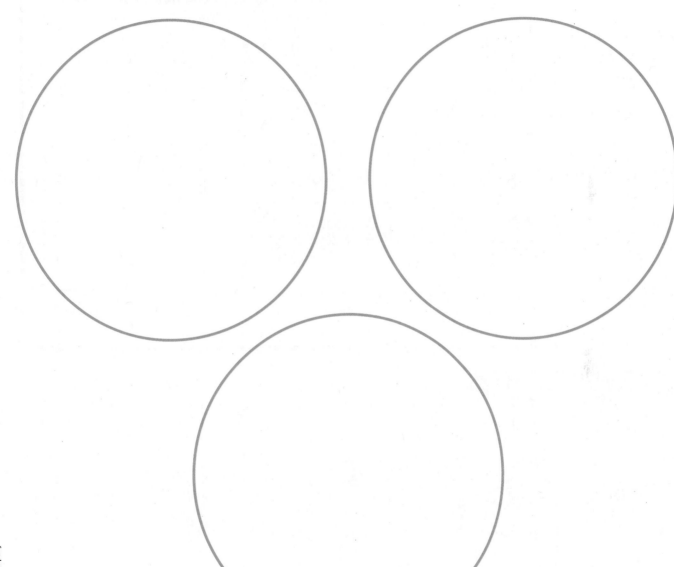

FOR THE TEACHER • Distribute play coins of dimes, nickels, and pennies and discuss their values. Have children sort the coins and draw them inside the three circles. Have children label the drawings with the numbers *1*, *5*, or *10* to indicate the cent value of each coin drawn.

Math Talk **Mathematical Practices**

A nickel has the same value as how many pennies? **Explain.**

Chapter 7

three hundred forty-five **345**

Model and Draw

 10 cents
10¢

 5 cents
5¢

 1 cent
1¢

dime

¢ is the **cent sign**.

nickel

penny

Count dimes by tens.

10¢, 20¢, 30¢

Count nickels by fives.

5¢, 10¢, 15¢

Count by tens. Count by fives. Count by ones.

10¢, 20¢, 25¢, 30¢, 31¢, 32¢

32¢

total value

Share and Show

 MATH BOARD

Count on to find the total value.

✓ 1.

_____

total value

✓ 2.

_____

total value

Name _____

Remember:
Write the cent sign
after the number.

On Your Own

Count on to find the total value.

3.

_____

☐
total value

4.

_____

☐
total value

5.

☐
total value

6.

☐
total value

7. **THINK SMARTER** Maggie had
5 nickels. She gave 2 nickels
to her sister. What is the total
value of the nickels that
Maggie has now?

_____

Problem Solving • Applications | WRITE ▶ Math

Solve. Write or draw to explain.

8. **MATHEMATICAL PRACTICE ①** **Analyze** Jackson has 4 pennies and 3 dimes. How much money does Jackson have?

_____

9. **MATHEMATICAL PRACTICE ④** **Use Models** Draw two ways to show 25¢. You can use dimes, nickels, and pennies.

10. **THINK SMARTER** Sue has 40¢. Circle coins to show this amount.

 TAKE HOME ACTIVITY • Draw pictures of five coins, using dimes, nickels, and pennies. Ask your child to find the total value.

FOR MORE PRACTICE: Standards Practice Book

© Houghton Mifflin Harcourt Publishing Company

Name _____

Quarters

Essential Question How do you find the total value of a group of coins?

Measurement and Data — 2.MD.8
MATHEMATICAL PRACTICES
MP.6, MP.7

Sort the coins. Then draw the coins.

┌─────────────────────────────────────┐
│   │
│   │
│   │
└─────────────────────────────────────┘

┌─────────────────────────────────────┐
│   │
│   │
│   │
└─────────────────────────────────────┘

┌─────────────────────────────────────┐
│   │
│   │
│   │
└─────────────────────────────────────┘

FOR THE TEACHER • Distribute play coins of quarters, dimes, and nickels and discuss their values. Have children sort the coins and draw them inside the three boxes. Have them label the drawings with 5¢, 10¢, or 25¢.

Math Talk **Mathematical Practices**

Describe how the value of a quarter is greater than the value of a dime.

three hundred forty-nine **349**

A **quarter** has a value of 25 cents.

25¢

Count by twenty-fives.   Count by tens.   Count by ones.

72¢

total value

25¢, 50¢, 60¢, 70¢, 71¢, 72¢

Share and Show

Count on to find the total value.

> Remember:
> ¢ is the cent sign.

1.

_____

total value

2.

_____

total value

3.

_____

total value

On Your Own

Count on to find the total value.

4.

_____

☐

total value

5.

_____

☐

total value

6.

☐

total value

7.

☐

total value

Draw and label a coin to solve.

8. **THINK SMARTER** Ed's coin has the same value as a group of 5 pennies and 4 nickels. What is his coin?

Problem Solving • Applications

 WRITE ▸ Math

MATHEMATICAL PRACTICE 6 Make Connections

Read the clue. Choose the name of a coin from the box to answer the question.

nickel	dime
quarter	penny

9. I have the same value as 5 pennies.

What coin am I?

_____

10. I have the same value as 25 pennies.

What coin am I?

_____

11. I have the same value as 2 nickels.

What coin am I?

_____

12. I have the same value as a group of 5 nickels.

What coin am I?

_____

13. **THINK SMARTER** Tom gives these coins to his brother.

Circle the value of the coins to complete the sentence.

Tom gives his brother

| 25¢ |
| 65¢ |
| 80¢ |

.

 TAKE HOME ACTIVITY • Have your child draw two quarters, two dimes, and two nickels, and then find the total value.

FOR MORE PRACTICE: Standards Practice Book

© Houghton Mifflin Harcourt Publishing Company

Name _____

Count Collections

Essential Question How do you order coins to help find the total value of a group of coins?

Measurement and Data—
2.MD.8
MATHEMATICAL PRACTICES
MP.4, MP.8

Line up the coins from greatest value to least value. Then draw the coins in that order.

greatest   least

greatest   least

Math Talk

Mathematical Practices

Describe how the values of the different kinds of coins compare.

FOR THE TEACHER • Give each child a mixture of four play coins. Have children order their coins and then draw them. Have children trade sets of coins and repeat.

© Houghton Mifflin Harcourt Publishing Company

Chapter 7

Order the coins from greatest value to least value.
Then find the total value.

Count the cents.
25, 50, 60, 61, 62

_____
total value

Share and Show

Draw and label the coins from greatest
to least value. Find the total value.

Remember: Write
the cent sign.

1.

_____

✓2.

_____

✓3.

_____

Name _____

Draw and label the coins from greatest
to least value. Find the total value.

4.

_____

5.

_____

6.

_____

7.

_____

8.

_____

Problem Solving • Applications  WRITE ▸ Math

Solve. Write or draw to explain.

9. **THINK SMARTER** Paulo had these coins.

He spent 1 quarter. How much
money does he have now?

_____

10. Rachel has 2 quarters, 3 dimes,
and 1 nickel in her bank. How
much money is in Rachel's bank?

_____

11. **GO DEEPER** Blake has only nickels and dimes.
He has double the number of nickels as dimes.
The total value of his coins is 60¢.
What coins does Blake have?

_____ nickels   _____ dimes

12. **THINK SMARTER** Malik has these coins in his pocket.
What is the total value of the coins?

_____

 TAKE HOME ACTIVITY • Have your child draw and label
coins with a total value of 32¢.

FOR MORE PRACTICE:
Standards Practice Book

Name _____

Show Amounts in Two Ways

Essential Question How do you choose coins to show a money amount in different ways?

Measurement and Data—
2.MD.8

MATHEMATICAL PRACTICES
MP.4, MP.8

Listen and Draw

Show the amount with coins. Draw the coins.
Write the amount.

```
...............................................
·                                             ·
·                                             ·
·                                             ·
·                                             ·
·                                             ·
·                                             ·
·                                             ·
...............................................
·                                             ·
·                                             ·
·                                             ·
·                                             ·
·                                             ·
·                                             ·
·                                             ·
...............................................
```

Math Talk **Mathematical Practices**

Can you show 10¢ with 3 coins? **Explain** how you know.

FOR THE TEACHER • Distribute play coins. Tell children to use coins to show 27 cents. Then have them draw the coins and write the amount. Repeat the activity for 51 cents.

Here are two ways to show 30¢.

Look at Matthew's way. If you trade 2 dimes and 1 nickel for 1 quarter, the coins will show Alicia's way.

Count the cents. Start with the dimes.

Count the cents. Start with the quarter.

Matthew

30¢

Alicia

30¢

Share and Show

MATH BOARD

Use coins. Show the amount in two ways. Draw and label the coins.

✓ 1.

61¢

✓ 2.

36¢

On Your Own

Use coins. Show the amount in two ways.
Draw and label the coins.

3.

55¢

4.

90¢

5.

75¢

6. THINK SMARTER   Teresa has 42¢.
She has no dimes. Draw to show
what coins she might have.

Problem Solving • Applications

 **④** Model Mathematics

Use coins to solve.

7. Lee buys a pen for 50¢. Draw coins to show two different ways to pay 50¢.

---

8. **MATHEMATICAL PRACTICE ①** Make Sense of Problems

Delia used 4 coins to buy a book for 40¢. Draw coins to show two ways to pay 40¢ with 4 coins.

9. **THINK SMARTER** Fill in the bubble next to all the groups of coins with a total value of 30¢.

○ 6 dimes

○ 1 quarter and 1 nickel

○ 2 nickels and 2 dimes

○ 3 nickels and 5 pennies

 TAKE HOME ACTIVITY • With your child, take turns drawing different collections of coins to show 57¢.

FOR MORE PRACTICE:
Standards Practice Book

Name _____

One Dollar

Essential Question How can you show the value of one dollar with coins?

Measurement and Data—2.MD.8
MATHEMATICAL PRACTICES
MP.4, MP.7

 **Listen and Draw**

Draw the coins. Write the total value.

_____

_____

FOR THE TEACHER • In the first box, have children draw eight nickels and then count to find the total value. In the second box, have children draw eight dimes and then count to find the total value.

Math Talk **Mathematical Practices**

How many pennies have the same value as 80¢? **Explain.**

One **dollar** has the same value as 100 cents.

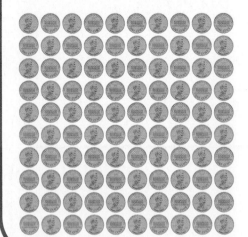

$1.00 = 100¢

dollar sign — decimal point

The decimal point separates the dollars from the cents.

Count 100 cents for one dollar.

Draw the coins to show $1.00. Write the total value.

1. nickels

$1.00

2. quarters

3. dimes

On Your Own

Circle coins to make $1.00.
Cross out the coins you do not use.

4.

5.

6.

7. **THINK** **SMARTER** Sara has these coins.
Draw more coins to show $1.00.

 TAKE HOME ACTIVITY • Have your child draw a group of
coins to show $1.00.

FOR MORE PRACTICE:
Standards Practice Book

✓ Mid-Chapter Checkpoint

Concepts and Skills

Count on to find the total value. (2.MD.8)

1.

   ☐ total value

2.

   ☐ total value

Use coins. Show the amount in two ways.
Draw and label the coins. (2.MD.8)

3.

   31¢

4. **THINK SMARTER** Mary used these coins to buy a folder. What is the total value of these coins? (2.MD.8)

   ☐ total value

Amounts Greater Than $1

Essential Question How do you show money amounts greater than one dollar?

Measurement and Data—
2.MD.8
MATHEMATICAL PRACTICES
MP.4, MP.7

Listen and Draw Real World

Draw and label the coins.
Write the total value.

_____
total value

Math Talk **Mathematical Practices**

Explain how you found the total value of the coins in the coin bank.

FOR THE TEACHER • Read the following problem: Dominic has 1 quarter, 2 dimes, 3 nickels, and 1 penny in his coin bank. How much money is in Dominic's bank? Have children draw and label coins to help them solve the problem.

Model and Draw

When you write amounts greater than one dollar, use a dollar sign and a decimal point.

$1.00

$1.27

total value

$1.50

total value

Share and Show

Circle the money that makes $1.00. Then write the total value of the money shown.

1.

_____

2.

_____

On Your Own

Circle the money that makes $1.00. Then write the total value of the money shown.

3.

_____

4.

_____

5.

_____

6. **THINK SMARTER** Martin used 3 quarters and 7 dimes to pay for a kite. How much money did he use?

_____

Problem Solving • Applications

Real World | **WRITE** ▶ **Math**

7. **GO DEEPER** Pam has fewer than 9 coins. The coins have a total value of $1.15. What coins could she have?

Draw the coins. Then write a list of her coins.

_____

_____

Personal Math Trainer

8. **THINK SMARTER +** Jason put this money in his bank.

Circle the amount to complete the sentence.

Jason put a total of $1.10 / $1.15 / $1.35 in his bank.

 TAKE HOME ACTIVITY • With your child, take turns drawing coins or a $1 bill and coins with a total value of $1.23.

FOR MORE PRACTICE: Standards Practice Book

© Houghton Mifflin Harcourt Publishing Company

Name _____

Problem Solving • Money

Essential Question How does acting it out help when solving problems about money?

Measurement and Data—
2.MD.8
MATHEMATICAL PRACTICES
MP.1, MP.4, MP.7

Kendra gave 2 dimes, 2 nickels, I quarter, and two $1 bills to her sister. How much money did Kendra give her sister?

⚷ Unlock the Problem

What do I need to find?	**What information do I need to use?**
how much money Kendra gave her sister	Kendra gave her sister 2 dimes,

Show how to solve the problem.
Draw to show the money that Kendra used.

Kendra gave her sister _____.

Chapter 7

three hundred sixty-nine **369**

Try Another Problem

Use play coins and bills to solve.
Draw to show what you did.

- What do I need to find?
- What information do I need to use?

I. Jacob has two $1 bills, 2 dimes, and 3 pennies in his pocket. How much money does Jacob have in his pocket? ________

2. Amber used 2 quarters, 1 nickel, 1 dime, and three $1 bills to buy a toy. How much money did Amber use to buy the toy? ________

Math Talk **Mathematical Practices**

Explain how you found the amount of money in Jacob's pocket.

Name _____

Use play coins and bills to solve.
Draw to show what you did.

☑3. Val used 3 quarters, 2 nickels, 2 pennies, and one $1 bill to buy a book. How much money did Val use to buy the book?

_____

☑4. Derek has two $1 bills, 2 quarters, and 6 dimes. How much money does he have?

_____

5.  Katy has 3 quarters, 2 nickels, 2 dimes, and 3 pennies. How many more pennies does she need to have $1.10?

_____ more pennies

Problem Solving • Applications

6. **MATHEMATICAL PRACTICE ①** **Make Sense of Problems**
Victor has some dollar bills, some quarters, and some nickels. Draw and label dollar bills, quarters, and nickels to show $2.25.

7. **THINK SMARTER** Ross used 3 quarters, 4 dimes, 3 nickels, and 5 pennies to buy a card. How much money did Ross use to buy the card? Draw to show how you solve the problem.

_____

TAKE HOME ACTIVITY • Ask your child to explain how he or she solved one problem in this lesson.

FOR MORE PRACTICE:
Standards Practice Book

Name _____

Time to the Hour and Half Hour

Essential Question How do you tell time to the hour and half hour on a clock?

Measurement and Data—
2.MD.7
MATHEMATICAL PRACTICES
MP.6, MP.8

Draw the hour hand to show each time.

FOR THE TEACHER • Call out times to the hour and to the half hour. Begin with 3:00. Have children draw the hour hand to show the time. Repeat the activity for half past 5:00, 11:00, and half past 8:00.

Math Talk **Mathematical Practices**

Describe where the hour hand points to show half past 4:00.

Chapter 7

Model and Draw

It takes 5 **minutes** for the minute hand to move from one number to the next number on a clock face.

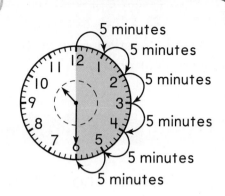

The clock hands on these clocks show 4:00 and 4:30. Write the times below the clocks.

4:00

4:30

The 30 tells you that the time is 30 minutes after the hour.

Share and Show

MATH BOARD

Look at the clock hands. Write the time.

I.

✓ 2.

✓ 3.

On Your Own

Look at the clock hands. Write the time.

4.

5.

6.

7.

8.

9.

10. Look at the time.
Draw the hour hand and the minute
hand to show the same time.

Problem Solving • Applications Real World

WRITE ▸ Math

11. **MATHEMATICAL PRACTICE 6** Make Connections

Allie eats lunch when the hour hand points halfway between the 11 and the 12, and the minute hand points to the 6. When does Allie eat lunch? Show the time on both clocks.

How do you know what time to write in the digital clock? Explain.

_____

_____

_____

12. **THINK SMARTER** Match the clocks that show the same time.

 TAKE HOME ACTIVITY • Have your child describe what he or she knows about a clockface.

FOR MORE PRACTICE:
Standards Practice Book

Name _____

Time to 5 Minutes

Essential Question How do you tell and show time to five minutes?

Measurement and Data—
2.MD.7
MATHEMATICAL PRACTICES
MP.6, MP.8

Listen and Draw (Real World)

Draw the hour hand and the minute hand to show the time.

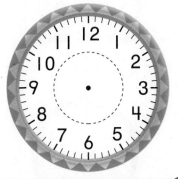

FOR THE TEACHER • Read the following story and have children draw the hour and minute hands to show each time. Sofia goes to music at 10:30. She goes to the playground at 11:00. She eats lunch at 11:30. Show the times Sofia does these things.

Math Talk **Mathematical Practices**

Describe where the minute hand points to show half past the hour.

Chapter 7

three hundred seventy-seven **377**

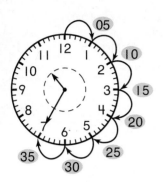

What does it mean when the minute hand points to the 7?

Count by fives until you reach the 7.

> Remember: The minute hand moves from one number to the next in 5 minutes.

The hour hand points between the 10 and the 11. The minute hand points to the 7.

The time is __10:35__.

> There are 60 minutes in 1 hour.

Share and Show

Look at the clock hands. Write the time.

1.

2.

3.

4.

✓ 5.

✓ 6.

Name _____

Look at the clock hands. Write the time.

7.

8.

9.

10.

11.

12.

MATHEMATICAL PRACTICE 4 Use Models Look at the time.
Draw the minute hand to show the same time.

13.

14.

15.

Problem Solving • Applications

WRITE ▶ Math

Draw the clock hands to show the time.
Then write the time.

16. **THINK SMARTER** My hour hand points
between the 8 and the 9.
In 35 minutes it will be the next
hour. What time is it?

17. How many minutes does it take for the
minute hand to travel around the clock
from the 12 to the 12?

_____

18. **THINK SMARTER** Angel eats lunch at 12:45. Angel
spent 10 minutes eating lunch. Draw the minute
hand on the clock to show when Angel finished
eating. Write the time.

_____ : _____

TAKE HOME ACTIVITY • Have your child draw a large blank
clock face and use two pencils as clock hands to show some
different times.

FOR MORE PRACTICE:
Standards Practice Book

Practice Telling Time

Essential Question What are the different ways you can read the time on a clock?

Measurement and Data—
2.MD.7
MATHEMATICAL PRACTICES
MP.6, MP.8

Listen and Draw Real World

Write the times on the digital clocks.
Then label the clocks with the children's names.

FOR THE TEACHER • First have children write the time for each analog clock. Then write *Luke, Beth, Ivy,* and *Rohan* on the board. Tell children to listen for each name to label the different times with. Luke plays football at 3:25. Beth eats lunch at 11:45. Ivy reads a book at 6:10. Rohan eats breakfast at 7:15.

Math Talk **Mathematical Practices**

Where would the minute hand point to show 15 minutes after the hour? **Explain.**

Chapter 7

three hundred eighty-one **381**

These are different ways to write and say the time.

15 minutes after 8
quarter past 8

30 minutes after 8
half past 8

Share and Show

Draw the minute hand to show the time. Write the time.

1. 15 minutes after 1

2. half past 9

3. quarter past 5

4. quarter past 10

5. 40 minutes after 3

6. half past 7

382 three hundred eighty-two

On Your Own

Draw the minute hand to show the time.
Write the time.

7. 15 minutes after 11

8. quarter past 4

9. 25 minutes after 8

10. 10 minutes after 6

11. half past 2

12. 45 minutes after 3

13. 5 minutes after 7

14. 30 minutes after 12

15. quarter past 10

Problem Solving • Applications

WRITE ▶ Math

16. **THINK SMARTER** Lily eats lunch at quarter past 12. Meg eats lunch at 12:30. Katie eats lunch at 12:15. Which girls eat lunch at the same time?

_____ and _____

17. **MATHEMATICAL PRACTICE 6** **Explain** Soccer practice starts at 4:30. Gabe arrives at soccer practice at 4:15. Does he arrive before or after practice starts? Explain.

_____

_____

_____

18. **THINK SMARTER** What time is shown on the clock? Fill in the bubble next to all the ways to write or say the time.

○ **3:25**

○ quarter past **5**

○ **5** minutes after **3**

○ **25** minutes after **3**

 TAKE HOME ACTIVITY • Name a time to 5 minutes. Ask your child to describe where the clock hands point at this time.

FOR MORE PRACTICE:
Standards Practice Book

A.M. and P.M.

Essential Question How do you use A.M. and P.M. to describe times?

Listen and Draw Real World

Draw the clock hands to show each time.
Then write each time.

Morning	Evening

FOR THE TEACHER • Have children draw a picture and write a label for the picture for an activity they do in the morning and for an activity they do in the evening. Then have them show the time they do each activity on the clocks.

Math Talk **Mathematical Practices**

Describe some activities that you do in both the morning and in the evening.

Model and Draw

Noon is 12:00 in the daytime.
Midnight is 12:00 at night.

Times after midnight and before noon are written with **a.m.**	Times after noon and before midnight are written with **p.m.**
11:00 a.m. is in the morning.	11:00 p.m. is in the evening.

Share and Show

MATH BOARD

Write the time. Then circle **a.m.** or **p.m.**

1. eat breakfast

7:15

a.m.

p.m.

2. go to art class

a.m.

p.m.

3. do homework

a.m.

p.m.

4. arrive at school

a.m.

p.m.

© Houghton Mifflin Harcourt Publishing Company • Image Credits: (tl) Getty Images/PhotoDisc (cr) Getty Images (bl) Getty Images/Stockdisc (br) Getty Images/PhotoDisc

Name _____

On Your Own

Write the time. Then circle **a.m.** or **p.m.**

5. go to the library

a.m.

p.m.

6. go to science class

a.m.

p.m.

7. eat lunch

a.m.

p.m.

8. look at the moon

a.m.

p.m.

9. **THINK SMARTER** Use the times in the list to complete the story.

Don got to school at _____.

His class went to the library

at _____. After school,

Don read a book at _____.

10:15 a.m.

3:20 p.m.

8:30 a.m.

Problem Solving • Applications

10. **GO DEEPER** Some times are shown on this time line.
Write a label for each dot that names something
you do at school during that part of the day.

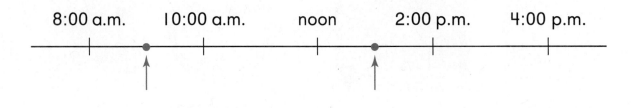

At what times would you say the
dots are placed on the time line?

_____ and _____

11. **THINK SMARTER +** The clock shows the time
Jane goes to recess. Write the time. Then
circle a.m. or p.m.

_____   a.m.

                  p.m.

Recess lasted one hour. Write the time recess
was over. Write a.m. or p.m.

_____

 TAKE HOME ACTIVITY • Name some activities and times.
Have your child say a.m. or p.m. for the times.

FOR MORE PRACTICE:
Standards Practice Book

© Houghton Mifflin Harcourt Publishing Company

Name _____

Units of Time

Essential Question How are different units of time related?

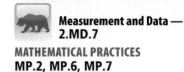

Measurement and Data — 2.MD.7

MATHEMATICAL PRACTICES
MP.2, MP.6, MP.7

Use the calendars to answer the questions.

			January			
Sunday	Monday	Tuesday	Wednesday	Thursday	Friday	Saturday
			1	2	3	4
5	6	7	8	9	10	11
12	13	14	15	16	17	18
19	20	21	22	23	24	25
26	27	28	29	30	31	

			February			
Sunday	Monday	Tuesday	Wednesday	Thursday	Friday	Saturday
						1
2	3	4	5	6	7	8
9	10	11	12	13	14	15
16	17	18	19	20	21	22
23	24	25	26	27	28	

			March			
Sunday	Monday	Tuesday	Wednesday	Thursday	Friday	Saturday
						1
2	3	4	5	6	7	8
9	10	11	12	13	14	15
16	17	18	19	20	21	22
23	24	25	26	27	28	29
30	31					

How many days are there in March? _____ days

How many Fridays are there in January? _____ Fridays

What day of the week is February 10? _____

What is the date of the third Sunday in March? _____

FOR THE TEACHER • Review the use of calendars with children. Have them answer the questions using the calendars shown on this page.

Math Talk

Mathematical Practices

Describe what a calendar shows.

Chapter 7

three hundred eighty-nine **389**

7 days is the same as I **week**.

January

Sunday	Monday	Tuesday	Wednesday	Thursday	Friday	Saturday
			1	2	3	4
5	6	7	8	9	10	11
12	13	14	15	16	17	18
19	20	21	22	23	24	25
26	27	28	29	30	31	

February

Sunday	Monday	Tuesday	Wednesday	Thursday	Friday	Saturday
						1
2	3	4	5	6	7	8
9	10	11	12	13	14	15
16	17	18	19	20	21	22
23	24	25	26	27	28	

March

Sunday	Monday	Tuesday	Wednesday	Thursday	Friday	Saturday
						1
2	3	4	5	6	7	8
9	10	11	12	13	14	15
16	17	18	19	20	21	22
23	24	25	26	27	28	29
30	31					

April

Sunday	Monday	Tuesday	Wednesday	Thursday	Friday	Saturday
		1	2	3	4	5
6	7	8	9	10	11	12
13	14	15	16	17	18	19
20	21	22	23	24	25	26
27	28	29	30			

May

Sunday	Monday	Tuesday	Wednesday	Thursday	Friday	Saturday
				1	2	3
4	5	6	7	8	9	10
11	12	13	14	15	16	17
18	19	20	21	22	23	24
25	26	27	28	29	30	31

June

Sunday	Monday	Tuesday	Wednesday	Thursday	Friday	Saturday
1	2	3	4	5	6	7
8	9	10	11	12	13	14
15	16	17	18	19	20	21
22	23	24	25	26	27	28
29	30					

July

Sunday	Monday	Tuesday	Wednesday	Thursday	Friday	Saturday
		1	2	3	4	5
6	7	8	9	10	11	12
13	14	15	16	17	18	19
20	21	22	23	24	25	26
27	28	29	30	31		

August

Sunday	Monday	Tuesday	Wednesday	Thursday	Friday	Saturday
					1	2
3	4	5	6	7	8	9
10	11	12	13	14	15	16
17	18	19	20	21	22	23
24	25	26	27	28	29	30
31						

September

Sunday	Monday	Tuesday	Wednesday	Thursday	Friday	Saturday
	1	2	3	4	5	6
7	8	9	10	11	12	13
14	15	16	17	18	19	20
21	22	23	24	25	26	27
28	29	30				

October

Sunday	Monday	Tuesday	Wednesday	Thursday	Friday	Saturday
			1	2	3	4
5	6	7	8	9	10	11
12	13	14	15	16	17	18
19	20	21	22	23	24	25
26	27	28	29	30	31	

November

Sunday	Monday	Tuesday	Wednesday	Thursday	Friday	Saturday
						1
2	3	4	5	6	7	8
9	10	11	12	13	14	15
16	17	18	19	20	21	22
23	24	25	26	27	28	29
30						

December

Sunday	Monday	Tuesday	Wednesday	Thursday	Friday	Saturday
	1	2	3	4	5	6
7	8	9	10	11	12	13
14	15	16	17	18	19	20
21	22	23	24	25	26	27
28	29	30	31			

From January I to December 31, there are about 52 weeks. This is I **year**.

> How many days are in each of these months?

Share and Show

✓ 1. Are there more days in July or in November? Explain.

_____

_____

✓ 2. In November, there are 4 weeks and _____ days.

Name _____

Look at the calendars in this lesson to solve.

3. List three months that each have 31 days.

_____

_____

4. List two months that have less than 31 days.

_____

_____

5. In October, there are 4 weeks and _____ days.

_____

Which is the greater amount of time? Circle the correct answer.

6. I week   or   I month

7. I year   or   I month

8. I day   or   I month

9. [THINK SMARTER] Brenda had a library book for 3 weeks. Ivan had a library book for 17 days. Who had a library book for a greater amount of time? Explain.

_____

_____

_____

Problem Solving • Applications

 Apply

10. We use the units below to measure how much time passes for different activities and events. List some things that would be measured in each of these units.

- hours _____

- months _____

- weeks _____

- minutes _____

11. **THINK SMARTER** Is the sentence true? Choose Yes or No.

9 days is more than 1 week.	○ Yes	○ No
10 days is longer than 2 weeks.	○ Yes	○ No
3 weeks is longer than 14 days.	○ Yes	○ No
One month is about 4 weeks long.	○ Yes	○ No
There are about 30 weeks in 1 year.	○ Yes	○ No

 TAKE HOME ACTIVITY • Have your child tell you about the different units of time in this lesson.

FOR MORE PRACTICE:
Standards Practice Book

✓ Chapter 7 Review/Test

1. Andrea pays $2.15 for a jump rope.

   Fill in the bubble next to all the ways that show $2.15.

   ○ two $1 bills, 1 dime, and 1 nickel

   ○ one $1 bill, 4 quarters, and 1 dime

   ○ two $1 bills and 1 quarter

   ○ one $1 bill, 3 quarters, and 4 dimes

2. The clock shows the time Michael eats breakfast.

   Write the time. Circle a.m. or p.m.

   _____ a.m.

                    p.m

   Tell how you knew whether to select a.m. or p.m.

   _____

   _____

   _____

3. Is the sentence true? Choose Yes or No.

There are about 52 weeks in 1 year.	○ Yes	○ No
19 days is longer than 2 weeks.	○ Yes	○ No
3 weeks is less than 20 days.	○ Yes	○ No
9 days is less than 1 week.	○ Yes	○ No

4. Tess gave Raul these coins. Tess says she gave Raul $1.00. Is Tess correct? Explain.

_____

_____

5. Write the time that is shown on this clock.

_____ : _____

6. What time is shown on the clock? Fill in the bubble next to all the ways to write or say the time.

○ 4:35

○ 7:20

○ 35 minutes past 4

○ quarter past 4

Name _____

7. Alicia has this money in her pocket.

Circle the amount to complete the sentence.

Alicia has a total of
$1.40
$1.60
$1.70
in her pocket.

---

8. Kate's father gave her these coins. Write the value of the coins. Explain how you found the the total value.

_____

_____

9. Write the times the clocks show.

_____   _____   _____

---

10. Ben has 30¢. Circle coins to show this amount.

---

11. Mia buys apples that costs 76¢.

Draw and label coins to show a total value of 76¢.

Length in Customary Units

Curious about Math

The Missouri River is the longest river in the United States.

What is the longest piece of furniture in your classroom? How would you find out?

Name _____

Compare Lengths

1. Order the pencils from shortest to longest.
   Write 1, 2, 3.

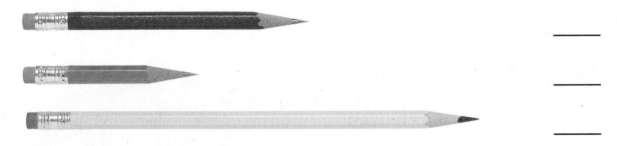

_____

_____

_____

Use Nonstandard Units to Measure Length

Use real objects and ■ to measure.

2. 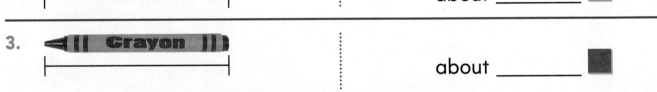   about _____ ■

3.    about _____ ■

Measure Length Twice: Nonstandard Units

Use ⬭ first. Then use ◼.
Measure the length of the pencil.

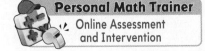

4. about _____ ⬭   5. about _____ ◼

This page checks understanding of important skills needed
for success in Chapter 8.

Vocabulary Builder

Review Words

length
longer
shorter
longest
shortest

Visualize It

Fill in the graphic organizer to describe the lengths of different objects.

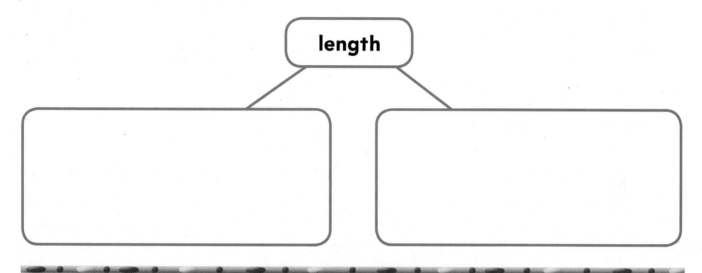

length

Understand Vocabulary

Use review words. Complete the sentences.

1. The blue pencil is the _____ pencil.

2. The red pencil is the _____ pencil.

3. The red pencil is _____ than the yellow pencil.

4. The blue pencil is _____ than the yellow pencil.

GO DIGITAL
• Interactive Student Edition
• Multimedia eGlossary

Game

Longer or Shorter?

Materials

• 9 🎲 • 9 🎲 • 🔵

Longer | Shorter

Play with a partner.

1 Each player chooses a picture on the board and then finds a real object that matches that picture.

2 Place the objects next to each other to find which is longer and which is shorter. If the objects are the same length, choose another object.

3 Spin the pointer on the spinner. The player with the object that matches the spinner puts a cube on that picture on the board.

4 Take turns until all the pictures have cubes. The player with more cubes on the board wins.

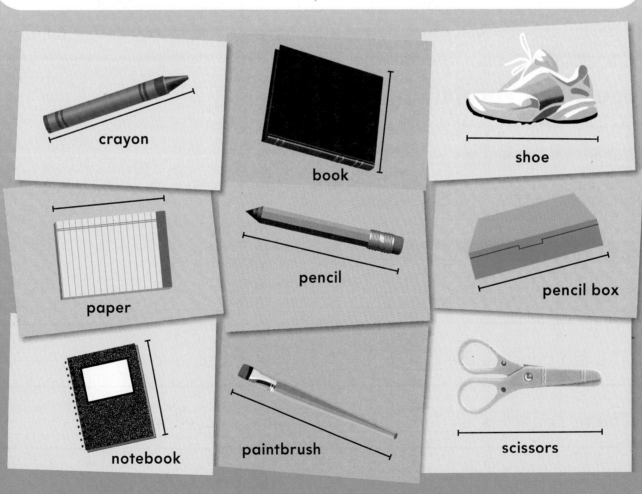

crayon

book

shoe

paper

pencil

pencil box

notebook

paintbrush

scissors

Name _____

Measure with Inch Models

Essential Question How can you use inch models to measure length?

Measurement and Data—
2.MD.1
MATHEMATICAL PRACTICES
MP.5, MP.6, MP.8

Listen and Draw Real World · Hands On

Use color tiles to measure the length.

_____ color tiles

_____ color tiles

_____ color tiles

© Houghton Mifflin Harcourt Publishing Company

HOME CONNECTION • Your child used color tiles as an introduction to measurement of length before using standard measurement tools.

Math Talk **Mathematical Practices**

Describe how to use color tiles to measure the length of an object.

A color tile is about 1 **inch** long.

About how many inches long is this string?

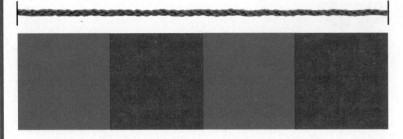

> Count the color tiles to find how many inches long the string is.

The string is 4 color tiles long.

So, the string is about ________ inches long.

Share and Show   MATH BOARD

Use color tiles. Measure the length of the object in inches.

1.

about _____ inches

2.

about _____ inches

✓ 3.

about _____ inches

✓ 4.

about _____ inches

On Your Own

Use color tiles. Measure the length of the object in inches.

5.

about _____ inches

6.

about _____ inches

7.

about _____ inches

8.

about _____ inches

9.

about _____ inches

10.

about _____ inches

Problem Solving • Applications  WRITE Math

11. **THINK SMARTER** Blue paper chains are 8 inches long. Red paper chains are 6 inches long. How many are needed to have 22 inches of paper chains?

_____ blue paper chains

_____ red paper chain

12. **MATHEMATICAL PRACTICE ②** Use Reasoning Liza has a ribbon that is 12 inches long. She needs to cut it into pieces that are each 4 inches long. How many pieces can she make?

_____ pieces

Personal Math Trainer

13. **THINK SMARTER +** Jeremy used color tiles to measure a string. Each tile is 1 inch long. How long is the string? Circle the number in the box to make the sentence true.

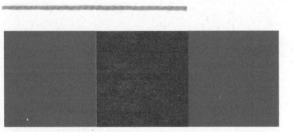

The string is about $\begin{array}{c} 2 \\ 3 \\ 4 \end{array}$ inches long.

 TAKE HOME ACTIVITY • Have your child use several of the same small item (such as paper clips) to measure the lengths of some objects at home.

FOR MORE PRACTICE:
Standards Practice Book

Name _____

Make and Use a Ruler

Essential Question Why is using a ruler similar to using a row of color tiles to measure length?

Measurement and Data—2.MD.1
MATHEMATICAL PRACTICES
MP.5, MP.6

 Listen and Draw Real World Hands On

Use color tiles. Make the given length. Trace along the edge to show the length.

4 inches

2 inches

3 inches

 Math Talk

Mathematical Practices

Describe how you knew how many color tiles to use for each length.

 HOME CONNECTION • Your child used color tiles as I-inch models to show different lengths. This activity helps to make inch units a more familiar concept.

Use a color tile to make a ruler on a paper strip.
Color 6 parts that are each about 1 inch long.

How to use your ruler:
Line up the left edge of an object with the first mark.

Share and Show

Measure the length with your ruler.
Count the inches.

1.

about _____ inches

☑ 2.

about _____ inches

☑ 3.

about _____ inches

On Your Own

Measure the length with your ruler.
Count the inches.

4.

about _____ inches

5.

about _____ inches

6.

about _____ inches

7.

about _____ inches

8.

about _____ inches

Problem Solving • Applications

9. **THINK SMARTER** Work with a classmate.
Use both of your rulers to measure
the length of a bulletin board or a window.
What is the length?

about _____ inches

10. **MATHEMATICAL PRACTICE 6** Explain Describe what you did in
Exercise 9. How did you measure a length that
is longer than your rulers?

_____

_____

_____

11. **THINK SMARTER** Measure the length of the yarn with your ruler.
Does the sentence describe the yarn. Choose Yes or No.

The yarn is 2 inches long.	○ Yes	○ No
The yarn is 3 inches long.	○ Yes	○ No
The yarn is less than 3 inches.	○ Yes	○ No
The yarn is longer than 2 inches.	○ Yes	○ No

 TAKE HOME ACTIVITY • Choose one object in this lesson. Have your
child find objects that are longer, about the same length, and shorter.

FOR MORE PRACTICE:
Standards Practice Book

Estimate Lengths in Inches

Essential Question How do you estimate the lengths of objects in inches?

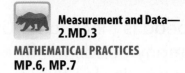

Measurement and Data—
2.MD.3
MATHEMATICAL PRACTICES
MP.6, MP.7

 **Listen and Draw**

Choose three objects. Measure their lengths with your ruler. Draw the objects and write their lengths.

about _____ inches

about _____ inches

about _____ inches

Math Talk **Mathematical Practices**

Describe how the three lengths compare. Which is the longest object?

FOR THE TEACHER • Provide a collection of small objects, 2 to 6 inches in length, for children to measure. Have them select one object, measure it, and return it before selecting another object.

Model and Draw

The bead is 1 inch long. Use this bead to help find how many beads will fit on the string. Which is the best estimate for the length of the string?

2 inches

(5 inches)

8 inches

2 inches is too short.

5 inches is about right.

8 inches is too long.

Share and Show

Circle the best estimate for the length of the string.

1.

1 inch   3 inches   5 inches

✓ 2.

2 inches   4 inches   6 inches

✓ 3.

4 inches   6 inches   8 inches

Name _____

On Your Own

Circle the best estimate for the length of the string.

4.

4 inches   7 inches   10 inches

5.

3 inches   6 inches   9 inches

6.

1 inch   3 inches   5 inches

7. **THINK SMARTER** Use the 1-inch mark. Estimate the length of each ribbon.

Estimates:

red ribbon: about _____ inches

blue ribbon: about _____ inches

Problem Solving • Applications 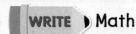 WRITE ▸ Math

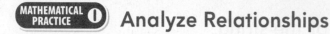

MATHEMATICAL PRACTICE ① Analyze Relationships

8. Sasha has a string that is the length of 5 beads. Each bead is 2 inches long. What is the length of the string?

_____ inches

9. Maurice has a string that is 15 inches long. He has beads that are each 3 inches long. How many beads will fit on the string?

_____ beads

10. **THINK SMARTER** Tameka has this string. She has many beads that are 1 inch long, like this blue bead. What is the best estimate for the length of the string? Draw more beads on the string to show your estimate.

_____ inches

 TAKE HOME ACTIVITY • With your child, estimate the lengths in inches of some small objects, such as books.

FOR MORE PRACTICE: Standards Practice Book

Measurement and Data—
2.MD.1
MATHEMATICAL PRACTICES
MP.5, MP.6

Name _____

Measure with an Inch Ruler

Essential Question How do you use an inch ruler to measure lengths?

Listen and Draw

Draw each worm to match the given length.

FOR THE TEACHER • Have children use the rulers that they made in Lesson 8.2 to draw a worm that is 1 inch long. Have children use the 1-inch-long worm as a guide to draw a worm that is 2 inches long and a worm that is 3 inches long, without using their rulers.

Math Talk **Mathematical Practices**

Describe how you decided how long to draw the 2-inch and 3-inch worms.

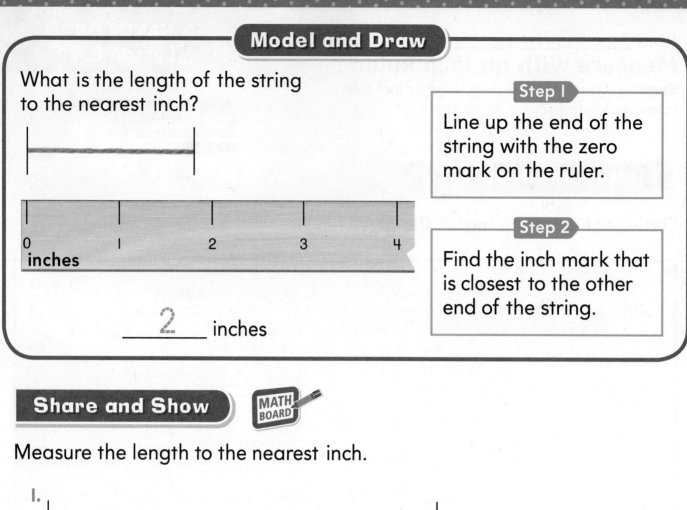

Model and Draw

What is the length of the string to the nearest inch?

Step 1
Line up the end of the string with the zero mark on the ruler.

Step 2
Find the inch mark that is closest to the other end of the string.

___2___ inches

Share and Show

MATH BOARD

Measure the length to the nearest inch.

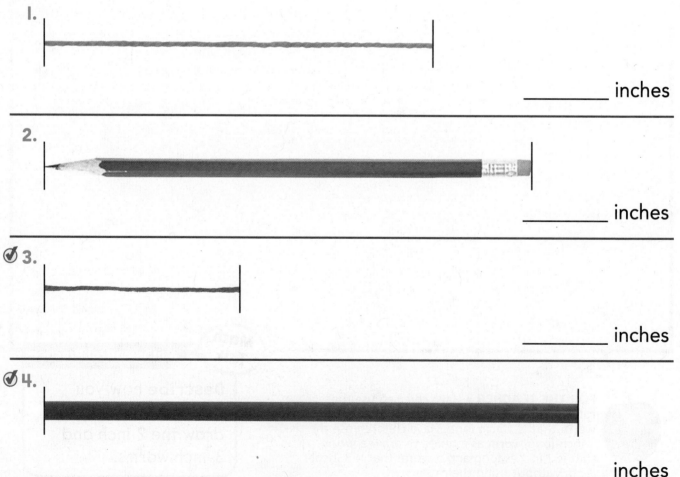

1.

_____ inches

2.

_____ inches

☑ 3.

_____ inches

☑ 4.

_____ inches

On Your Own

Measure the length to the nearest inch.

5.

_____ inches

6.

_____ inches

7.

_____ inches

8.

_____ inches

9.

_____ inches

10.

_____ inches

Problem Solving • Applications

WRITE ▸ Math

11. **THINK SMARTER** How much longer is the red string than the blue string?

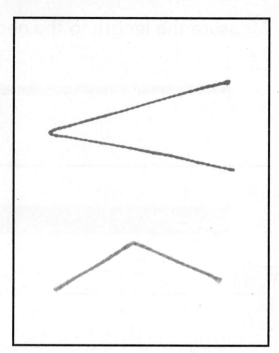

_____ inches longer

12. **THINK SMARTER** If the red and blue strings were straight and placed end to end, what would the total length be?

_____ inches

13. **THINK SMARTER** Mrs. Grant's pencil is 5 inches long. Is this Mrs. Grant's pencil? Use an inch ruler to find out. Use the numbers and words on the tiles to make the sentences true.

| 3 | 4 | 5 | is | is not |

The pencil is _____ inches long.

This pencil _____ Mrs. Grant's pencil.

TAKE HOME ACTIVITY • Have your child measure the lengths of some objects to the nearest inch using a ruler or a similar measuring tool.

FOR MORE PRACTICE: Standards Practice Book

Name _____

Problem Solving • Add and Subtract in Inches

Essential Question How can drawing a diagram help when solving problems about length?

Measurement and Data—
2.MD.5, 2.MD.6
MATHEMATICAL PRACTICES
MP.1, MP.2, MP.4

There is a paper clip chain that is 16 inches long. Aliyah removes 9 inches of paper clips from the chain. How long is the paper clip chain now?

Unlock the Problem (Real World)

What do I need to find?

how long the paper

clip chain is now

What information do I need to use?

The chain is _____ inches long.

_____ inches of paper clips are removed from the chain.

Show how to solve the problem.

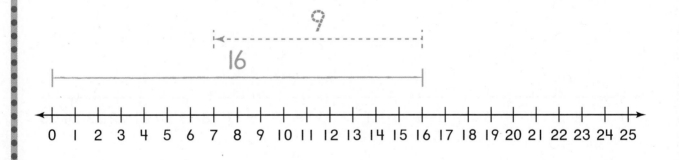

_____

The paper clip chain is _____ inches long now.

HOME CONNECTION • Your child drew a diagram to represent a problem about lengths. The diagram can be used to choose the operation for solving the problem.

© Houghton Mifflin Harcourt Publishing Company

Chapter 8

Draw a diagram. Write a number sentence using a ▆ for the missing number. Solve.

1. Carmen has a string that is 13 inches long and a string that is 8 inches long. How many inches of string does she have?

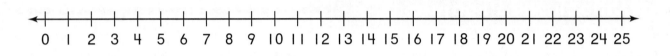

_____

Carmen has _____ inches of string.

2. Eli has a cube train that is 24 inches long.
He removes 9 inches of cubes from the train.
How long is Eli's cube train now?

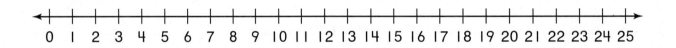

_____

Eli's cube train is _____ inches long now.

Math Talk | **Mathematical Practices**

Describe how your diagram shows what happened in the second problem.

Name _____

Draw a diagram. Write a number sentence using
a ▩ for the missing number. Solve.

☑3. Lee has a paper strip chain that is 25 inches
long. He unhooks 13 inches from the chain.
How long is Lee's paper strip chain now?

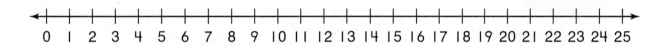

_____

Lee's paper strip chain is _____ inches long now.

4. **THINK SMARTER** Sue has two ribbons that have the
same length. She has 18 inches of ribbon in all.
How long is each ribbon?

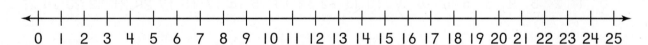

Each ribbon is _____ inches long.

 TAKE HOME ACTIVITY • Have your child explain how he or she
used a diagram to solve a problem in this lesson.

FOR MORE PRACTICE:
Standards Practice Book

Name _____

✓ Mid-Chapter Checkpoint

Concepts and Skills

Use color tiles. Measure the length of the object in inches. (2.MD.1)

1.

about _____ inches

The bead is one inch long. Circle the best
estimate for the length of the string. (2.MD.3)

2.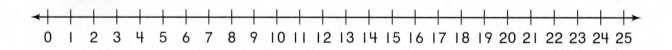

1 inch   2 inches   5 inches

Draw a diagram. Write a number sentence using
a ▇ for the missing number. Solve.

3. A mark is 17 inches long. Katy erases 9 inches
   from the mark. How long is the mark now? (2.MD.5, 2.MD.6)

<---+--->
    0 1 2 3 4 5 6 7 8 9 10 11 12 13 14 15 16 17 18 19 20 21 22 23 24 25

_____

The mark is _____ inches long now.

4. **THINK SMARTER** Use an inch ruler. What is the
   length of the string to the nearest inch? (2.MD.1)

_____ inches

Name _____

Measure in Inches and Feet

Essential Question Why is measuring in feet different from measuring in inches?

 Measurement and Data—2.MD.2
MATHEMATICAL PRACTICES
MP.5, MP.6, MP.7

Listen and Draw

Draw or write to describe how you did each measurement.

First measurement

Second measurement

Math Talk

Describe how the length of a sheet of paper and the length of a paper clip are different.

FOR THE TEACHER • Have pairs of children stand apart and measure the distance between them with sheets of paper folded in half lengthwise. Then have them measure the same distance using large paper clips.

12 inches is the same as 1 **foot**.
A 12-inch ruler is 1 foot long.
You can measure lengths in inches
and also in feet.

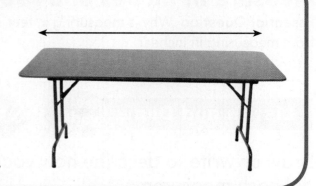

The real table is about 60 inches long.
The real table is also about 5 feet long.

Share and Show

Measure to the nearest inch.
Then measure to the nearest foot.

Find the real object.	Measure.
desk 1.	_____ inches _____ feet
window 2.	_____ inches _____ feet
door MR. MARTIN'S CLASS 3.	_____ inches _____ feet

Name _____

Measure to the nearest inch.
Then measure to the nearest foot.

Find the real object.	Measure.
chalkboard 	_____ inches _____ feet
5. **poster** 	_____ inches _____ feet
6. **teacher's desk** 	_____ inches _____ feet
7. **easel** 	_____ inches _____ feet
8. **bulletin board** 	_____ inches _____ feet

4.

Chapter 8 • Lesson 6

Problem Solving • Applications

9. **THINK SMARTER** Estimate the length of a real shelf in inches and in feet. Then measure.

 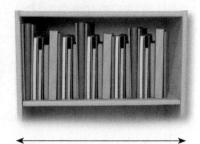

Estimates:

_____ inches

_____ feet

Measurements:

_____ inches

_____ feet

10. **MATHEMATICAL PRACTICE 6** Explain

Look at your measurements for the shelf. Why is the number of inches different from the number of feet?

_____

_____

_____

_____

11. **THINK SMARTER** Use the words on the tiles that makes the sentence true.

| inches | feet |

A book shelf is 4 _____ long.

Deb's necklace is 20 _____ long.

A marker is 3 _____ long.

Jim's bicycle is 4 _____ long.

 TAKE HOME ACTIVITY • Have your child measure the distance of a few footsteps in inches and then in feet.

FOR MORE PRACTICE: Standards Practice Book

© Houghton Mifflin Harcourt Publishing Company

Name _____

Estimate Lengths in Feet

Essential Question How do you estimate the lengths of objects in feet?

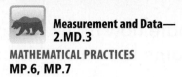

Measurement and Data—
2.MD.3

MATHEMATICAL PRACTICES
MP.6, MP.7

Listen and Draw

Look for 3 classroom objects that are about the same length as a 12-inch ruler. Draw and label the objects.

Math Talk
Mathematical Practices

Which objects have a greater length than the ruler? **Explain.**

FOR THE TEACHER • Provide a collection of objects for children to choose from. Set a 12-inch ruler on the table with the objects for children to use as a visual comparison.

Chapter 8

four hundred twenty-five **425**

Estimate how many 12-inch rulers will be about the same length as this bulletin board.

> Think about how many rulers will fit end-to-end.

_____ rulers, or _____ feet

Find each object. Estimate how many 12-inch rulers will be about the same length as the object.

☑ 1. bookshelf

Estimate: _____ rulers, or _____ feet

_____

☑ 2. chair

Estimate: _____ rulers, or _____ feet

On Your Own

Find each object. Estimate how many 12-inch rulers
will be about the same length as the object.

3. desktop

Estimate: _____ rulers, or _____ feet

4. wall map

Estimate: _____ rulers, or _____ feet

5. window

Estimate: _____ rulers, or _____ feet

6. teacher's desk

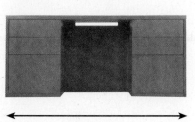

Estimate: _____ rulers, or _____ feet

Problem Solving • Applications

WRITE ▶ Math

7. **THINK SMARTER** Estimate the distance from your desk to the door in feet. Then estimate the same distance in inches.

_____ feet

_____ inches

Explain how you made your estimates for the number of feet and for the number of inches.

_____

_____

_____

8. **THINK SMARTER** Match the object with the estimate of its length in feet.

1 foot	3 feet	7 feet
•	•	•
•	•	•
jump rope	12-inch ruler	baseball bat

 TAKE HOME ACTIVITY • With your child, estimate the lengths of some objects in feet.

FOR MORE PRACTICE: Standards Practice Book

Name _____

Choose a Tool

Essential Question How do you choose a measuring tool to use when measuring lengths?

Measurement and Data—2.MD.1
MATHEMATICAL PRACTICES
MP.5, MP.8

Listen and Draw Real World   Hands On

Draw or write to describe how you measured the distances with the yarn.

Distance 1

Distance 2

FOR THE TEACHER • Have each small group use a 1-yard piece of yarn to measure a distance marked on the floor with masking tape. Have groups repeat the activity to measure another distance that is different from the first one.

Math Talk   **Mathematical Practices**

Which distance was longer? **Explain** how you know.

Chapter 8

four hundred twenty-nine **429**

Model and Draw

You can use different tools to measure lengths and distances.

inch ruler

An inch ruler can be used to measure shorter lengths.

yardstick

A **yardstick** shows 3 feet. It can be used to measure greater lengths and distances.

measuring tape

A **measuring tape** can be used to measure lengths and distances that are not flat or straight.

Share and Show

MATH BOARD

| inch ruler |
| yardstick |
| measuring tape |

Choose the best tool for measuring the real object. Then measure and record the length or distance.

☑ 1. the length of a book

Tool: _____

Length: _____

☑ 2. the distance around a cup

Tool: _____

Distance: _____

On Your Own

inch ruler
yardstick
measuring tape

Choose the best tool for measuring the real object.
Then measure and record the length or distance.

3. the length of a chalkboard

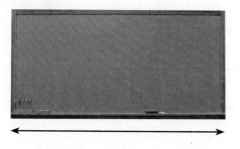

Tool: _____

Length: _____

4. the length of a marker

Tool: _____

Length: _____

5. the distance around a globe

Tool: _____

Distance: _____

6. the length of a classroom wall

Tool: _____

Length: _____

Problem Solving • Applications Real World

 WRITE Math

7. **THINK SMARTER** Rachel wants to measure the length of a sidewalk. Should she use an inch ruler or a yardstick? Explain.

Rachel should use _____ because

_____

_____

_____

8. **MATHEMATICAL PRACTICE ③** Apply

What is an object that you would measure with a measuring tape? Explain why you would use this tool.

_____

_____

_____

Personal Math Trainer

9. **THINK SMARTER +** Jim measures the length of a picnic table with an inch ruler. Is Jim using the best tool for measuring? Explain.

_____

_____

_____

🏠 **TAKE HOME ACTIVITY** • Have your child name some objects that he or she would measure using a yardstick.

FOR MORE PRACTICE: Standards Practice Book

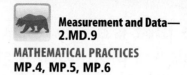

Name _____

Display Measurement Data

Essential Question How can a line plot be used to show measurement data?

Measurement and Data—
2.MD.9
MATHEMATICAL PRACTICES
MP.4, MP.5, MP.6

Use an inch ruler. Measure and record each length.

_____ inches

_____ inches

_____ inches

Math Talk **Mathematical Practices**

Describe how the lengths of the three strings are different.

HOME CONNECTION • Your child practiced measuring different lengths in inches in preparation for collecting measurement data in this lesson.

Chapter 8

four hundred thirty-three **433**

A **line plot** is a way to show data. On this line plot, each **X** stands for the length of one pencil in inches.

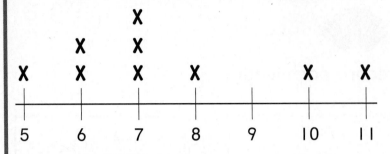

Lengths of Pencils in Inches

How many pencils are just 6 inches long? How many different pencils are shown in this data?

Share and Show

☑ 1. Use an inch ruler. Measure and record the lengths of 5 books in inches.

1st book: _____ inches		
2nd book: _____ inches		
3rd book: _____ inches		
4th book: _____ inches		
5th book: _____ inches		

☑ 2. Write a title for the line plot. Then write the numbers and draw the **X**s.

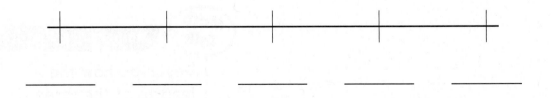

On Your Own

3. Use an inch ruler. Measure and record the lengths of 5 pencils in inches.

1st pencil: _____ inches
2nd pencil: _____ inches
3rd pencil: _____ inches
4th pencil: _____ inches
5th pencil: _____ inches

4. Write a title for the line plot. Then write the numbers and draw the **X**s.

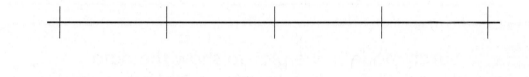

5. Use an inch ruler. Measure and record the lengths of 4 crayons in inches. Then complete the line plot.

1st crayon: _____ inches
2nd crayon: _____ inches
3rd crayon: _____ inches
4th crayon: _____ inches

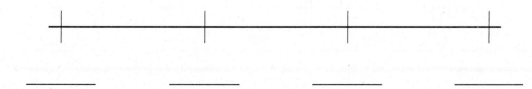

Problem Solving • Applications WRITE ▸ Math

6. **THINK SMARTER** Use the data in the list to complete the line plot.

Lengths of Ribbons
6 inches
5 inches
7 inches
6 inches

_____

_____

7. **THINK SMARTER** Sarah made a line plot to show the data about the length of leaves. Is Sarah's line plot correct? Tell why or why not.

The Length of Leaves	
4 inches	6 inches
5 inches	4 inches
3 inches	5 inches
4 inches	

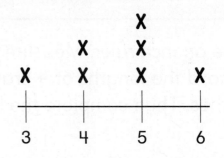

Lengths of Leaves in Inches

_____

_____

_____

🏠 **TAKE HOME ACTIVITY** • Have your child describe how to make a line plot.

FOR MORE PRACTICE:
Standards Practice Book

© Houghton Mifflin Harcourt Publishing Company

√ Chapter 8 Review/Test

1. Josh wants to measures the distance around a soccer ball.

Circle the best choice of tool.

inch ruler   yardstick   measuring tape

Explain your choice of tool.

_____

_____

2. Luke has a string that is 6 inches long and a string that is 11 inches long. How many inches of string does Luke have?

Draw a diagram. Write a number sentence using a ▨ for the missing number. Solve.

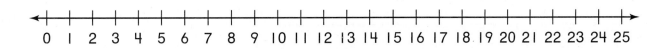

_____

Luke has _____ inches of string.

3. Use an inch ruler. What is the length of the lip balm to the nearest inch?

Circle the number in the box to make the sentence true.

The lip balm is
$$\boxed{\begin{array}{c} 2 \\ 3 \\ 4 \end{array}}$$
inches long.

---

4. Tom uses tiles to measure a string. Each tile is
1 inch long. Tom says the string is 3 inches long.
Is he correct? Explain.

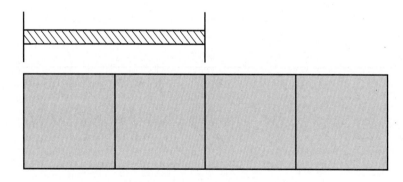

_____

_____

Name _____

5. Dalia made a line plot to show the lengths of her ribbons. How many ribbons are shown in the line plot?

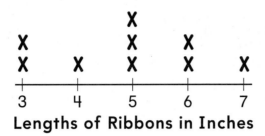

Lengths of Ribbons in Inches

The line plot shows _____ ribbons.

Suppose Dalia cut one of the ribbons that is 6 inches long into two pieces that are each 3 inches long. Explain how she should change the line plot.

_____

_____

6. Use the words on the tiles to make the sentence true.

The table is 3 _____ long.

The belt is 30 _____ long.

The hallway is 15 _____ long.

inches	feet

7. Use the 1-inch mark. Estimate the length of each object.

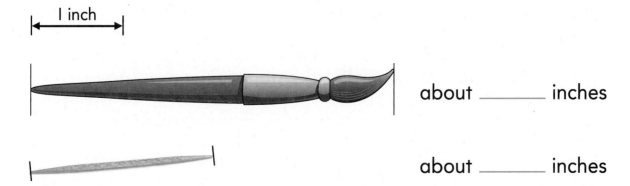

about _____ inches

about _____ inches

8. Use an inch ruler. What is the length of the paper clip to the nearest inch?

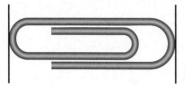

_____ inches

9. Estimate how many 12-inch rulers will be about the same height as a classroom door. Does the sentence describe the door? Choose Yes or No.

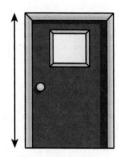

The door is about 8 feet high.	○ Yes	○ No
The door is less than 3 rulers high.	○ Yes	○ No
The door is more than 20 feet high.	○ Yes	○ No
The door is less than 15 rulers high.	○ Yes	○ No

What is your estimate of how wide the door is?

_____

Length in Metric Units

A wind farm is a group of wind turbines used to make electricity. One way to measure the distance between two wind turbines is by counting footsteps. What is another way?

Show What You Know ✓

Compare Lengths

1. Order the strings from shortest to longest.
   Write 1, 2, 3.

_____ _____

_____

_____

Use Nonstandard Units to Measure Length

Use real objects and ■ to measure.

2. about _____ ■

3. about _____ ■

Measure Length Twice: Nonstandard Units

Use 🔩 first. Then use ⊂▭⊃.
Measure the length of the ribbon.

4. about _____ 🔩

5. about _____ ⊂▭⊃

This page checks understanding of important
skills needed for success in Chapter 9.

Personal Math Trainer
Online Assessment
and Intervention

© Houghton Mifflin Harcourt Publishing Company

Name _____

Vocabulary Builder

Visualize It

Fill in the graphic organizer. Think of an object and write about how you can **measure** the **length** of that object.

length

_____
_____

_____
_____

Understand Vocabulary

Use the color tiles to **estimate** the length of each straw.

1.

about _____ tiles

2.

about _____ tiles

 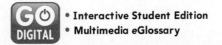
• Interactive Student Edition
• Multimedia eGlossary

Game

Estimating Length

Materials

- 12 ⬤
- 12 🔘
- 15 ▪️
- 15 ▪️

Play with a partner.

1. Take turns choosing a picture. Find the real object.

2. Each player estimates the length of the object in cubes and then makes a cube train for his or her estimate.

3. Compare the cube trains to the length of the object. The player with the closer estimate puts a counter on the picture. If there is a tie, both players put a counter on the picture.

4. Repeat until all pictures are covered. The player with more counters on the board wins.

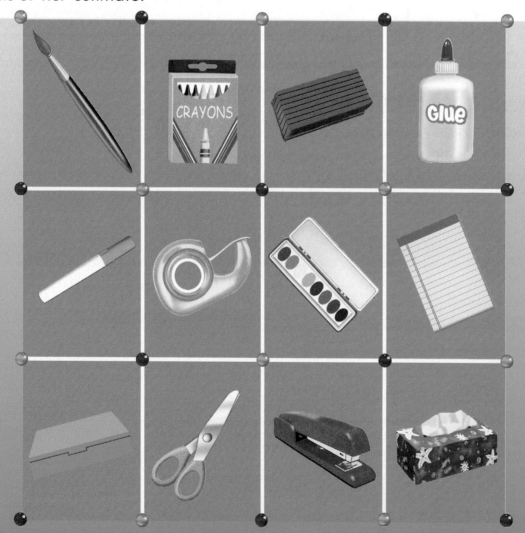

Name _____

Measure with a Centimeter Model

Essential Question How do you use a centimeter model to measure the lengths of objects?

Measurement and Data—2.MD.1

MATHEMATICAL PRACTICES
MP.5, MP.6, MP.8

Listen and Draw

Use 🟦 to measure the length.

_____

_____ unit cubes

_____ unit cubes

_____ unit cubes

HOME CONNECTION • Your child used unit cubes as an introduction to measurement of length before using metric measurement tools.

Math Talk **Mathematical Practices**

Describe how to use unit cubes to measure an object's length.

Chapter 9

A unit cube is about 1 **centimeter** long.

About how many centimeters long is this string?

The string is about _____ centimeters long.

> You can make a mark for each centimeter to keep track and to count.

Share and Show

Use a unit cube. Measure the length in centimeters.

1.

about _____ centimeters

_____

✓ 2.

about _____ centimeters

✓ 3.

about _____ centimeters

Name _____

Use a unit cube. Measure the length in centimeters.

4.

about _____ centimeters

5.

about _____ centimeters

6.

about _____ centimeters

7.

about _____ centimeters

8.

about _____ centimeters

Problem Solving • Applications  WRITE Math

Solve. Write or draw to explain.

9. **THINK SMARTER** Mrs. Duncan measured
the lengths of a crayon and a pencil.
The pencil is double the length of the crayon.
The sum of their lengths is 24 centimeters.
What are their lengths?

crayon: _____

pencil: _____

Personal Math Trainer

10. **THINK SMARTER +** Marita uses unit cubes to
measure the length of a straw.
Circle the number in the box that makes
the sentence true.

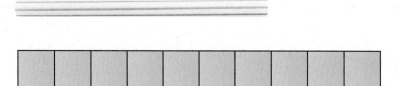

The straw is | 3 |
              | 7 | centimeters long.
              | 10 |

 TAKE HOME ACTIVITY • Have your child compare the lengths
of other objects to those in this lesson.

FOR MORE PRACTICE:
Standards Practice Book

Estimate Lengths in Centimeters

Essential Question How do you use known lengths to estimate unknown lengths?

Measurement and Data—2.MD.3
MATHEMATICAL PRACTICES
MP.6, MP.7

Listen and Draw Real World   Hands On

Find three classroom objects that are shorter than your 10-centimeter strip. Draw the objects. Write estimates for their lengths.

about _____ centimeters

about _____ centimeters

about _____ centimeters

Math Talk   **Mathematical Practices**

Which object has a length closest to 10 centimeters? **Explain.**

HOME CONNECTION • Your child used a 10-centimeter strip of paper to practice estimating the lengths of some classroom objects.

This pencil is about 10 centimeters long. Which is the most reasonable estimate for the length of the ribbon?

7 centimeters

13 centimeters

20 centimeters

> The ribbon is longer than the pencil. 7 centimeters is not reasonable.

> The ribbon is not twice as long as the pencil. 20 centimeters is not reasonable.

The ribbon is a little longer than the pencil.
So, 13 centimeters is the most reasonable estimate.

Share and Show MATH BOARD

☑ 1. The yarn is about 5 centimeters long. Circle the best estimate for the length of the crayon.

10 centimeters

15 centimeters

20 centimeters

☑ 2. The string is about 12 centimeters long. Circle the best estimate for the length of the straw.

3 centimeters

7 centimeters

11 centimeters

Name _____

3. The rope is about 8 centimeters long. Circle the best estimate for the length of the paper clip.

2 centimeters

4 centimeters

8 centimeters

4. The pencil is about 11 centimeters long.
Circle the best estimate for the length of the chain.

6 centimeters

10 centimeters

13 centimeters

5. The hair clip is about 7 centimeters long.
Circle the best estimate for the length of the yarn.

10 centimeters

17 centimeters

22 centimeters

6. The ribbon is about 13 centimeters long.
Circle the best estimate for the length of the string.

5 centimeters

11 centimeters

17 centimeters

Problem Solving • Applications  WRITE ▸ Math

7. **THINK SMARTER** For each question, circle the best estimate.

About how long is a new crayon?

5 centimeters

10 centimeters

20 centimeters

About how long is a new pencil?

20 centimeters

40 centimeters

50 centimeters

---

8. **MATHEMATICAL PRACTICE ①** **Analyze** Mr. Lott has 250 more centimeters of tape than Mrs. Sanchez. Mr. Lott has 775 centimeters of tape. How many centimeters of tape does Mrs. Sanchez have?

_____ centimeters

---

9. **THINK SMARTER** This feather is about 7 centimeters long. Rachel says the yarn is about 14 centimeters long. Is Rachel correct? Explain.

_____

_____

 TAKE HOME ACTIVITY • Give your child an object that is about 5 centimeters long. Have him or her use it to estimate the lengths of some other objects.

FOR MORE PRACTICE:
Standards Practice Book

Name _____

Measure with a Centimeter Ruler

Essential Question How do you use a centimeter ruler to measure lengths?

 Measurement and Data— 2.MD.1
MATHEMATICAL PRACTICES
MP.5, MP.6

Listen and Draw Real World   Hands On

Find three small objects in the classroom.
Use unit cubes to measure their lengths.
Draw the objects and write their lengths.

_____ centimeters

_____ centimeters

_____ centimeters

Math Talk **Mathematical Practices**

Describe how the three lengths compare. Which object is shortest?

 HOME CONNECTION • Your child used unit cubes to measure the lengths of some classroom objects as an introduction to measuring lengths in centimeters.

Chapter 9

four hundred fifty-three **453**

What is the length of the crayon to the nearest centimeter?

Remember: Line up the left edge of the object with the zero mark on the ruler.

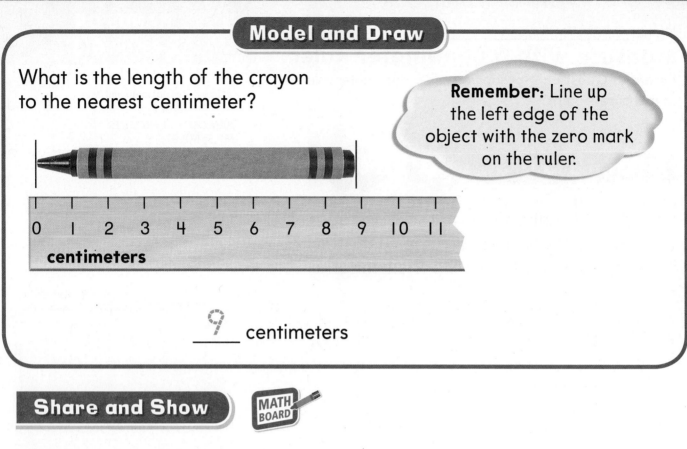

0 1 2 3 4 5 6 7 8 9 10 11
centimeters

_9_ centimeters

Share and Show

MATH BOARD

Measure the length to the nearest centimeter.

1.

_____ centimeters

2.

_____ centimeters

3.

_____ centimeters

On Your Own

Measure the length to the nearest centimeter.

4.

_____ centimeters

5.

_____ centimeters

6.

_____ centimeters

7.

_____ centimeters

8.

_____ centimeters

Problem Solving • Applications

WRITE Math

9. **THINK SMARTER** The crayon was on the table next to the centimeter ruler. The left edge of the crayon was not lined up with the zero mark on the ruler.

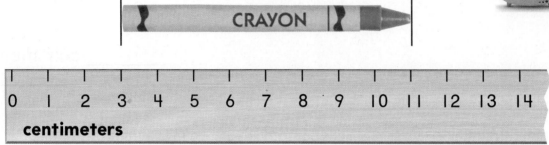

What is the length of the crayon?
Explain how you found your answer.

_____

_____

_____

10. **THINK SMARTER** This is Lee's string. Hana's string is 7 centimeters long. Whose string is longer? Use a centimeter ruler to find out. Explain.

_____

_____

TAKE HOME ACTIVITY • Have your child measure the lengths of some objects using a centimeter ruler.

FOR MORE PRACTICE:
Standards Practice Book

Name _____

Problem Solving • Add and Subtract Lengths

Essential Question How can drawing a diagram help when solving problems about lengths?

Measurement and Data—
2.MD.6, 2.MD.5
MATHEMATICAL PRACTICES
MP.1, MP.2, MP.4

Nate had 23 centimeters of string.
He gave 9 centimeters of string to Myra.
How much string does Nate have now?

⚷ Unlock the Problem Real World

What do I need to find?

how much string

Nate has now

What information do I need to use?

Nate had _____ centimeters of string.

He gave _____ centimeters of string to Myra.

Show how to solve the problem.

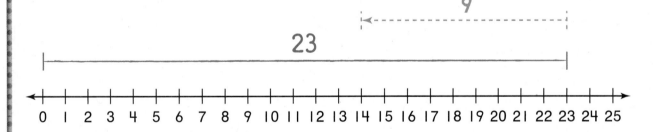

_____

Nate has _____ centimeters of string now.

HOME CONNECTION • Your child drew a diagram to represent a problem about lengths. The diagram can be used to choose the operation for solving the problem.

Chapter 9

four hundred fifty-seven **457**

Draw a diagram. Write a number sentence using a ▮ for the missing number. Then solve.

1. Ellie has a ribbon that is 12 centimeters long. Gwen has a ribbon that is 9 centimeters long. How many centimeters of ribbon do they have?

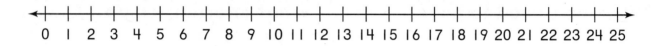

_____

They have _____ centimeters of ribbon.

2. A string is 24 centimeters long. Justin cuts 8 centimeters off. How long is the string now?

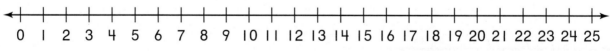

_____

Now the string is

_____ centimeters long.

Math Talk **Mathematical Practices**

Explain how your diagram shows what happened in the first problem.

Share and Show

Draw a diagram. Write a number sentence using a ▢ for the missing number. Then solve.

☑3. A chain of paper clips is 18 centimeters long. Sondra adds 6 centimeters of paper clips to the chain. How long is the chain now?

_____

The chain is _____ centimeters long now.

4. **THINK SMARTER** A ribbon was 22 centimeters long. Then Martha cut a piece off to give to Tao. Now the ribbon is 5 centimeters long. How many centimeters of ribbon did Martha give to Tao?

Martha gave _____ centimeters of ribbon to Tao.

TAKE HOME ACTIVITY • Have your child explain how he or she used a diagram to solve one problem in this lesson.

FOR MORE PRACTICE:
Standards Practice Book

✓ Mid-Chapter Checkpoint

Concepts and Skills

Use a unit cube. Measure the length in centimeters. (2.MD.1)

1.

about _____ centimeters

2.

about _____ centimeters

3. The pencil is about 11 centimeters long. Circle the best estimate for the length of the string. (2.MD.3)

7 centimeters

10 centimeters

16 centimeters

4. **THINK SMARTER** Use a centimeter ruler. What is the length of this ribbon to the nearest centimeter? (2.MD.1)

_____ centimeters

Name _____

Centimeters and Meters

Essential Question How is measuring in meters different from measuring in centimeters?

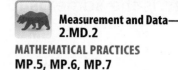

Draw or write to describe how you did each measurement.

1st measurement

2nd measurement

FOR THE TEACHER • Have each small group use a 1-meter piece of yarn to measure a distance marked on the floor with masking tape. Then have them measure the same distance using a sheet of paper folded in half lengthwise.

Math Talk **Mathematical Practices**

Describe how the lengths of the yarn and the sheet of paper are different.

Chapter 9

Model and Draw

I **meter** is the same as 100 centimeters.

The real door is about 200 centimeters tall.
The real door is also about 2 meters tall.

Share and Show

Measure to the nearest centimeter.
Then measure to the nearest meter.

Find the real object.	Measure.
chair 1.	_____ centimeters _____ meters
teacher's desk ☑ 2.	_____ centimeters _____ meters
wall ☑ 3.	_____ centimeters _____ meters

Name _____

On Your Own

Measure to the nearest centimeter.
Then measure to the nearest meter.

Find the real object.	Measure.
4. **chalkboard** 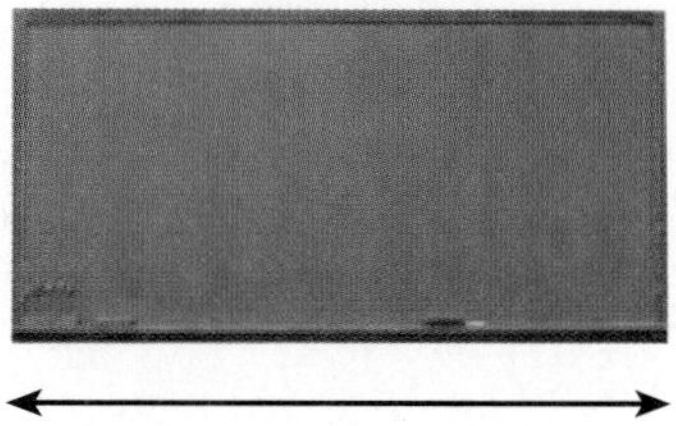	_____ centimeters _____ meters
5. **bookshelf** 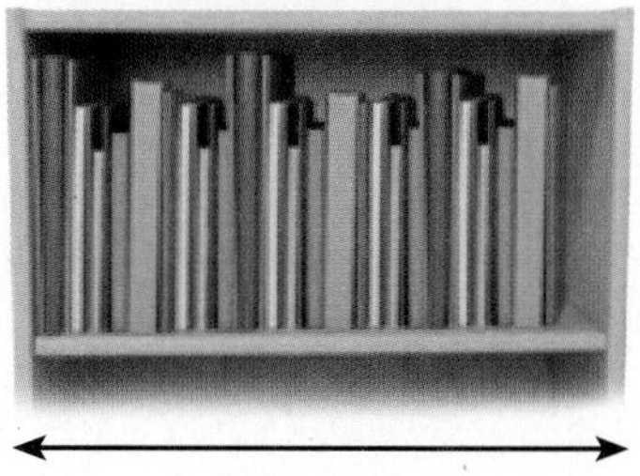	_____ centimeters _____ meters
6. **table** 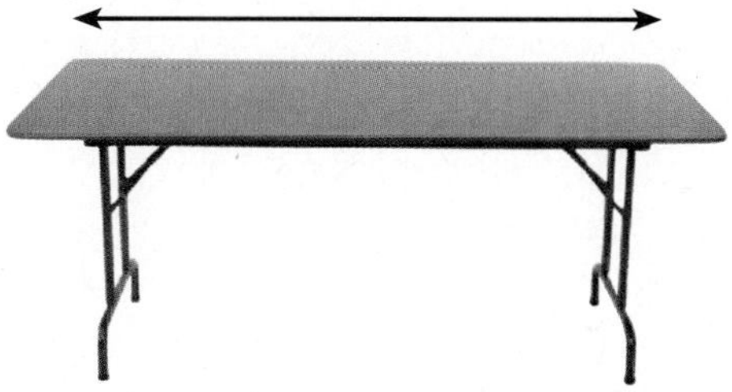	_____ centimeters _____ meters

7. **GO DEEPER** Write these lengths in order from shortest to longest.

200 centimeters
10 meters
1 meter

_____

Problem Solving • Applications  WRITE ▸ Math

8. **THINK SMARTER** Mr. Ryan walked next to a barn. He wants to measure the length of the barn. Would the length be a greater number of centimeters or a greater number of meters? Explain your answer.

_____

_____

_____

9. **THINK SMARTER** Write the word on the tile that makes the sentence true.

centimeters	meters

A bench is 2 _____ long.

A pencil is 15 _____ long.

A paper clip is 3 _____ long.

A bed is 3 _____ long.

 TAKE HOME ACTIVITY • Have your child describe how centimeters and meters are different.

FOR MORE PRACTICE:
Standards Practice Book

Estimate Lengths in Meters

Essential Question How do you estimate the lengths of objects in meters?

Measurement and Data—
2.MD.3
MATHEMATICAL PRACTICES
MP.6, MP.7

Listen and Draw (Real World)

Find an object that is about 10 centimeters long.
Draw and label it.

Is there a classroom object that is about
50 centimeters long? Draw and label it.

FOR THE TEACHER • Provide a collection of objects for children to choose from. Above the table of displayed objects, draw and label a 10-centimeter line segment and a 50-centimeter line segment.

Math Talk

Mathematical Practices

Describe how the lengths of the two real objects compare.

Estimate. About how many meter sticks will match the width of a door?

A 1-meter measuring stick is about 100 centimeters long.

about _____ meters

Find the real object.
Estimate its length in meters.

☑ 1. bookshelf

about _____ meters

☑ 2. bulletin board

about _____ meters

On Your Own

Find the real object.
Estimate its length in meters.

3. teacher's desk

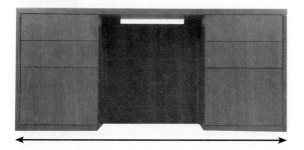

about _____ meters

4. wall

about _____ meters

5. window

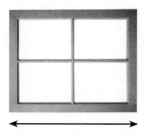

about _____ meters

6. chalkboard

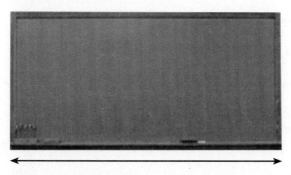

about _____ meters

Problem Solving • Applications

WRITE Math

7. **THINK SMARTER** In meters, estimate the distance from your teacher's desk to the door of your classroom.

about _____ meters

Explain how you made your estimate.

_____

_____

_____

_____

8. **THINK SMARTER** Estimate the length of an adult's bicycle. Fill in the bubble next to all the sentences that are true.

○ The bicycle is about 2 meters long.

○ The bicycle is about 200 centimeters long.

○ The bicycle is less than 1 meter long.

○ The bicycle is about 2 centimeters long.

○ The bicycle is more than 200 meters long.

 TAKE HOME ACTIVITY • With your child, estimate the lengths of some objects in meters.

FOR MORE PRACTICE:
Standards Practice Book

Measure and Compare Lengths

Essential Question How do you find the difference between the lengths of two objects?

Measurement and Data—
2.MD.4
MATHEMATICAL PRACTICES
MP.2, MP.4

Measure and record each length.

_____ centimeters

_____ centimeters

Math Talk **Mathematical Practices**

Name a classroom object that is longer than the paintbrush. **Explain** how you know.

HOME CONNECTION • Your child measured these lengths as an introduction to measuring and then comparing lengths.

How much longer is the pencil than the crayon?

_____8_____ centimeters

_____5_____ centimeters

_____8_____ − _____5_____ = _____
centimeters   centimeters   centimeters

The pencil is _____ centimeters longer than the crayon.

Share and Show

MATH BOARD

Measure the length of each object. Complete the number sentence to find the difference between the lengths.

☑ **1.**

_____ centimeters

_____ centimeters

_____ − _____ = _____
centimeters   centimeters   centimeters

The string is _____ centimeters longer than the straw.

☑ **2.**

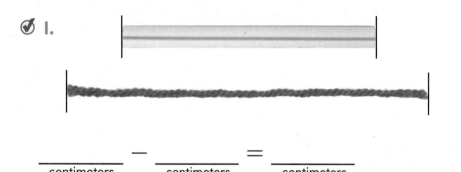

_____ centimeters

_____ centimeters

_____ − _____ = _____
centimeters   centimeters   centimeters

The paintbrush is _____ centimeters longer than the toothpick.

470 four hundred seventy

On Your Own

Measure the length of each object. Complete the number sentence to find the difference between the lengths.

3.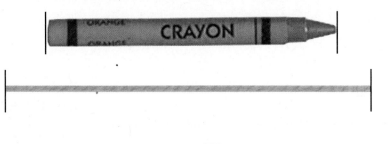

_____ centimeters

_____ centimeters

_____ − _____ = _____
centimeters · · centimeters · · centimeters

The yarn is _____ centimeters longer than the crayon.

4.

_____ centimeters

_____ centimeters

_____ − _____ = _____
centimeters · · centimeters · · centimeters

The string is _____ centimeters longer than the paper clip.

5. **THINK SMARTER** Use a centimeter ruler. Measure the length of your desk and the length of a book.

desk: _____ centimeters

book: _____ centimeters

Which is shorter? _____

How much shorter is it? _____

Problem Solving • Applications  WRITE Math

 Analyze Relationships

6. Mark has a rope that is 23 centimeters long. He cuts 15 centimeters off. What is the length of the rope now?

_____ centimeters

7. The yellow ribbon is 15 centimeters longer than the green ribbon. The green ribbon is 29 centimeters long. What is the length of the yellow ribbon?

_____ centimeters

Personal Math Trainer

8. THINK SMARTER + Measure the length of each object. Which object is longer? How much longer? Explain.

_____

_____

_____

TAKE HOME ACTIVITY • Have your child tell you how he or she solved one of the problems in this lesson.

FOR MORE PRACTICE:
Standards Practice Book

© Houghton Mifflin Harcourt Publishing Company

✓ Chapter 9 Review/Test

1. Michael uses unit cubes to measure the length of the yarn. Circle the number in the box that makes the sentence true.

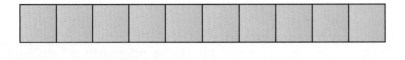

The yarn is | 2 4 6 | centimeters long.

2. The paper clip is about 4 centimeters long. Robin says the string is about 7 centimeters long. Gale says the string is about 20 centimeters long.

Which girl has the better estimate? Explain.

_____

_____

3. Sandy's paper chain is 14 centimeters long. Tim's paper chain is 6 centimeters long. How many centimeters of paper chain do they have? Draw a diagram. Write a number sentence using a ▢ for the missing number. Then solve.

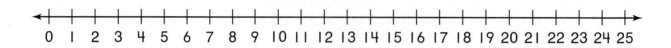

0 1 2 3 4 5 6 7 8 9 10 11 12 13 14 15 16 17 18 19 20 21 22 23 24 25

_____

The paper chain is _____ centimeters long now.

---

4. Write the word on the tile that makes the sentence true.

centimeters	meters

A hallway is 4 _____ long.

A marker is 15 _____ long.

A toothpick is 5 _____ long.

A sofa is 2 _____ long.

5. Estimate the length of a real car. Fill in the bubble next to all the sentences that are true.

○ The car is about 4 meters long.

○ The car is less than I meter long.

○ The car is less than 6 meters long.

○ The car is about 20 centimeters long.

○ The car is more than 150 meters long.

6. Measure the length of each object. Does the sentence describe the objects? Choose Yes or No.

_____ centimeters

GREEN

_____ centimeters

The marker is II centimeters longer than the crayon.	○ Yes	○ No
The crayon is 4 centimeters shorter than the marker.	○ Yes	○ No
The total length of the marker and the crayon is I8 centimeters.	○ Yes	○ No

7. Ethan's rope is 25 centimeters long. Ethan cuts the rope and gives a piece to Hank. Ethan's rope is now 16 centimeters long. How many centimeters of rope does Hank have?

Draw a diagram. Write a number sentence using a ▨ for the missing number. Then solve.

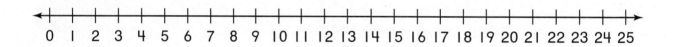

_____

Hank has _____ centimeters of rope.

---

8. Measure the length of the paintbrush to the nearest centimeter. Circle the number in the box that makes the sentence true.

The paintbrush is about

12
13
14

centimeters long.

Curious
about
Math

Look at the different kinds of balloons.

What are some ways you can sort these balloons?

Show What You Know ✓

Read a Picture Graph

Use the picture graph.

Fruit We Like				
● orange	●	●	●	●
🍐 pear	🍐	🍐		

1. How many children chose pear? _____ children

2. Circle the fruit that more children chose.

Read a Tally Chart

Complete the tally chart.

Color We Like		Total
green	III	
red	IIII I	
blue	IIII III	

3. How many children chose red?

_____ children

4. Which color did the fewest children choose?

_____

Addition and Subtraction Facts

Write the sum or difference.

5. $10 - 4 =$ _____

6. $4 + 5 =$ _____

7. $6 + 5 =$ _____

8. $9 - 3 =$ _____

9. $5 + 7 =$ _____

10. $11 - 3 =$ _____

This page checks understanding of important skills needed for success in Chapter 10.

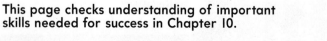

Personal Math Trainer
Online Assessment and Intervention

Vocabulary Builder

Visualize It

Draw **tally marks** to show each number.

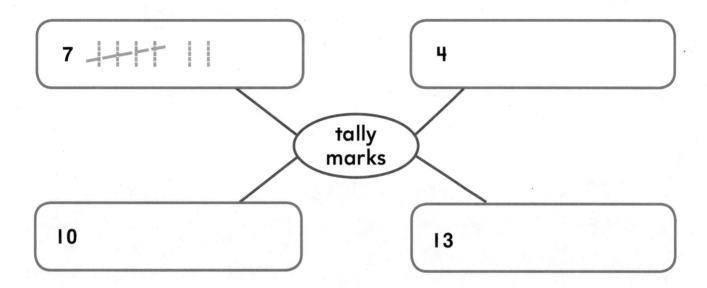

Understand Vocabulary

Write a number to complete the sentence.

1. 10 apples is **more than** _____ apples.

_____

2. 6 bananas is **fewer than** _____ bananas.

_____

3. _____ grapes is **more than** 6 grapes.

_____

4. _____ oranges is **fewer than** 5 oranges.

Game

Making Tens

Materials
- 🎲
- 25 ▪
- small bag

Play with a partner.

1. Put 25 ▪ in a bag.
2. Toss the 🎲. Take that many ▪ and put them on your ten frame. Take turns.

3. When you have 10 ▪ on your ten frame, make a tally mark on the tally chart. Then put the 10 ▪ back in the bag.

4. The first player to make 10 tally marks wins.

Player 1				

Player 2				

Making Tens	
Player	**Tally**
Player 1	
Player 2	

Name _____

Collect Data

Essential Question How do you use a tally chart to record data from a survey?

Lesson 10.1

Measurement and Data—2.MD.10

MATHEMATICAL PRACTICES
MP.1, MP.4, MP.6

Listen and Draw

Take turns choosing a cube from the bag.
Draw a tally mark in the chart for each cube.

Cube Colors	
Color	**Tally**
blue	
red	
green	

HOME CONNECTION • Your child made tally marks to record the color of cubes taken from a bag. This activity prepares children for using and recording data in this chapter.

Math Talk Mathematical Practices

Explain how tally marks help you keep track of what has been taken.

© Houghton Mifflin Harcourt Publishing Company

Chapter 10

You can take a **survey** to collect **data**.
You can record the data with tally marks.

Greg asked his classmates which lunch was their favorite.

Favorite Lunch	
Lunch	**Tally**
pizza	IIII
sandwich	||||| I
salad	III
pasta	|||||

The tally marks in the tally chart show the children's answers. Each tally mark stands for one child's choice.

Share and Show

1. Take a survey. Ask 10 classmates which pet is their favorite. Use tally marks to show their choices.

✓ 2. How many classmates chose dog?

_____ classmates

✓ 3. Which pet did the fewest classmates choose?

_____

Favorite Pet	
Pet	**Tally**
cat	
dog	
fish	
bird	

4. Did more classmates choose cat or dog? _____

How many more? _____ more classmates

On Your Own

5. Take a survey. Ask 10 classmates which indoor game is their favorite. Use tally marks to show their choices.

Favorite Indoor Game	
Game	Tally
board	
card	
computer	
puzzle	

6. How many classmates chose board game?

_____ classmates

7. Which game did the most classmates choose?

_____

8. **GO DEEPER** Did more classmates choose a card game or a computer game?

_____

How many more? _____ more classmates

9. Which game did the fewest classmates choose?

_____

10. **MATHEMATICAL PRACTICE 3** Apply How many classmates did not choose a board game or a puzzle? Explain how you know.

_____

_____

_____

_____

Problem Solving • Applications (Real World)

11. **THINK SMARTER** Maeko asked her classmates to choose their favorite subject. She made this tally chart.

How many more classmates chose math than reading?

_____ more classmates

Favorite Subject	
Subject	Tally
reading	‖‖‖ I
math	‖‖‖ IIII
science	‖‖‖ ‖‖‖

Write a question about the data in the chart. Then write the answer to your question.

_____

_____

_____

12. **THINK SMARTER** Fill in the bubble next to all the sentences that describe data in the tally chart.

○ 10 children voted for lunch.

○ 13 children voted for breakfast.

○ More children voted for dinner than for lunch.

○ A total of 35 children voted for their favorite meal.

Favorite Meal	
Meal	Tally
breakfast	‖‖‖ III
lunch	‖‖‖ ‖‖‖
dinner	‖‖‖ ‖‖‖ II

 TAKE HOME ACTIVITY • With your child, take a survey about favorite games and make a tally chart to show the data.

FOR MORE PRACTICE:
Standards Practice Book

Name _____

Read Picture Graphs

Essential Question How do you use a picture graph to show data?

Measurement and Data—
2.MD.10
MATHEMATICAL PRACTICES
MP.1, MP.2, MP.6

Use the tally chart to solve the problem.
Draw or write to show what you did.

Favorite Hobby	
Hobby	**Tally**
crafts	⊮ I
reading	IIII
music	⊮
sports	⊮ II

_____ more children

Math Talk

Mathematical Practices

Can the chart be used to find how many girls chose music? **Explain.**

FOR THE TEACHER • Read the following problem. Mr. Martin's class made this tally chart. How many more children in his class chose sports than chose reading as their favorite hobby?

Chapter 10

four hundred eighty-five **485**

A **picture graph** uses pictures to show data.

Number of Soccer Games							
March	⚽	⚽	⚽	⚽			
April	⚽	⚽	⚽				
May	⚽	⚽	⚽	⚽	⚽	⚽	
June	⚽	⚽	⚽	⚽	⚽	⚽	⚽

Key: Each ⚽ stands for 1 game.

A **key** tells how many each picture stands for.

Share and Show

Use the picture graph to answer the questions.

Favorite Snack								
pretzels	☺	☺	☺	☺	☺	☺	☺	☺
grapes	☺	☺	☺	☺	☺	☺	☺	
popcorn	☺	☺	☺					
apples	☺	☺	☺	☺	☺	☺		

Key: Each ☺ stands for 1 child.

☑ 1. Which snack was chosen by the fewest children? _____

☑ 2. How many more children chose pretzels
than apples? _____ more children

Name _____

Use the picture graph to answer the questions.

Number of Pencils									
Alana	✏	✏	✏						
Kiana	✏	✏	✏	✏	✏				
Dante	✏	✏	✏	✏					
Brad	✏	✏	✏	✏	✏	✏	✏	✏	

Key: Each ✏ stands for 1 pencil.

3. How many pencils do Alana and Brad have? _____ pencils

4. How many more pencils does Kiana
   have than Alana has? _____ more pencils

5. *THINK SMARTER* Mrs. Green has the same
   number of pencils as the four children.
   How many pencils does she have?

   _____ pencils

Math
on the
Spot

6. **MATHEMATICAL PRACTICE ④** Use Graphs Christy has 7 pencils.
   Write two sentences to describe how her number
   of pencils compares to the data in the picture graph.

   _____

   _____

   _____

   _____

Problem Solving • Applications WRITE ▸ Math

Favorite Balloon Color

green	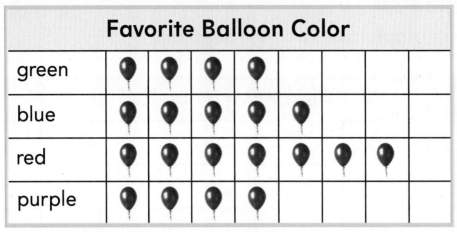							
blue								
red								
purple								

Key: Each 🎈 stands for 1 child.

7. **GO DEEPER** Which three colors were chosen
by a total of 13 children? _____

8. **THINK SMARTER** Use the numbers on the tiles to
complete the sentence about the picture graph.

1	2	3
4	5	6

Number of Pets

Scott	◆	◆	◆	
Andre	◆			
Maddie	◆	◆		

Key: Each ◆ stands for 1 pet.

Scott has ____ pets.

Andre has ____ fewer pets than Scott.

Maddie and Scott have ____ more pets than Andre.

 TAKE HOME ACTIVITY • Have your child explain how
he or she solved one of the problems in this lesson.

FOR MORE PRACTICE:
Standards Practice Book

© Houghton Mifflin Harcourt Publishing Company • Image Credits: ©Getty Images

Name _____

Make Picture Graphs

Essential Question How do you make a picture graph to show data in a tally chart?

Measurement and Data—
2.MD.10
MATHEMATICAL PRACTICES
MP.1, MP.4, MP.6

Listen and Draw

Take turns choosing a cube from the bag.
Draw a smiley face in the graph for each cube.

Cube Colors					
blue					
red					
green					
orange					

Key: Each ☺ stands for 1 cube.

Math Talk **Mathematical Practices**

Explain how you know that the number of smiley faces for blue matches the number of blue cubes.

HOME CONNECTION • Your child made a graph by recording smiley faces for the colors of cubes taken from a bag. This activity prepares children for working with picture graphs in this lesson.

Each picture in the graph stands for 1 flower.
Draw pictures to show the data in the tally chart.

Number of Flowers Picked	
Name	**Tally**
Jessie	III
Inez	ЖHt
Paulo	IIIII

Number of Flowers Picked					
Jessie	⬭	⬭	⬭		
Inez					
Paulo					

Key: Each ⬭ stands for 1 flower.

Share and Show

1. Use the tally chart to complete the picture graph.
   Draw a ☺ for each child.

Favorite Sandwich	
Sandwich	**Tally**
cheese	ЖHt
ham	II
tuna	IIII
turkey	III

Favorite Sandwich					
cheese					
ham					
tuna					
turkey					

Key: Each ☺ stands for 1 child.

✔ 2. How many children chose tuna? _____ children

✔ 3. How many more children chose cheese
     than ham? _____ more children

On Your Own

4. Use the tally chart to complete the picture graph.
   Draw a ☺ for each child.

Favorite Fruit	
Fruit	**Tally**
apple	IIII
plum	II
banana	IIII
orange	III

Favorite Fruit					
apple					
plum					
banana					
orange					

Key: Each ☺ stands for 1 child.

5. How many children chose banana? _____ children

6. How many fewer children chose plum
   than banana? _____ fewer children

7. **THINK SMARTER** How many children chose
   a fruit that was not a plum?

   _____ children

8. **GO DEEPER** Which three fruits were
   chosen by a total of 10 children?

   _____

TAKE HOME ACTIVITY • Ask your child to explain how to
read the picture graph on this page.

FOR MORE PRACTICE:
Standards Practice Book

✓ Mid-Chapter Checkpoint

Concepts and Skills

Use the picture graph to answer the questions. (2.MD.10)

Favorite Season									
spring	☺	☺	☺	☺	☺	☺			
summer	☺	☺	☺	☺	☺	☺	☺	☺	
fall	☺	☺	☺	☺					
winter	☺	☺	☺	☺	☺	☺	☺		

Key: Each ☺ stands for 1 child.

1. Which season did the fewest children choose?

_____

2. How many more children chose spring than fall?

_____ more children

3. How many children chose a season that was not winter?

_____ children

4. THINK SMARTER How many children chose a favorite season?

_____ children

Draw tally marks to show this number.

_____

Name _____

Read Bar Graphs

Essential Question How is a bar graph used to show data?

Measurement and Data—2.MD.10
Also 2.MD.6
MATHEMATICAL PRACTICES
MP.1, MP.2, MP.6

Listen and Draw *Real World*

Use the picture graph to solve the problem.
Draw or write to show what you did.

Red Trucks Seen Last Week							
Morgan	■	■	■				
Terrell	■	■	■	■	■	■	
Jazmin	■	■	■	■	■	■	■
Carlos	■	■	■	■			

Key: Each ■ stands for 1 red truck.

_____ red trucks

Math Talk

Mathematical Practices

Describe how the data in the graph for Terrell and for Jazmin are different.

FOR THE TEACHER • Read this problem to children. Morgan made a picture graph to show the number of red trucks that she and her friends saw last week. How many red trucks did the four children see last week?

Chapter 10

A **bar graph** uses bars to show data.
Look at where the bars end.
This tells how many.

There are
8 children playing
soccer.

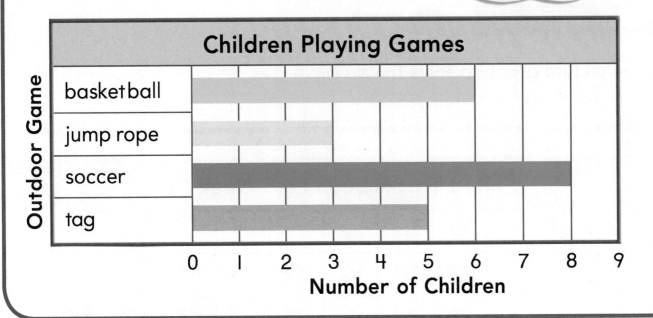

Children Playing Games

Outdoor Game

basketball

jump rope

soccer

tag

0 1 2 3 4 5 6 7 8 9

Number of Children

Share and Show

Use the bar graph.

1. How many green marbles are
    in the bag?

    _____ green marbles

2. How many more blue marbles
    than purple marbles are in
    the bag?

    _____ more blue marbles

3. How many marbles are in the bag?

    _____ marbles

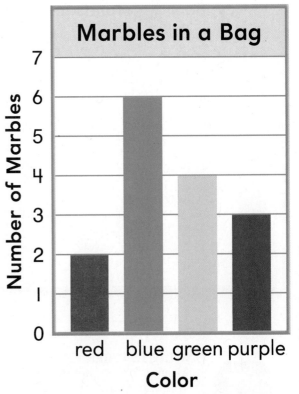

Marbles in a Bag

Number of Marbles

7
6
5
4
3
2
1
0

red   blue green purple

Color

Name _____

Use the bar graph.

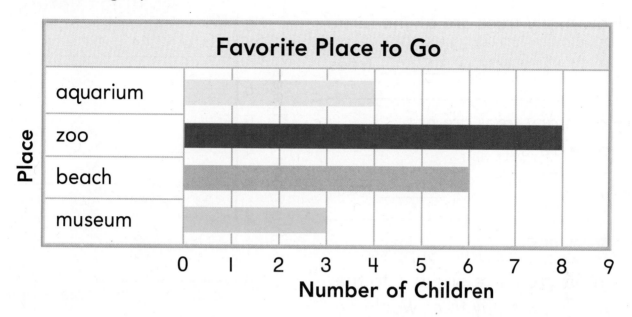

Favorite Place to Go

4. How many children chose the beach?

_____ children

5. Which place did the fewest children choose?

_____

6. How many more children chose the zoo than the aquarium?

_____ more children

7. GO DEEPER How many children chose a place that was not the zoo?

_____ children

8. THINK SMARTER Greg chose a place that has more votes than the aquarium and the museum together. Which place did Greg choose?

_____

Problem Solving • Applications    Math

Use the bar graph.

9. How many trees are at the farm?

_____ trees

10. How many trees are not apple trees?

_____ trees

11. **MATHEMATICAL PRACTICE 6** **Explain** Suppose 7 more trees are brought to the farm. How many trees would be at the farm then? Explain.

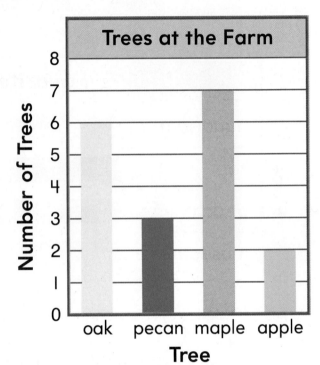

Trees at the Farm

Number of Trees

oak   pecan maple apple

Tree

12. **THINK SMARTER** Use the data in the bar graph about trees to finish the sentences.

There are ____ fewer apple trees than oak trees. Explain.

 TAKE HOME ACTIVITY • Ask your child to explain how to read a bar graph.

FOR MORE PRACTICE: Standards Practice Book

Name _____

Make Bar Graphs

Essential Question How do you make a bar graph to show data?

Measurement and Data—2.MD.10
Also 2.MD.6
MATHEMATICAL PRACTICES
MP.3, MP.4, MP.6

Listen and Draw Real World

Use the bar graph to solve the problem.
Draw or write to show what you did.

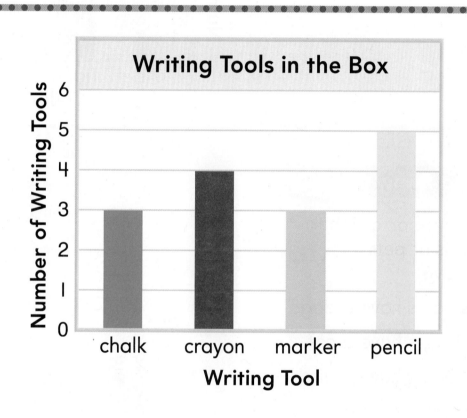

_____ writing tools

Math Talk **Mathematical Practices**

Describe how the information in the graph for crayon and for marker is different.

FOR THE TEACHER • Read the following problem. Barry made this bar graph. How many writing tools are in the box?

Abel read 2 books, Jiang read 4 books, Cara read 1 book, and Jamila read 3 books.

Complete the bar graph to show this data.

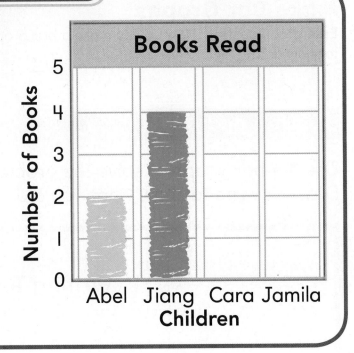

Share and Show

Ella is making a bar graph to show the kinds of pets her classmates have.

- 5 classmates have a dog.
- 7 classmates have a cat.
- 2 classmates have a bird.
- 3 classmates have fish.

✓ 1. Write labels and draw bars to complete the graph.

_____

✓ 2. How will the graph change if one more child gets a bird?

_____

_____

_____

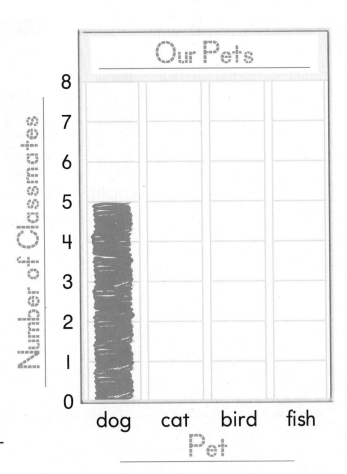

498 four hundred ninety-eight

On Your Own

Dexter asked his classmates which pizza topping is their favorite.

- 4 classmates chose peppers.
- 7 classmates chose meat.
- 5 classmates chose mushrooms.
- 2 classmates chose olives.

3. Write a title and labels for the bar graph.

_____

4. Draw bars in the graph to show the data.

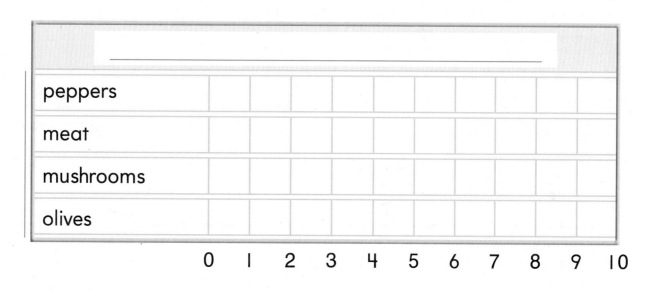

peppers											
meat											
mushrooms											
olives											

0   1   2   3   4   5   6   7   8   9   10

_____

5. Which topping did the most classmates choose? _____

6. **THINK SMARTER** Did more classmates choose peppers and olives than meat? Explain.

_____

_____

_____

Problem Solving • Applications

Cody asked his classmates which zoo animal is their favorite.

- 6 classmates chose bear.
- 4 classmates chose lion.
- 7 classmates chose tiger.
- 3 classmates chose zebra.

7. Use the data to complete the bar graph. Write a title and labels. Draw bars.

_____

8. **GO DEEPER** How many fewer classmates chose lion than classmates that chose the other zoo animals?

_____ fewer classmates

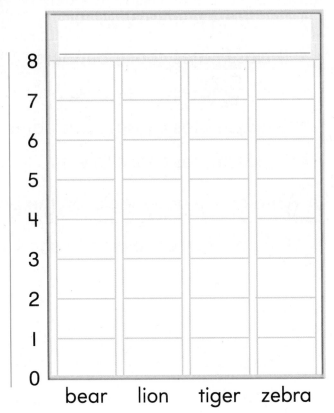

_____

Personal Math Trainer

9. **THINK SMARTER +** Look at the bar graph above.

Suppose 2 of Cody's classmates chose zebra instead of bear. Explain how the bar graph would change.

_____

_____

_____

 TAKE HOME ACTIVITY • Ask your child to describe how to make a bar graph to show data.

FOR MORE PRACTICE: Standards Practice Book

© Houghton Mifflin Harcourt Publishing Company

Name _____

Problem Solving • Display Data

Essential Question How does making a bar graph help when solving problems about data?

Measurement and Data—2.MD.10
MATHEMATICAL PRACTICES
MP.1, MP.3, MP.4

Maria recorded the rainfall in her town for four months. How did the amount of rainfall change from September to December?

September	4 inches
October	3 inches
November	2 inches
December	1 inch

🔑 Unlock the Problem

What do I need to find?	**What information do I need to use?**
how the amount of ___rainfall___ changed from September to December	the amount of ___rainfall___ in each of the four months

Show how to solve the problem.

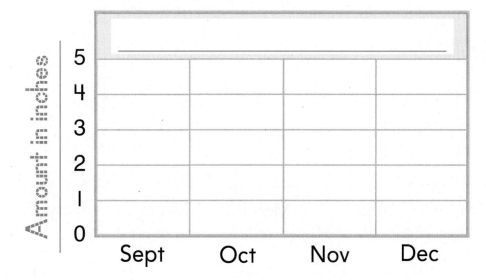

The amount of rainfall _____

_____

HOME CONNECTION • Your child made a bar graph to show the data. Making a graph helps your child organize data to solve problems.

Try Another Problem

Make a bar graph to solve the problem.

I. Matthew measured the height of his plant once a week for four weeks. Describe how the height of the plant changed from May 1 to May 22.

- What do I need to find?
- What information do I need to use?

May 1	2 inches
May 8	3 inches
May 15	5 inches
May 22	7 inches

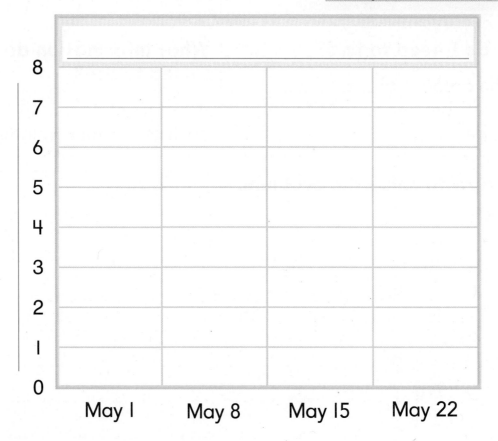

The height of the plant _____

_____

 Math Talk **Mathematical Practices**

How many inches did the plant grow from May 1 to May 22? **Explain.**

502 five hundred two

Name _____

Make a bar graph to solve the problem.

✓2. Bianca wrote the number of hours that she practiced playing guitar in June. Describe how the amount of practice time changed from Week 1 to Week 4.

Week 1	1 hour
Week 2	2 hours
Week 3	4 hours
Week 4	5 hours

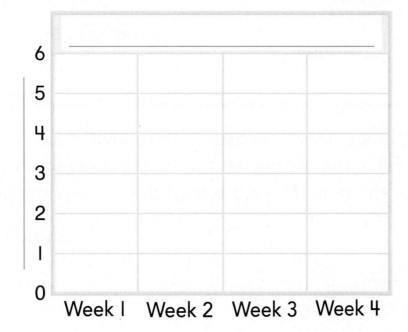

The amount of practice time _____

_____

3. **THINK SMARTER** If Bianca's practice time is 4 hours in Week 5, how does her practice time change from Week 1 to Week 5?

_____

_____

_____

Problem Solving • Applications

WRITE ▶ Math

4. How many strings are 9 inches long?

_____ strings

5. GO DEEPER How many strings are more than 6 inches long?

_____ strings

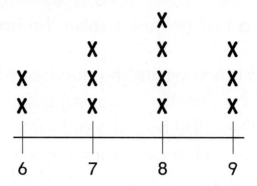

Lengths of Strings in Inches

Personal Math Trainer

6. THINK SMARTER ➕ David measured the snowfall for four weeks. Fill in the bubble next to all the sentences that describe the data. Make a bar graph to solve the problem.

Week 1	1 inch
Week 2	2 inches
Week 3	3 inches
Week 4	4 inches

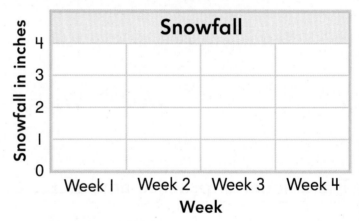

○ There were 2 inches of snow in Week 2.

○ The amount of snowfall increased each week.

○ Snowfall decreased from Week 3 to Week 4.

○ There were a total of 4 inches of snow in Week 2 and Week 3.

○ There were 3 more inches of snow in Week 4 than in Week 1.

 TAKE HOME ACTIVITY • Have your child explain how he or she solved one of the problems in this lesson.

FOR MORE PRACTICE:
Standards Practice Book

Name ________________________________

Chapter 10 Review/Test

1. Hara asked her friends their favorite yogurt flavor. Use the data on the card to make a tally chart.

lime - 2 people
peach - 3 people
berry - 5 people
vanilla - 7 people

Favorite Yogurt Flavor	
Yogurt	**Tally**
peach	
berry	
lime	
vanilla	

2. Does the sentence describe the data in the tally chart above? Choose Yes or No.

7 children like berry and peach	○ Yes	○ No
More children like peach than lime	○ Yes	○ No
More children like vanilla than any other flavor.	○ Yes	○ No

3. Hara asked 5 more friends. 3 friends like berry and 2 friends like lime. Which flavor do most children choose now? Explain.

____

____

____

GO DIGITAL Assessment Options Chapter Test

4. Teresa counted the leaves on her plant once a month for four months. Describe how the number of leaves on the plant changed from May 1 to August 1. Make a bar graph to solve the problem.

May 1	2 leaves
June 1	4 leaves
July 1	6 leaves
August 1	8 leaves

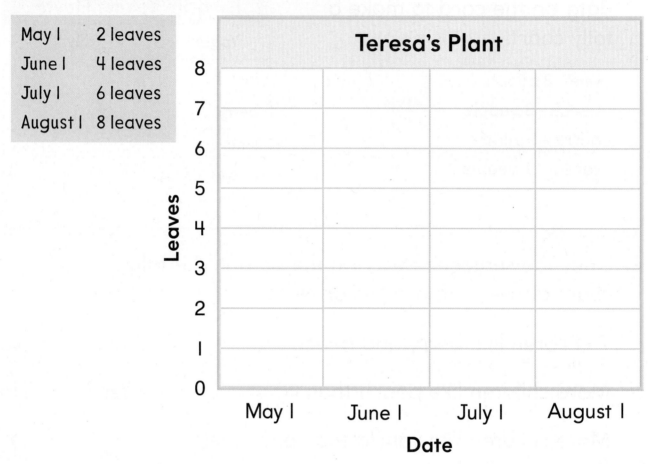

Teresa's Plant

The number of leaves on the plant _____

_____

---

5. If Teresa counts 1 more leaf on September 1, how does the number of leaves change from May 1 to September 1?

_____

_____

6. Use the tally chart to complete the picture graph. Draw a ☺ for each child.

Favorite Recess Game	
tag	I
hopscotch	ЖЖ
kickball	III
jacks	II

Favorite Recess Game					
tag					
hopscotch					
kickball					
jacks					

Key: Each ☺ stands for I child.

7. How many children chose hopscotch?

_____ children

8. How many fewer children chose tag than kickball?

_____ fewer children

9. Which two games were chosen by a total of 4 children?

_____

10. Mr. Sanchez asked the children in his class to name their favorite kind of book. Use the data to complete the bar graph.

8 children like fiction
4 children like science
6 children like history
9 children like poetry

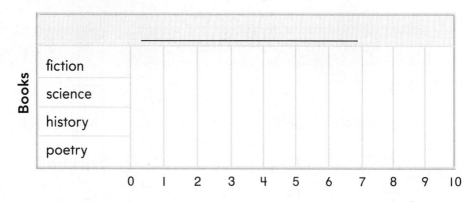

Books

| fiction |
| science |
| history |
| poetry |

0 1 2 3 4 5 6 7 8 9 10

11. Fill in the bubble next to all the sentences that describe the data in the bar graph above.

○ 8 children chose fiction.

○ Fewer children chose fiction than history.

○ 3 more children chose history than science.

○ More children chose poetry than any other kind of book.

12. Did more children choose science and history than poetry? Explain.

_____

_____

13. How many children chose a book that is not fiction?

_____ children

A Farmer's Job

by Tami Morton

CRITICAL AREA Describing and analyzing shapes

509

A farmer's job is never done. Farmers are busy during all of the seasons of the year. They grow fruits and vegetables for people to eat.
What shapes do you see?

_____

Social Studies

Why is a farmer's work important?

In the spring, farmers get the fields ready.

They plow the fields and fertilize the soil.

They plant their seeds.

What shapes do you see?

_____

Social Studies

How is a farmer's work today
different from long ago?

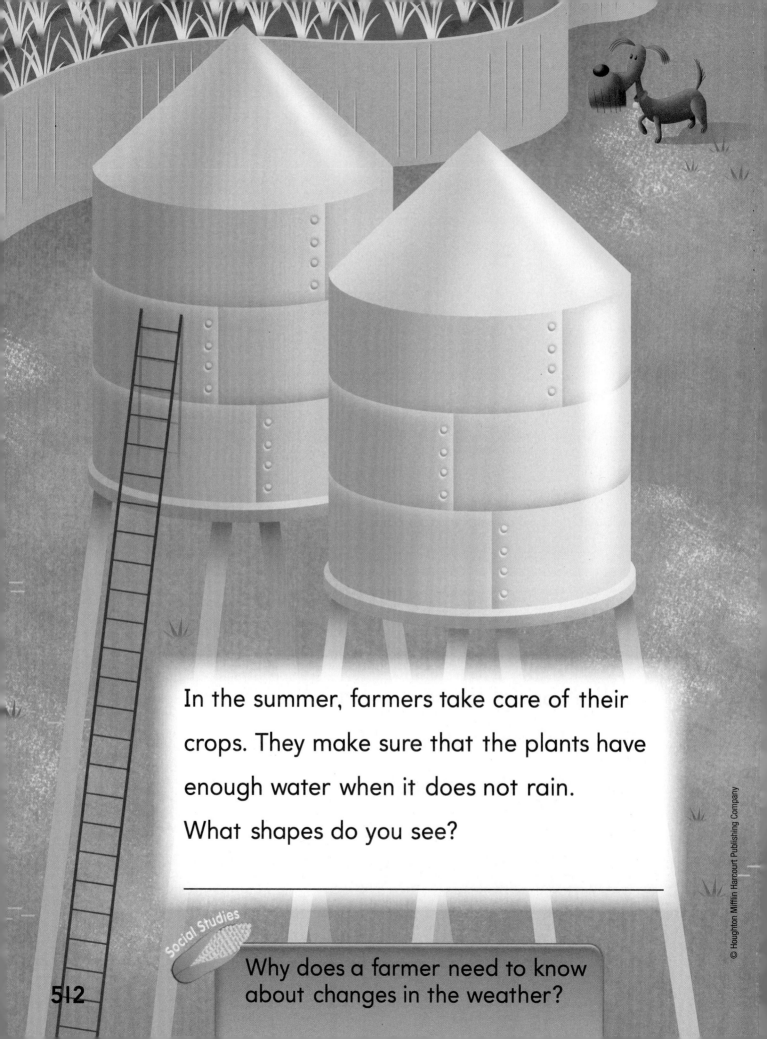

In the summer, farmers take care of their crops. They make sure that the plants have enough water when it does not rain. What shapes do you see?

_____

Social Studies

Why does a farmer need to know about changes in the weather?

512

In the fall, farmers harvest many fruits and vegetables. They sell most of these fruits and vegetables to other people. What shapes do you see?

_____

Why does a farmer grow more fruits and vegetables than his or her family can eat?

Social Studies

In the winter, farmers clear the fields
and get ready for the next season.

They plan what they are going to plant.

They check their machines.

A farmer's job is never done.

What shapes do you see?

_____

Social Studies

Why are the seasons
important to a farmer?

Name _____

Write About the Story

Look at the pictures of the farm objects. Draw a picture and write your own story about the objects. Tell about the shapes that the objects look like.

Vocabulary Review

cylinder	cube
cone	circle
sphere	triangle
square	rectangle
rectangular prism	

WRITE ▶ Math

_____

_____

_____

_____

_____

_____

What shape do you see?

Draw a line to match the shape with the name.

•   •   •

•   •   •

cylinder   rectangular prism   circle

Circle each shape that has a curved surface.

cylinder   rectangular prism

cube   cone

sphere

Write a riddle about a shape. Ask a classmate to read the riddle and name the shape.

Geometry and Fraction Concepts

Curious about Math

Hot air rises. A balloon filled with hot air will float up into the sky.

Some balloons look as though they have two-dimensional shapes on them. Name some two-dimensional shapes. Then draw some examples of them.

Name _____

Equal Parts

Circle the shape that has two equal parts.

1.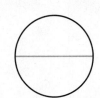

2.

Identify Three-Dimensional Shapes

3. Circle each ⬮.

4. Circle each ▱.

Identify Shapes

Circle all the shapes that match the shape name.

5. triangle

6. rectangle

This page checks understanding of important skills needed for success in Chapter 11.

© Houghton Mifflin Harcourt Publishing Company • Image Credits: (tcl) ©Photodisc/Getty Images; (tcr) ©Lawrence Manning/Corbis

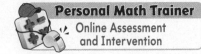

Personal Math Trainer
Online Assessment
and Intervention

Vocabulary Builder

Review Words
equal parts
shape
rectangle
triangle
square

Visualize It

Draw pictures to complete the graphic organizer.

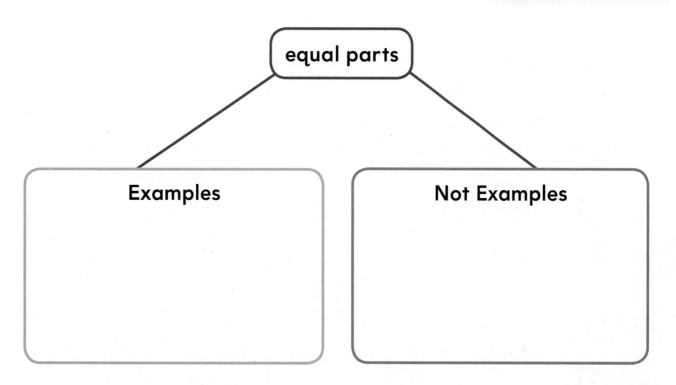

Understand Vocabulary

Draw a **shape** to match the shape name.

rectangle ⋮ triangle ⋮ square

GO
DIGITAL
• **Interactive Student Edition**
• **Multimedia eGlossary**

Count the Sides

Materials • 1 • 10 ● • 10 ○

Play with a partner.

① Toss the 🎲. If you toss a 1 or a 2, toss the 🎲 again.

② Look for a shape that has the same number of sides as the number you tossed.

③ Put one of your counters on that shape.

④ Take turns. Cover all the shapes. The player with more counters on the board wins.

Name _____

Three-Dimensional Shapes

Essential Question What objects match three-dimensional shapes?

Geometry–2.G.1

MATHEMATICAL PRACTICES
MP.6

Listen and Draw Real World

Draw a picture of an object with the same shape shown.

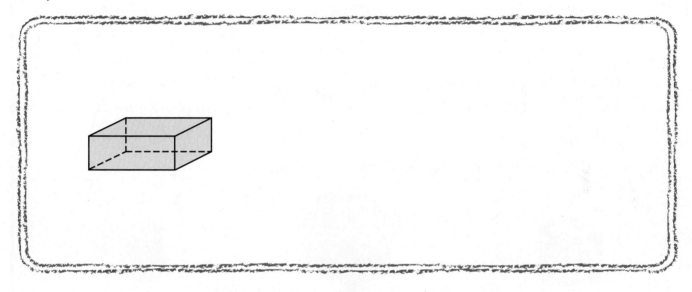

FOR THE TEACHER • Have children look at the first shape and name some real objects that have this shape, such as a cereal box. Have each child draw a picture of a real-life object that has the same shape. Repeat for the second shape.

Math Talk **Mathematical Practices**

Describe how the shapes are alike.
Describe how they are different.

Chapter 11

These are three-dimensional shapes.

cube

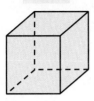

rectangular prism

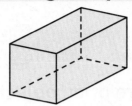

sphere

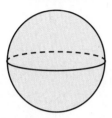

cylinder

cone

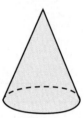

Which of these objects has the shape of a cube?

Share and Show

Circle the objects that match the shape name.

☑ I. sphere

☑ 2. cube

522 five hundred twenty-two

Name _____

Circle the objects that match the shape name.

3. cylinder

4. rectangular prism

5. cone

6. cube

7. **THINK SMARTER** Circle the shapes that have a curved surface.
Draw an X on the shapes that do not have a curved surface.

Math on the Spot

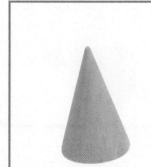    

Problem Solving • Applications

8. **MATHEMATICAL PRACTICE 6** Make Connections

Reba traced around the bottom of each block.
Match each block with the shape Reba drew.

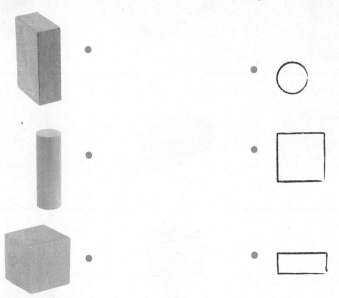

9. **THINK SMARTER** Match the shapes.

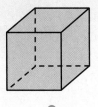 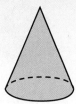 

 TAKE HOME ACTIVITY • Ask your child to name an object that has the shape of a cube.

FOR MORE PRACTICE:
Standards Practice Book

Attributes of Three-Dimensional Shapes

Essential Question How would you describe the faces of a rectangular prism and the faces of a cube?

 Geometry—2.G.1

MATHEMATICAL PRACTICES
MP.4, MP.5, MP.6

Listen and Draw

Circle the cones. Draw an X on the sphere.

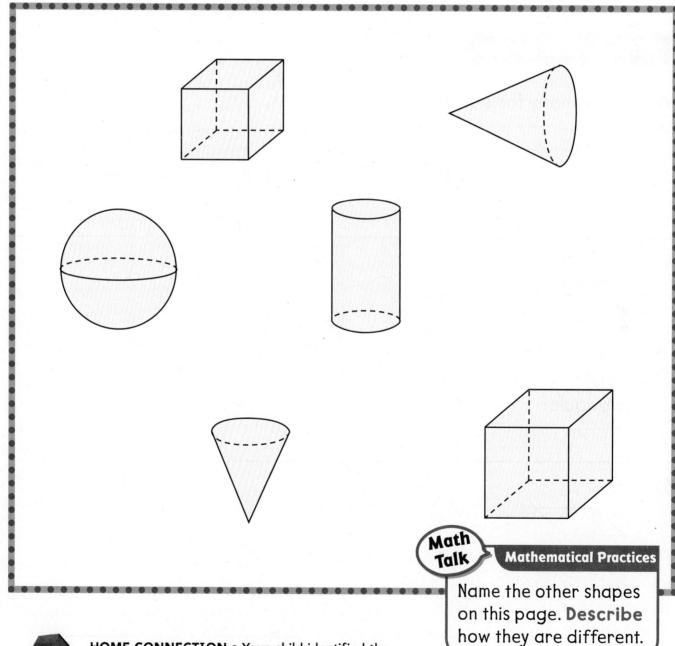

Math Talk **Mathematical Practices**

Name the other shapes on this page. **Describe** how they are different.

 **HOME CONNECTION** • Your child identified the shapes on this page to review some of the different kinds of three-dimensional shapes.

Chapter 11

The **faces** of a cube are squares.

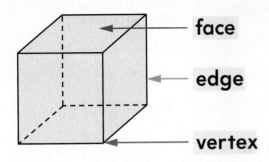

face

edge

vertex

The **vertices** are the corner points of the cube.

Share and Show

Write how many for each.

	faces	edges	vertices
☑ 1. rectangular prism	_____	_____	_____
☑ 2. cube	_____	_____	_____

On Your Own

3. **GO DEEPER** Use dot paper.
   Follow these steps to draw a cube.

Step 1 Draw a square. Make each side 4 units long.

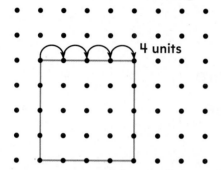

4 units

Step 2 Draw edges from 3 vertices, like this.

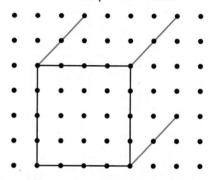

Step 3 Draw 2 more edges.

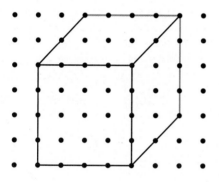

Step 4 Draw 3 dashed edges to show the faces that are not seen.

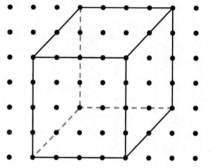

4. **THINK SMARTER** Trace all the faces of a rectangular prism on a sheet of paper. Write to tell about the shapes that you drew.

_____

_____

Problem Solving • Applications  WRITE ▸ Math

5. **MATHEMATICAL PRACTICE 6** **Make Connections** Marcus traced around the faces of a three-dimensional shape. Circle the name of the shape he used.

cylinder

cube

sphere

cone

6. **THINK SMARTER** Use the words on the tiles to label the parts of the cube.

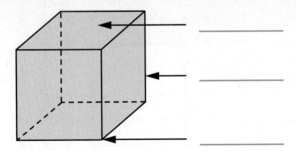

edge   face   vertex

Describe the faces of a cube.

_____

_____

 TAKE HOME ACTIVITY • Have your child tell you about the faces on a cereal box or another kind of box.

FOR MORE PRACTICE:
Standards Practice Book

© Houghton Mifflin Harcourt Publishing Company

Name _____

Build Three-Dimensional Shapes

Essential Question How can you build a rectangular prism?

Geometry—2.G.1

MATHEMATICAL PRACTICES
MP.4, MP.6

Listen and Draw Real World

Circle the shapes with curved surfaces. Draw an X on the shapes with flat surfaces.

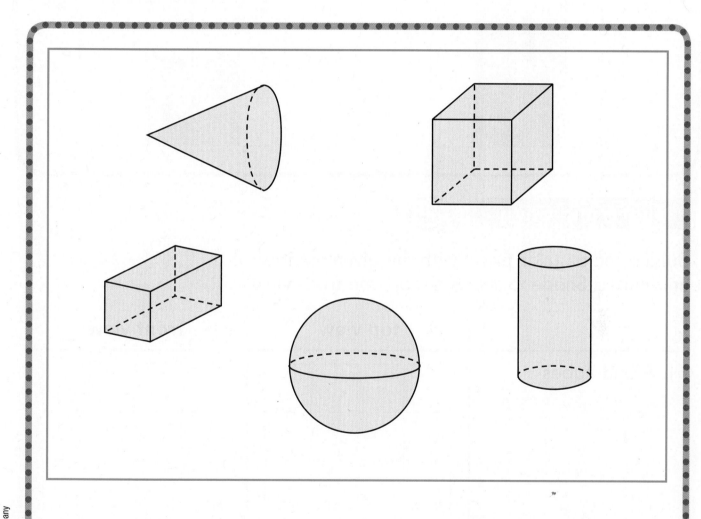

Math Talk

Mathematical Practices

Name the shapes you drew an X on. **Describe** how they are different.

HOME CONNECTION • Your child sorted the shapes on this page using the attributes of the shapes.

Build this rectangular prism
using 12 unit cubes.

The shading shows the top and front views.

top view

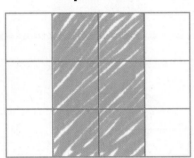

front view

Share and Show

Build a rectangular prism with the given number of
unit cubes. Shade to show the top and front views.

	top view	front view
✓1. 9 unit cubes		
✓2. 16 unit cubes		

On Your Own

Build a rectangular prism with the given number of unit cubes. Shade to show the top and front views.

	top view	front view
3. 24 unit cubes		

4. **THINK SMARTER** The top, side, and front views of a rectangular prism are shown. Build the prism. How many unit cubes are used to build the solid?

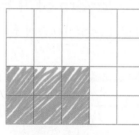

top view   front view   side view

_____ unit cubes

5. **MATHEMATICAL PRACTICE ①** **Analyze** Jen uses 18 cubes to build a rectangular prism. The top and front views are shown. Shade to show the side view.

top view   front view   side view

Problem Solving • Applications Real World | WRITE ▸ Math

Solve. Write or draw to explain.

6. **GO DEEPER** Tomas built this rectangular prism.
How many unit cubes did he use?

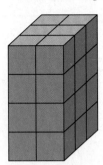

_____ cubes

---

7. **MATHEMATICAL PRACTICE ⑦** Look for Structure
Theo builds the first layer of
a rectangular prism using 4 cubes.
He adds 3 more layers of 4 cubes each.
How many cubes are used for the prism?   _____ cubes

Personal Math Trainer

8. **THINK SMARTER ✦** Tyler built this rectangular
prism using unit cubes. Then he took it
apart and used all of the cubes to build
two new prisms. Fill in the bubble next
to the two prisms he built.

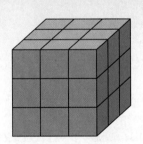

○ 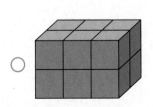   ○ 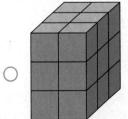   ○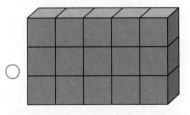

 TAKE HOME ACTIVITY • Ask your child to show how he or
she solved an exercise in the lesson.

FOR MORE PRACTICE:
Standards Practice Book

Name _____

Two-Dimensional Shapes

Essential Question What shapes can you name just by knowing the number of sides and vertices?

Geometry—2.G.1

MATHEMATICAL PRACTICES
MP.4, MP.7

Listen and Draw

Use a ruler. Draw a shape with 3 straight sides.
Then draw a shape with 4 straight sides.

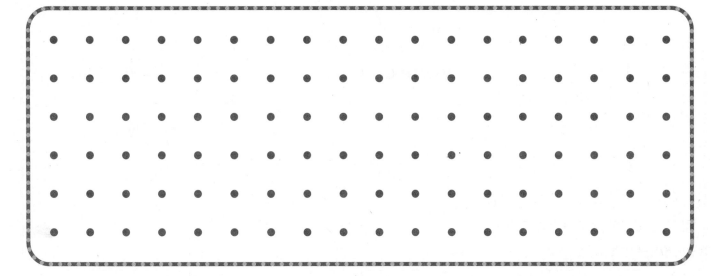

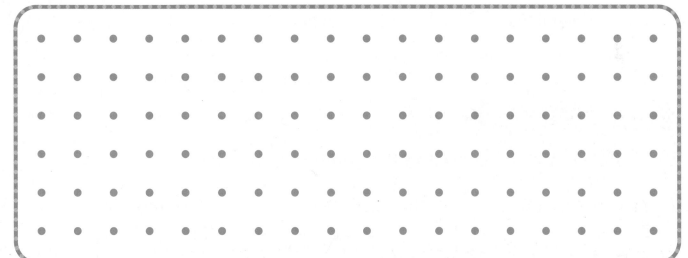

© Houghton Mifflin Harcourt Publishing Company

 FOR THE TEACHER • Have children use rulers as straight edges for drawing the sides of shapes. Have children draw a two-dimensional shape with 3 sides and then a two-dimensional shape with 4 sides.

Math Talk **Mathematical Practices**

Describe how your shapes are different from the shapes a classmate drew.

Chapter 11

five hundred thirty-three **533**

Model and Draw

You can count **sides** and **vertices** to name two-dimensional shapes. Look at how many sides and vertices each shape has.

triangle

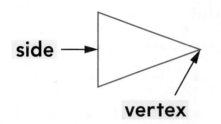 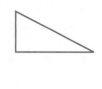

$\underline{3}$ sides

$\underline{3}$ vertices

quadrilateral	pentagon	hexagon
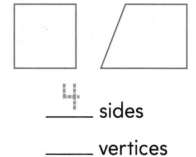	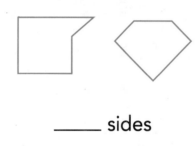	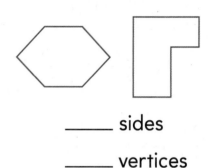
$\underline{4}$ sides	_____ sides	_____ sides
_____ vertices	_____ vertices	_____ vertices

Share and Show

 MATH BOARD

Write the number of sides and the number of vertices.

1. triangle

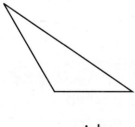

_____ sides

_____ vertices

✓ 2. hexagon

_____ sides

_____ vertices

✓ 3. pentagon

_____ sides

_____ vertices

On Your Own

Write the number of sides and the number of vertices. Then write the name of the shape.

pentagon
triangle
hexagon
quadrilateral

4.

_____ sides

_____ vertices

_____

5.

_____ sides

_____ vertices

_____

6.

_____ sides

_____ vertices

_____

7.

_____ sides

_____ vertices

_____

8.

_____ sides

_____ vertices

_____

9.

_____ sides

_____ vertices

_____

Go DEEPER Draw more sides to make the shape.

10. pentagon

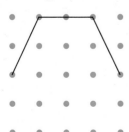

11. quadrilateral

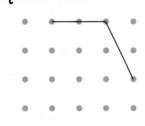

12. hexagon

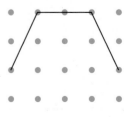

Problem Solving • Applications

WRITE) Math

Solve. Draw or write to explain.

13. **THINK SMARTER** Alex draws a hexagon and two pentagons. How many sides does Alex draw altogether?

_____ sides

14. **MATHEMATICAL PRACTICE ④** Use Diagrams

Ed draws a shape that has 4 sides. It is not a square. It is not a rectangle. Draw a shape that could be Ed's shape.

15. **THINK SMARTER** Count the sides and vertices of each two-dimensional shape. Draw each shape where it belongs in the chart.

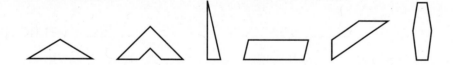

Quadrilateral	Hexagon	Triangle

 TAKE HOME ACTIVITY • Ask your child to draw a shape that is a quadrilateral.

FOR MORE PRACTICE:
Standards Practice Book

Angles in Two-Dimensional Shapes

Essential Question How do you find and count angles in two-dimensional shapes?

 Geometry—2.G.1

MATHEMATICAL PRACTICES
MP.4, MP.6, MP.7

Listen and Draw Hands On

Use a ruler. Draw two different triangles.
Then draw two different rectangles.

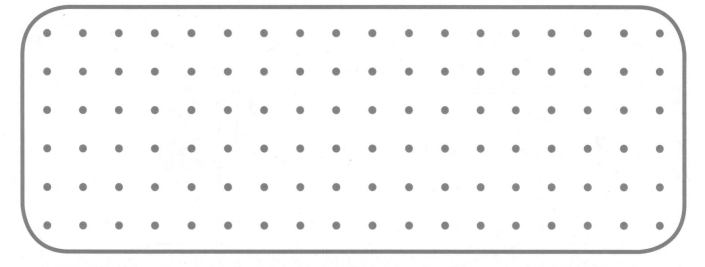

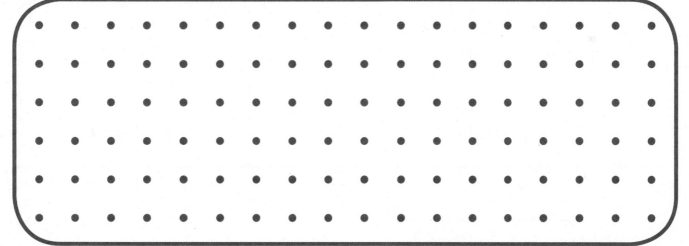

FOR THE TEACHER • Have children use pencils and rulers (or other straight edges) to draw the shapes. Have them draw two different triangles in the green box and two different rectangles in the purple box.

Math Talk

Mathematical Practices

Describe a triangle and a rectangle. Tell about their sides and vertices.

When two sides of a shape meet,
they form an **angle**.

angle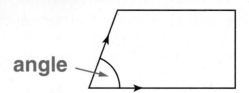

This shape has 3 angles.

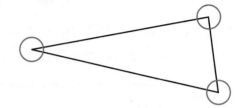

Share and Show

Circle the angles in each shape.
Write how many.

1.

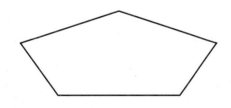

_____ angles

2.

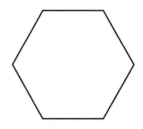

_____ angles

3.

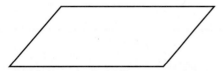

_____ angles

4.

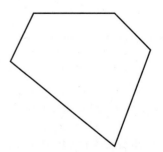

_____ angles

On Your Own

Circle the angles in each shape. Write how many.

5.

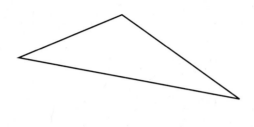

_____ angles

6.

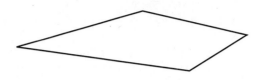

_____ angles

7.

_____ angles

8.

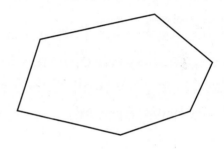

_____ angles

9. THINK SMARTER Draw more sides to make the shape. Write how many angles.

Math on the Spot

pentagon

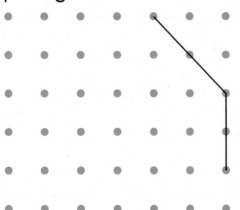

_____ angles

quadrilateral

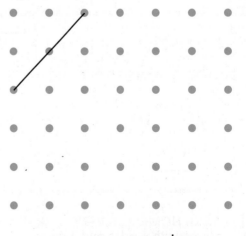

_____ angles

Problem Solving • Applications  WRITE ▸ Math

10. Draw two shapes that have 7 angles in all.

11. **MATHEMATICAL PRACTICE 4** **Use Diagrams**

Ben drew 3 two-dimensional shapes that had 11 angles in all. Draw shapes Ben could have drawn.

12. **THINK SMARTER** Fill in the bubble next to all the shapes that have 5 angles.

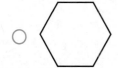 ○   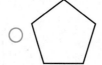 ○   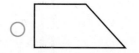 ○   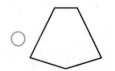 ○

 TAKE HOME ACTIVITY • Ask your child to draw a shape with 4 sides and 4 angles.

FOR MORE PRACTICE:
Standards Practice Book

Name _____

Sort Two-Dimensional Shapes

Essential Question How do you use the number of sides and angles to sort two-dimensional shapes?

Geometry—2.G.1

MATHEMATICAL PRACTICES
MP.4, MP.6

Listen and Draw

Make the shape with pattern blocks. Draw and color the blocks you used.

Use one block.

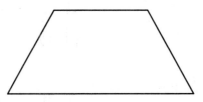

Use two blocks.

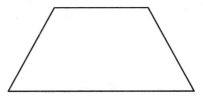

Use three blocks.

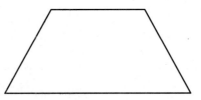

FOR THE TEACHER • Tell children that the shape shown three times on the page is a trapezoid. Have children use pattern blocks to make the trapezoid three times: with one pattern block, with two pattern blocks, and then with three pattern blocks.

 Math Talk

Mathematical Practices

Describe how you could sort the blocks you used.

Chapter 11

Model and Draw

Which shapes match the rule?

Shapes with more than 3 sides

Shapes with fewer than 5 angles

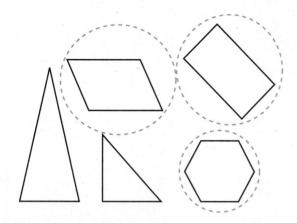
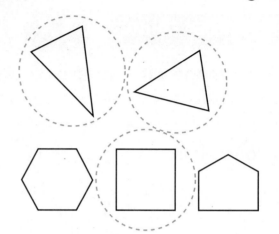

Share and Show

Circle the shapes that match the rule.

1. Shapes with 5 sides

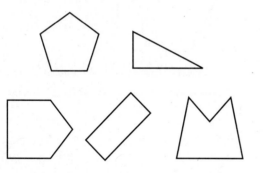

2. Shapes with more than 3 angles

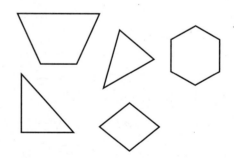

3. Shapes with fewer than 4 angles

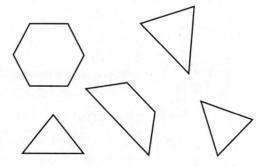

4. Shapes with fewer than 5 sides

Name _____

Circle the shapes that match the rule.

5. Shapes with 4 sides

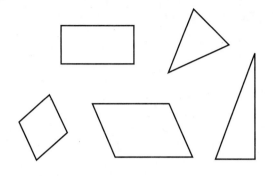

6. Shapes with more than 4 angles

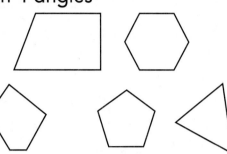

7. Shapes with fewer than 4 angles

8. Shapes with fewer than 5 sides

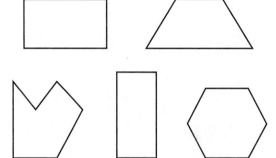

9. *THINK SMARTER* Draw three shapes that match the rule. Circle them. Then draw two shapes that do not match the rule.

Shapes with fewer than 5 angles

Problem Solving • Applications    WRITE ▸ Math

10.  **Make Connections**

Sort the shapes.

• Use red to color the shapes with more than 4 sides.

• Use blue to color the shapes with fewer than 5 angles.

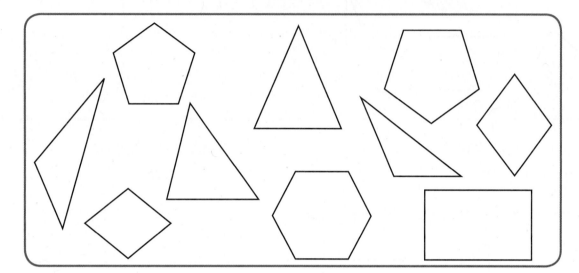

11. **THINK SMARTER** Draw each shape where it belongs in the chart.

Shapes with 4 or Fewer Sides	Shapes with More than 4 sides

 TAKE HOME ACTIVITY • Ask your child to draw some shapes that each have 4 angles.

FOR MORE PRACTICE:
Standards Practice Book

Name _____

Partition Rectangles

Essential Question How do you find the total number of same-size squares that will cover a rectangle?

Geometry—2.G.2
Also 2.OA.4
MATHEMATICAL PRACTICES
MP.5, MP.8

Listen and Draw

Put several color tiles together. Trace around the shape to draw a two-dimensional shape.

HOME CONNECTION • After putting together tiles, your child traced around them to draw a two-dimensional shape. This activity is an introduction to partitioning a rectangle into several same-size squares.

Math Talk **Mathematical Practices**

Is there a different shape that can be made with the same number of tiles? **Explain.**

Trace around color tiles. How many
square tiles cover this rectangle?

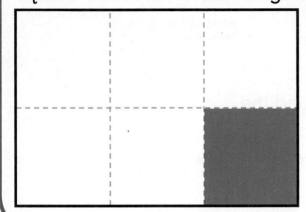

Number of rows: _2_

Number of columns: _3_

Total: _____ square tiles

Share and Show

Use color tiles to cover the rectangle.
Trace around the square tiles. Write how many.

☑ 1.

Number of rows: _____

Number of columns: _____

Total: _____ square tiles

☑ 2.

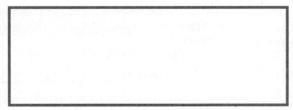

Number of rows: _____

Number of columns: _____

Total: _____ square tiles

On Your Own

Use color tiles to cover the rectangle.
Trace around the square tiles. Write how many.

3.

Number of rows: _____

Number of columns: _____

Total: _____ square tiles

4.

Number of rows: _____

Number of columns: _____

Total: _____ square tiles

---

5. **THINK SMARTER** Mary started to cover this rectangle with ones blocks. **Explain** how you would estimate the number of ones blocks that would cover the whole rectangle.

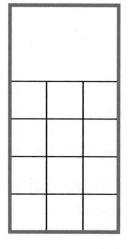

_____

_____

_____

TAKE HOME ACTIVITY • Have your child describe what he or she did in this lesson.

FOR MORE PRACTICE:
Standards Practice Book

 **Mid-Chapter Checkpoint**

Concepts and Skills

Circle the objects that match the shape name. (2.G.1)

I. cylinder				
2. cube				

Write the number of sides and the number of vertices. (2.G.1)

3. quadrilateral

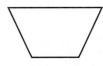

____ sides

____ vertices

4. pentagon

____ sides

____ vertices

5. hexagon

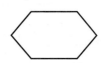

____ sides

____ vertices

6. **THINK SMARTER** How many angles does this shape have? (2.G.1)

____ angles

Equal Parts

Essential Question What are halves, thirds, and fourths of a whole?

Geometry—2.G.3

MATHEMATICAL PRACTICES
MP.6, MP.8

Listen and Draw

Put pattern blocks together to match the shape of the hexagon. Trace the shape you made.

Math Talk **Mathematical Practices**

Describe how the shapes you used are different from the shapes a classmate used.

FOR THE TEACHER • Have children place a yellow hexagon pattern block on the workspace and make the same shape by using any combination of pattern blocks. Discuss how they know if the outline of the blocks they used is the same shape as the yellow hexagon.

Chapter 11

The green rectangle is the whole.
It can be divided into equal parts.

There are 2 halves.
Each part is a half.

There are 3 thirds.
Each part is a third.

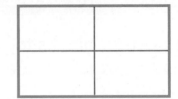

There are 4 fourths.
Each part is a fourth.

Share and Show

MATH BOARD

Write how many equal parts there are in the whole.
Write **halves**, **thirds**, or **fourths** to name the equal parts.

1.

____ equal parts

_____

2.

____ equal parts

_____

3.

____ equal parts

_____

4.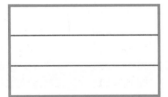

____ equal parts

_____

✓ 5.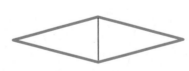

____ equal parts

_____

✓ 6.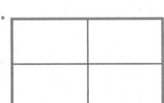

____ equal parts

_____

Name _____

Write how many equal parts there are in the whole.
Write **halves**, **thirds**, or **fourths** to name the equal parts.

7.

____ equal parts

_____

8.

____ equal parts

_____

9.

____ equal parts

_____

10.

____ equal parts

_____

11.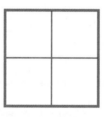

____ equal parts

_____

12.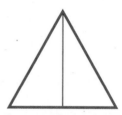

____ equal parts

_____

13. **THINK SMARTER** Draw to show halves.
Explain how you know that the
parts are halves.

_____

_____

_____

Problem Solving • Applications  WRITE • Math

14. **MATHEMATICAL PRACTICE 6** **Make Connections** Sort the shapes.

- Draw an X on shapes that do **not** show equal parts.

- Use red to color the shapes that show thirds.

- Use blue to color the shapes that show fourths.

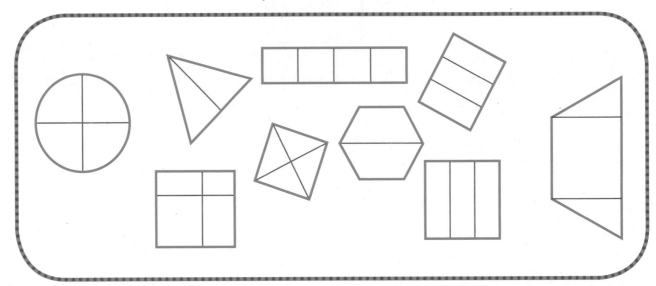

Personal Math Trainer

15. *THINK SMARTER* + Draw lines to show fourths three different ways.

Explain how you know that the parts are fourths.

_____

_____

 TAKE HOME ACTIVITY • Ask your child to fold one sheet of paper into halves and another sheet of paper into fourths.

FOR MORE PRACTICE:
Standards Practice Book

Show Equal Parts of a Whole

Essential Question How do you know if a shape shows halves, thirds, or fourths?

Geometry—2.G.3

MATHEMATICAL PRACTICES
MP.5, MP.6

Listen and Draw

Circle the shapes that show equal parts.

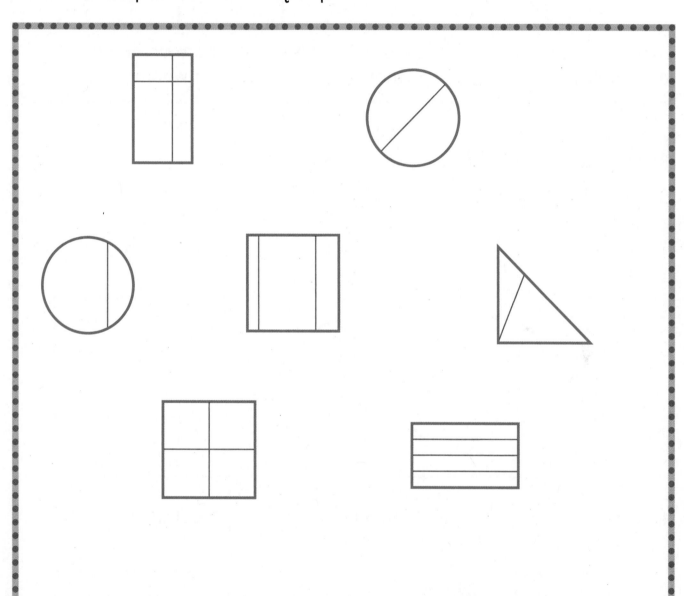

HOME CONNECTION • Your child completed this sorting activity with shapes to review the concept of equal parts.

Math Talk

Mathematical Practices

Does the triangle show halves? **Explain.**

Model and Draw

You can draw to show equal parts of a whole.

halves 2 equal parts	thirds 3 equal parts	fourths 4 equal parts
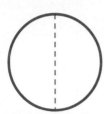		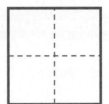
There are 2 halves in a whole.	There are 3 thirds in a whole.	There are 4 fourths in a whole.

Share and Show

Draw to show equal parts.

1. thirds

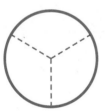

2. halves

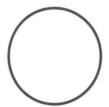

3. fourths

4. halves

⊘5. fourths

⊘6. thirds

Name _____

Draw to show equal parts.

7. halves

8. fourths

9. thirds

10. thirds

11. halves

12. fourths

13. halves

14. thirds

15. fourths

16. Does this shape show thirds?
Explain.

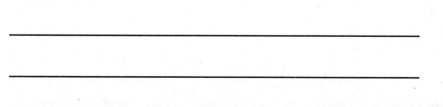

_____

_____

_____

_____

Problem Solving • Applications WRITE Math

17. Colton and three friends want to share a pizza equally. Draw to show how the pizza should be divided.

Math on the Spot

18. GO DEEPER There are two square pizzas. Each pizza is cut into fourths. How many pieces of pizza are there?

_____ pieces

19. THINK SMARTER Fill in the bubble next to the shapes that show thirds. Explain your answer.

○ 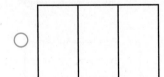　○ 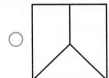　○ 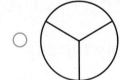　○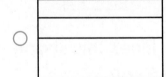

_____

_____

 TAKE HOME ACTIVITY • Have your child describe how to show equal parts of a shape.

FOR MORE PRACTICE:
Standards Practice Book

Describe Equal Parts

Essential Question How do you find a half of, a third of, or a fourth of a whole?

 Geometry—2.G.3

MATHEMATICAL PRACTICES
MP.4, MP.6

Listen and Draw

Find shapes that show fourths and color them green.
Find shapes that show halves and color them red.

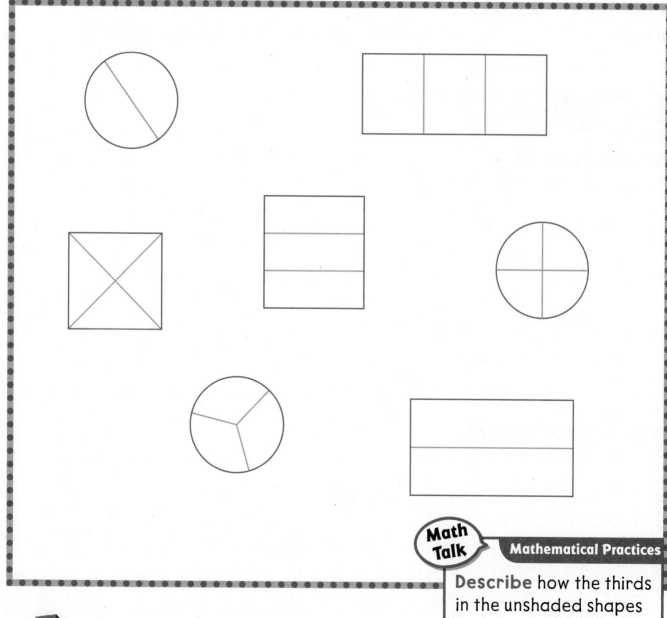

Math Talk **Mathematical Practices**

Describe how the thirds in the unshaded shapes compare to each other.

HOME CONNECTION • Your child identified the number of equal parts in shapes to review describing equal parts of a whole.

Chapter 11

These are some ways to show and describe an equal part of a whole.

I of 4 equal parts is called a **quarter of** that shape.

2 equal parts

A **half of** the shape is green.

3 equal parts

A **third of** the shape is green.

4 equal parts

A **fourth of** the shape is green.

Share and Show

Draw to show thirds.
Color a third of the shape.

1.

2.

☑ 3.

Draw to show fourths.
Color a fourth of the shape.

4.

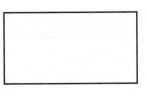

5.

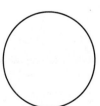

☑ 6.

On Your Own

Draw to show halves.
Color a half of the shape.

7.

8.

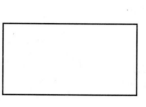

9.

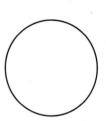

Draw to show thirds.
Color a third of the shape.

10.

11.

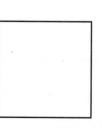

12.

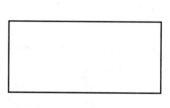

Draw to show fourths.
Color a fourth of the shape.

13.

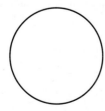

14.

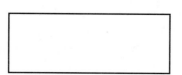

15.

Problem Solving • Applications

16. **THINK SMARTER** Two posters are the same size. A third of one poster is red, and a fourth of the other poster is blue.

Is the red part or the blue part larger? Draw and write to explain.

_____

_____

_____

_____

17. **THINK SMARTER** Draw to show halves, thirds, and fourths. Color a half, a third, or a fourth of the shape.

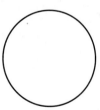 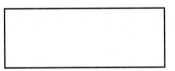 

TAKE HOME ACTIVITY • Draw a square. Have your child draw to show thirds and color a third of the square.

FOR MORE PRACTICE:
Standards Practice Book

Name _____

Problem Solving • Equal Shares

Essential Question How can drawing a diagram
help when solving problems about equal shares?

Geometry—2.G.3

MATHEMATICAL PRACTICES
MP.1, MP.4, MP.6

There are two sandwiches that are the same
size. Each sandwich is divided into fourths, but
the sandwiches are cut differently. How might
the two sandwiches be cut?

Unlock the Problem

What do I need to find?

how the sandwiches

could be cut

What information do I need to use?

There are _____ sandwiches.
Each sandwich is divided

into _____.

Show how to solve the problem.

HOME CONNECTION • Your child drew a diagram to represent and solve
a problem about dividing a whole in different ways to show equal shares.

© Houghton Mifflin Harcourt Publishing Company

Draw to show your answer.

- What do I need to find?
- What information do I need to use?

1. Marquis has two square sheets of paper that are the same size. He wants to cut each sheet into halves. What are two different ways he can cut the sheets of paper?

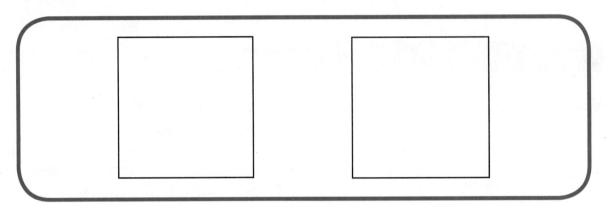

2. Shanice has two pieces of cloth that are the same size. She needs to divide each piece into thirds. What are two different ways she can divide the pieces of cloth?

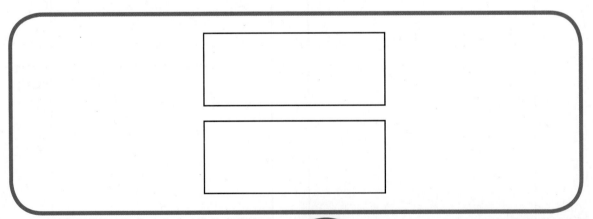

Math Talk

Mathematical Practices

In Problem 2, **explain** how a third of the two pieces of cloth are alike and how they are different.

Name _____

Draw to show your answer.

☑3. Brandon has two pieces of toast that are the same size. What are two different ways he can divide the pieces of toast into halves?

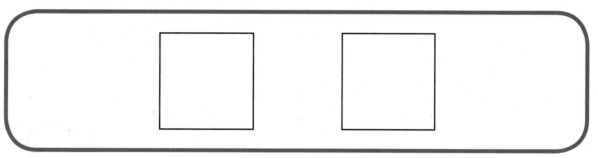

☑4. Mr. Rivera has two small trays of pasta that are the same size. What are two different ways he can cut the pasta into fourths?

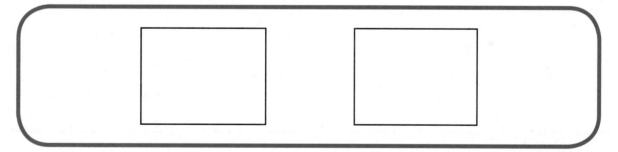

5. _THINK SMARTER_ Erin has two ribbons that are the same size. What are two different ways she can divide the ribbons into thirds?

Problem Solving • Applications | WRITE ▶ Math

Solve. Write or draw to explain.

6. **MATHEMATICAL PRACTICE ④ Use Diagrams** David needs to divide two pieces of paper into the same number of equal shares. Look at how the first paper is divided. Show how to divide the second paper a different way.

---

7. **GO DEEPER** Mrs. Lee cut two sandwiches into halves. How many equal shares does she have?

_____ equal shares

8. **THINK SMARTER** Emma wants to cut a piece of paper into fourths. Fill in the bubble next to all the ways she could cut the paper.

  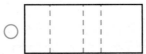 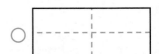

 TAKE HOME ACTIVITY • Ask your child to draw two rectangles and show two different ways to divide them into fourths.

FOR MORE PRACTICE: Standards Practice Book

✓ Chapter 11 Review/Test

I. Match the shapes.

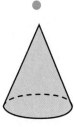 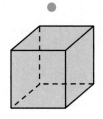  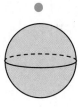

---

2. Do the sentences describe a cube?
Choose Yes or No.

A cube has 4 faces.   ○ Yes   ○ No

A cube has 8 vertices.   ○ Yes   ○ No

A cube has 14 edges.   ○ Yes   ○ No

Each face of a cube is a square.   ○ Yes   ○ No

Rewrite each sentence with a mistake to make
it a true sentence.

_____

_____

3. Draw lines to show thirds.

Explain how you know that the parts are thirds.

_____

_____

4. Will and Ana have gardens that are the same size.
They divide their gardens into fourths. What are
two different ways they can divide the gardens?
Draw to show your answer.

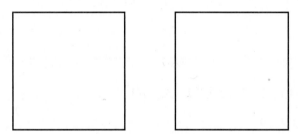

5. Draw to show halves, thirds, and fourths.
Color a half, a third, and a fourth.

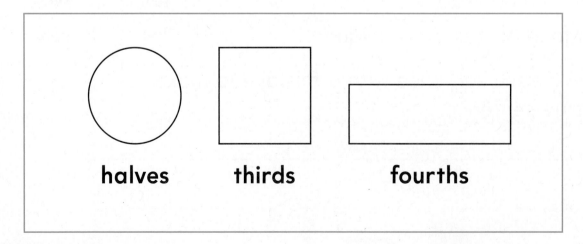

halves   thirds   fourths

6. Max wants to cover the rectangle with blue tiles. Explain how you would estimate the number of blue tiles he would need to cover the rectangle.

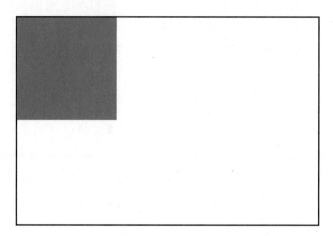

_____

_____

---

7. Jenna built this rectangular prism. Circle the number of unit cubes Jenna used.

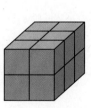 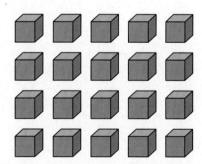

---

8. Rachel makes a pentagon and a quadrilateral with toothpicks. She uses one toothpick for each side of a shape. How many toothpicks does Rachel need?

_____ toothpicks

9. Kevin drew 2 two-dimensional shapes that had 9 angles in all. Draw the shapes Kevin could have drawn.

10. Fill in the bubble next to the shapes that show fourths.

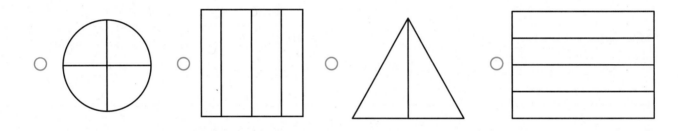

11. Draw each shape where it belongs in the chart.

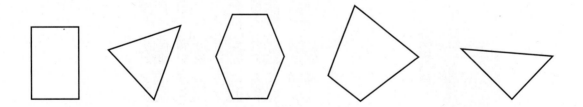

Shapes with 3 or Fewer Angles	Shapes with More than 3 Angles

Picture Glossary

addend sumando

$$5 + 8 = 13$$

addends

a.m. a.m.

Times after midnight and before noon are written with **a.m.**

11:00 a.m. is in the morning.

angle ángulo

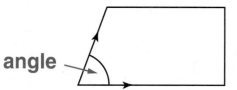

angle

bar graph gráfica de barras

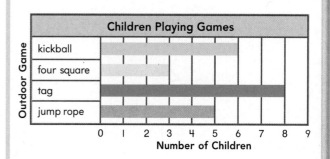

cent sign símbolo de centavo

53¢

cent sign

centimeter centímetro

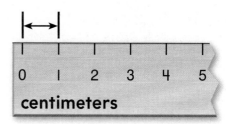

centimeters

column columna

column

$$
\begin{array}{r}
3\boxed{3} \\
3\boxed{4} \\
+3\boxed{2}
\end{array}
$$

compare comparar

Use these symbols when you **compare**: $>$, $<$, $=$.

$$241 > 234$$

$$123 < 128$$

$$247 = 247$$

cone cono

cube cubo

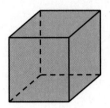

cylinder cilindro

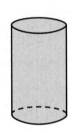

data datos

Favorite Lunch	
Lunch	Tally
pizza	IIII
sandwich	HHT I
salad	III
pasta	HHT

The information in this chart is called **data**.

decimal point punto decimal

$1.00
↑
decimal point

---

difference diferencia

$9 - 2 = 7$
↑
difference

---

digit dígito

0, 1, 2, 3, 4, 5, 6, 7, 8, and 9 are **digits**.

---

dime moneda de 10¢

A **dime** has a value of 10 cents.

dollar dólar

One **dollar** is worth 100 cents.

---

dollar sign símbolo de dólar

$1.00
↑
dollar sign

---

edge arista

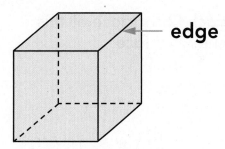
edge

An **edge** is formed where two faces of a three-dimensional shape meet.

estimate estimación

> An **estimate** is an amount that tells about how many.

even par

> 2, 4, 6, 8, 10, . . .
>
> even numbers

face cara

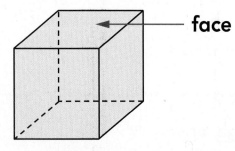

face

> Each flat surface of this cube is a **face**.

foot pie

> 1 **foot** is the same length as 12 inches.

fourth of cuarto de

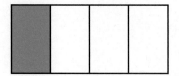

> A **fourth of** the shape is green.

fourths cuartos

> This shape has 4 equal parts. These equal parts are called **fourths**.

half of mitad de

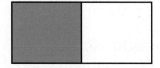

> A **half of** the shape is green.

halves mitades

This shape has 2 equal parts. These equal parts are called **halves**.

hexagon hexágono

A two-dimensional shape with 6 sides is a **hexagon**.

hour hora

There are 60 minutes in 1 **hour**.

hundred centena

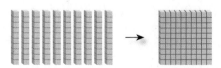

There are 10 tens in 1 **hundred**.

inch pulgada

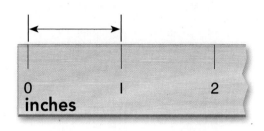

inches

is **equal to** (=) es igual a

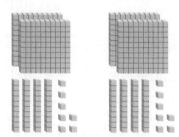

247 is equal to 247.
247 = 247

is greater than (>) es mayor que

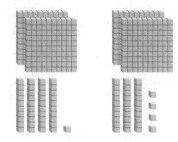

241 is greater than 234.
241 > 234

is less than (<) es menor que

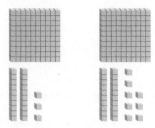

123 **is less than** 128.

123 < 128

key clave

Number of Soccer Games						
March	⚽	⚽	⚽	⚽		
April	⚽	⚽	⚽			
May	⚽	⚽	⚽	⚽	⚽	
June	⚽	⚽	⚽	⚽	⚽	⚽	⚽

Key: Each ⚽ stands for 1 game.

The **key** tells how many each picture stands for.

line plot diagrama de puntos

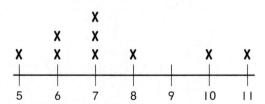

Lengths of Paintbrushes in Inches

measuring tape cinta métrica

meter metro

1 **meter** is the same length as 100 centimeters.

midnight medianoche

Midnight is 12:00 at night.

minute minuto

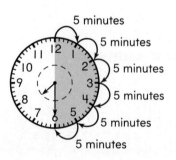

There are 30 **minutes** in a half hour.

nickel moneda de 5¢

A **nickel** has a value of 5 cents.

penny moneda de 1¢

A **penny** has a value of 1 cent.

noon mediodía

Noon is 12:00 in the daytime.

pentagon pentágono

A two-dimensional shape with 5 sides is a **pentagon**.

odd impar

1, 3, 5, 7, 9, 11, . . .

odd numbers

picture graph gráfica con dibujos

Number of Soccer Games						
March	⚽	⚽	⚽	⚽		
April	⚽	⚽	⚽			
May	⚽	⚽	⚽	⚽	⚽	⚽
June	⚽	⚽	⚽	⚽	⚽	⚽	⚽

Key: Each ⚽ stands for 1 game.

p.m. p.m.

Times after noon and before midnight are written with **p.m.**

11:00 p.m. is in the evening.

quarter of cuarta parte de

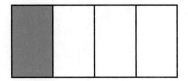

A **quarter of** the shape is green.

quadrilateral cuadrilátero

A two-dimensional shape with 4 sides is a **quadrilateral**.

quarter past y cuarto

15 minutes after 8
quarter past 8

quarter moneda de 25¢

A **quarter** has a value of 25 cents.

rectangular prism prisma rectangular

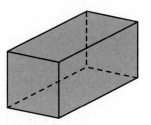

regroup reagrupar

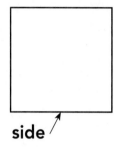

You can trade 10 ones for
1 ten to **regroup**.

side lado

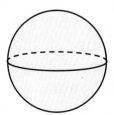

This shape has 4 **sides**.

sphere esfera

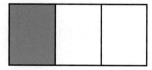

sum suma o total

$$9 + 6 = 15$$

sum

survey encuesta

Favorite Lunch	
Lunch	Tally
pizza	IIII
sandwich	ЖН I
salad	III
pasta	ЖН

A **survey** is a collection
of data from answers to
a question.

third of un tercio de

A **third of** the shape
is green.

thirds tercios

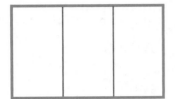

This shape has 3 equal parts. These equal parts are called **thirds**.

thousand millar

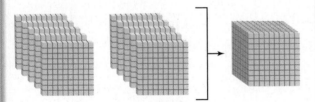

There are 10 hundreds in 1 **thousand**.

week semana

7 days is the same as 1 **week**.

vertex/vertices vértice/vértices

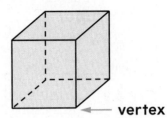

← vertex

A corner point of a three-dimensional shape is a **vertex**.

vertex

This shape has 5 **vertices**.

yardstick regla de 1 yarda

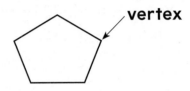

A **yardstick** is a measuring tool that shows 3 feet.

year año

From January 1 to December 31, there are about 52 weeks. This is 1 **year**.

Correlations

© Houghton Mifflin Harcourt Publishing Company

 CALIFORNIA COMMON CORE STATE STANDARDS

Standards You Will Learn		Student Edition Lessons
Mathematical Practices		
MP.1	Make sense of problems and persevere in solving them.	Lessons 1.7, 3.6, 3.8, 3.9, 3.10, 4.7, 4.9, 4.10, 5.9, 5.10, 5.11, 6.7, 7.7, 8.5, 9.4, 10.1, 10.2, 10.3, 10.4, 10.6, 11.11
MP.2	Reason abstractly and quantitatively.	Lessons 2.11, 3.5, 3.9, 4.9, 4.10, 5.9, 5.10, 5.11, 7.12, 8.5, 9.4, 9.7, 10.2, 10.4
MP.3	Construct viable arguments and critique the reasoning of others.	Lessons 1.1, 2.8, 4.6, 4.7, 5.5, 5.10, 10.5, 10.6
MP.4	Model with mathematics.	Lessons 1.4, 1.7, 2.3, 2.11, 3.8, 3.9, 3.11, 4.1, 4.2, 4.5, 4.9, 4.10, 5.4, 5.9, 5.10, 5.11, 6.7, 7.3, 7.4, 7.5, 7.6, 7.7, 8.5, 8.9, 9.4, 9.7, 10.1, 10.3, 10.5, 10.6, 11.2, 11.3, 11.4, 11.5, 11.6, 11.10, 11.11
MP.5	Use appropriate tools strategically.	Lessons 1.1, 3.7, 3.10, 4.4, 5.1, 5.2, 5.3, 5.8, 6.1, 8.1, 8.2, 8.4, 8.6, 8.8, 8.9, 9.1, 9.3, 9.5, 11.2, 11.7, 11.9
MP.6	Attend to precision.	Lessons 1.3, 1.5, 1.6, 1.8, 1.9, 2.1, 2.5, 2.8, 2.12, 3.4, 3.11, 4.1, 4.2, 4.3, 4.6, 4.8, 4.11, 4.12, 5.5, 5.7, 6.1, 6.2, 6.3, 6.4, 6.5, 6.8, 6.9, 6.10, 6.11, 7.1, 7.2, 7.8, 7.9, 7.10, 7.11, 7.12, 8.1, 8.2, 8.3, 8.4, 8.6, 8.7, 8.9, 9.1, 9.2, 9.3, 9.5, 9.6, 10.1, 10.2, 10.3, 10.4, 10.5, 11.1, 11.2, 11.3, 11.5, 11.6, 11.8, 11.9, 11.10, 11.11
MP.7	Look for and make use of structure.	Lessons 1.1, 1.2, 1.3, 1.6, 1.7, 1.8, 1.9, 2.1, 2.2, 2.3, 2.4, 2.5, 2.6, 2.7, 2.8, 2.9, 2.10, 3.1, 3.2, 3.3, 3.5, 3.10, 4.4, 4.5, 4.7, 4.8, 5.3, 5.4, 5.6, 5.7, 7.1, 7.2, 7.5, 7.6, 7.7, 7.11, 7.12, 8.3, 8.6, 8.7, 9.2, 9.5, 9.6, 11.4, 11.5

Standards You Will Learn

Mathematical Practices		
MP.8	Look for and express regularity in repeated reasoning.	Lessons 1.2, 1.5, 1.6, 2.1, 2.2, 2.4, 2.12, 3.1, 3.2, 3.3, 3.4, 3.5, 3.7, 4.3, 4.6, 4.11, 4.12, 5.1, 5.2, 5.5, 5.8, 6.2, 6.3, 6.4, 6.5, 6.6, 6.8, 6.9, 6.10, 6.11, 6.12, 7.3, 7.4, 7.8, 7.9, 7.10, 8.1, 8.8, 9.1, 11.7, 11.8

Domain: Operations and Algebraic Thinking

Represent and solve problems involving addition and subtraction.

2.OA.1	Use addition and subtraction within 100 to solve one- and two-step word problems involving situations of adding to, taking from, putting together, taking apart, and comparing, with unknowns in all positions, e.g., by using drawings and equations with a symbol for the unknown number to represent the problem.	Lessons 3.8, 3.9, 4.9, 4.10, 5.9, 5.10, 5.11

Add and subtract within 20

2.OA.2	Fluently add and subtract within 20 using mental strategies. By end of Grade 2, know from memory all sums of two one-digit numbers.	Lessons 3.1, 3.2, 3.3, 3.4, 3.5, 3.6, 3.7

Work with equal groups of objects to gain foundations for multiplication.

2.OA.3	Determine whether a group of objects (up to 20) has an odd or even number of members, e.g., by pairing objects or counting them by 2s; write an equation to express an even number as a sum of two equal addends.	Lessons 1.1, 1.2
2.OA.4	Use addition to find the total number of objects arranged in rectangular arrays with up to 5 rows and up to 5 columns; write an equation to express the total as a sum of equal addends.	Lesson 3.11

Standards You Will Learn

Domain: Number and Operations in Base Ten		
Understand place value.		
2.NBT.1	Understand that the three digits of a three-digit number represent amounts of hundreds, tens, and ones; e.g., 706 equals 7 hundreds, 0 tens, and 6 ones. Understand the following as special cases:	Lessons 2.2, 2.3, 2.4, 2.5
	a. 100 can be thought of as a bundle of ten tens — called a "hundred."	Lesson 2.1
	b. The numbers 100, 200, 300, 400, 500, 600, 700, 800, 900 refer to one, two, three, four, five, six, seven, eight, or nine hundreds (and 0 tens and 0 ones).	Lesson 2.1
2.NBT.2	Count within 1000; skip-count by 2s, 5s, 10s, and 100s.	Lessons 1.8, 1.9, 3.10
2.NBT.3	Read and write numbers to 1000 using base-ten numerals, number names, and expanded form.	Lessons 1.3, 1.4, 1.5. 1.6, 1.7, 2.6, 2.7, 2.8
2.NBT.4	Compare two three-digit numbers based on meanings of the hundreds, tens, and ones digits, using >, =, and < symbols to record the results of comparisons.	Lessons 2.11, 2.12
Use place value understanding and properties of operations to add and subtract.		
2.NBT.5	Fluently add and subtract within 100 using strategies based on place value, properties of operations, and/or the relationship between addition and subtraction.	Lessons 4.1, 4.2, 4.3, 4.4, 4.5, 4.6, 4.7, 4.8, 5.1, 5.2, 5.3, 5.4, 5.5, 5.6, 5.7, 5.8
2.NBT.6	Add up to four two-digit numbers using strategies based on place value and properties of operations.	Lessons 4.11, 4.12

Standards You Will Learn

Domain: Number and Operations in Base Ten

Use place value understanding and properties of operations to add and subtract.

2.NBT.7	Add and subtract within 1000, using concrete models or drawings and strategies based on place value, properties of operations, and/or the relationship between addition and subtraction; relate the strategy to a written method. Understand that in adding or subtracting three-digit numbers, one adds or subtracts hundreds and hundreds, tens and tens, ones and ones; and sometimes it is necessary to compose or decompose tens or hundreds.	Lessons 6.1, 6.2, 6.3, 6.4, 6.5, 6.7, 6.8, 6.9, 6.10. 6.11
2.NBT.7.1	Use estimation strategies to make reasonable estimates in problem solving.	Lessons 6.6, 6.12
2.NBT.8	Mentally add 10 or 100 to a given number 100–900, and mentally subtract 10 or 100 from a given number 100–900.	Lessons 2.9, 2.10
2.NBT.9	Explain why addition and subtraction strategies work, using place value and the properties of operations.	Lesson 6.9

Domain: Measurement and Data

Measure and estimate lengths in standard units.

2.MD.1	Measure the length of an object by selecting and using appropriate tools such as rulers, yardsticks, meter sticks, and measuring tapes.	Lessons 8.1, 8.2, 8.4, 8.8, 9.1, 9.3
2.MD.2	Measure the length of an object twice, using length units of different lengths for the two measurements; describe how the two measurements relate to the size of the unit chosen.	Lessons 8.6, 9.5

Standards You Will Learn

Domain: Measurement and Data

Measure and estimate lengths in standard units.

2.MD.3	Estimate lengths using units of inches, feet, centimeters, and meters.	Lessons 8.3, 8.7, 9.2, 9.6
2.MD.4	Measure to determine how much longer one object is than another, expressing the length difference in terms of a standard length unit.	Lesson 9.7

Relate addition and subtraction to length.

2.MD.5	Use addition and subtraction within 100 to solve word problems involving lengths that are given in the same units, e.g., by using drawings (such as drawings of rulers) and equations with a symbol for the unknown number to represent the problem.	Lessons 8.5, 9.4
2.MD.6	Represent whole numbers as lengths from 0 on a number line diagram with equally spaced points corresponding to the numbers 0, 1, 2, ..., and represent whole-number sums and differences within 100 on a number line diagram.	Lessons 8.5, 9.4

Work with time and money.

2.MD.7	Tell and write time from analog and digital clocks to the nearest five minutes, using a.m. and p.m. Know relationships of time (e.g., minutes in an hour, days in a month, weeks in a year).	Lessons 7.8, 7.9, 7.10, 7.11, 7.12
2.MD.8	Solve word problems involving combinations of dollar bills, quarters, dimes, nickels, and pennies, using $ and ¢ symbols appropriately. *Example: If you have 2 dimes and 3 pennies, how many cents do you have?*	Lessons 7.1, 7.2, 7.3, 7.4, 7.5, 7.6, 7.7

Standards You Will Learn

Domain: Measurement and Data		
Represent and interpret data.		
2.MD.9	Generate measurement data by measuring lengths of several objects to the nearest whole unit, or by making repeated measurements of the same object. Show the measurements by making a line plot, where the horizontal scale is marked off in whole-number units.	Lesson 8.9
2.MD.10	Draw a picture graph and a bar graph (with single-unit scale) to represent a data set with up to four categories. Solve simple put-together, take-apart, and compare problems using information presented in a bar graph.	Lessons 10.1, 10.2, 10.3, 10.4, 10.5, 10.6
Domain: Geometry		
Reason with shapes and their attributes.		
2.G.1	Recognize and draw shapes having specified attributes, such as a given number of angles or a given number of equal faces. Identify triangles, quadrilaterals, pentagons, hexagons, and cubes.	Lessons 11.1, 11.2, 11.3, 11.4, 11.5, 11.6
2.G.2	Partition a rectangle into rows and columns of same-size squares and count to find the total number of them.	Lesson 11.7
2.G.3	Partition circles and rectangles into two, three, or four equal shares, describe the shares using the words *halves, thirds, half of, a third of,* etc., and describe the whole as two halves, three thirds, four fourths. Recognize that equal shares of identical wholes need not have the same shape.	Lessons 11.8, 11.9, 11.10, 11.11

Index

Halves, 549–552, 553–556, 557–560, 561–564

Hands On activities. See Activities

Hands On lessons, 13–16, 65–68, 157–160, 305–308, 309–312, 345–348, 349–352, 357–360, 401–404, 405–408, 413–416, 421, 424, 445–448, 453–456, 461–464, 469–472, 489–491, 545–547

Hexagons, 533–536, 538–539

Home Activity. See Family Involvement; Take Home Activity

Hundred chart, 10, 41, 45

Hundreds
counting patterns with, 45–48, 89–92, 94–96
defined, 58
grouping tens as, 57–60
place value, 57–60, 61–64, 65–68, 69–72, 73–76, 77–80, 81–83, 85–88, 101–104

Inches, 401–403, 405–408, 409–412, 413–416, 417–419, 421–424, 433–436

Inverse relationship
of addition and subtraction, 137–140, 141–143, 257–260,
between size of units and number of units needed to measure, 421–424, 461–464

Key, used in a picture graph, 485–488, 489–491, 493

Length
add and subtract, 417–419, 457–459
choosing tools for measuring, 429–432

comparing, 469–472
data displayed in line plots, 433–436
estimation of, 409–412, 425–428, 449–452, 465–468
in feet, 421–424, 425–428
in inches, 401–404, 405–408, 409, 413–416, 417–419, 421–424
inverse relationship between size of units and number of units needed to measure, 421–424, 461–464
in meters, 461–464, 465–468

Line plots, 433–436

Listen and Draw
Listen and Draw appears in most Student Edition lessons. Some examples are: 21, 37, 281, 297, 493, 553
Math Story, 109–116, 333–339, 509–516

Look for Structure, 40, 135, 532

Make a Graph strategy, 501–504

Make a Model strategy, 97–100, 305–308

Make Arguments, 15, 87, 315

Make Connections, 28, 36, 139, 160, 180, 268, 352, 376, 524, 528, 544, 552

Make Sense of Problems, 24, 184, 188, 192, 208, 212, 308, 312, 360, 372

Manipulatives and Materials
base-ten blocks, 25, 33, 65–68, 97–100, 173, 185, 189, 241, 289, 293, 305–308, 309
centimeter rulers, 453–456, 462–464, 469–472
color tiles, 401–403, 406, 545–547
connecting cubes, 13–14, 17, 481, 489
counters (two-color), 157–160, 161
inch rulers, 414–416, 422–424, 425–428, 430–431, 433–436
measuring tape, 430–432
pattern blocks, 541, 549
play money 345, 349, 353, 357–360, 361–363
unit cubes 445–448, 453
yardstick, 430–431

© Houghton Mifflin Harcourt Publishing Company

S